Especially for Mormons

Volume Two

Stan and Sharon Miller

Kellirae Arts
Provo, Utah

16th Printing, 1998

KELLIRAE ARTS
P.O. BOX 300
PROVO, UTAH 84603

FOREWORD

The short sayings of wise and good men are of great value, like the dust of gold and the sparks of diamonds.

—Tillotson

The first volume of ESPECIALLY FOR MORMONS, published originally in 1971, has been distributed all around the globe. We have received many gratifying letters from our readers thanking us for bringing some of their favorite quotes, poems and stories together in one cover. Many have also encouraged us to continue gathering these writings, most of which are heretofore unpublished, and bring them to public availability.

Hence, here is ESPECIALLY FOR MORMONS, Volume Two. This collection is not intended as a sequel to our original publication, but simply as additional material which may be inspirational and worthwhile in Gospel application.

As was indicated in Volume One, we have long felt that there is a wealth of excellent material available which is especially suited to the Latter-day Saint audience. With Volume Two we have still barely begun to uncover uncounted "quotes worth requoting." But we present here some of our favorites from non-Latter-day Saint writers as well as those of Latter-day Saint authors.

To

Myles and Elsie Jones
Henry and Beverly Miller. . .

. . .Our parents whose loving examples have created ESPECIALLY FOR MORMONS.

ACKNOWLEDGEMENTS

Attempt has been made to acknowledge each contributor by name. However in many instances authorship was indeterminate. We express deepest appreciation to each person whose writings appear herein. We are sure each shares our desire to have their writings reach and inspire as many people as possible.

Most of all, we extend appreciation to so many friends who have expressed encouragement in this book's preparation. All of our readers are our friends, and so to you we lovingly present ESPECIALLY FOR MORMONS, Volume Two.

INDEX OF SUBJECTS

Age	1
America	7
Bible	13
Boys	14
Character	16
Chastity	24
Christ	27
Christmas	36
Death	57
Determination	69
Endurance	89
Especially for Mormons	96
Example	109
Faith	112
Family	117
Father	125
Free Agency	128
Friendship	130
Goals	137
Gossip	139
Gratitude	143
Habit	145
Happiness	146
Honor	152
Human Relations	154
Humor	161
Judging	174
Kindness	181
Life	184
Love	196
Man's Worth	209
Marriage	221
Missionary Work	229
Mother	234
Opportunity	242
Prayer	246
Preparation	252
Prophets	255
Regret	264
Sabbath	274
Sacrament	277
Service	284
Smiling	290
Success	292
Teaching	299
Testimony	305
Thanksgiving	307
Time	309
Tithing	314
Values	318
Woman	336
Word of Wisdom	345
Work	348
Work for the Dead	352
Youth	355

AGE

Middle age is when you know all the answers and nobody ever asks you the questions.

* * * * *

People don't grow old. They merely get old by not growing.

* * * * *

Young folks ought to know that we old folks know more about being young than they know about being old.

* * * * *

Men and women are what happened to little boys and girls.

* * * * *

To be seventy years young is sometimes far more cheerful and hopeful than to be forty years old.

* * * * *

The harvest of old age is the memory and rich store of blessings laid up in earlier life.

* * * * *

The tragedy of life is not that it ends so soon, but that we wait so long to begin it.

* * * * *

You can take no credit for beauty at sixteen. But if you are beautiful at sixty, it would be your own soul's doing.

* * * * *

The belief that youth is the happiest time of life is founded on a fallacy. The happiest person is the person who thinks the most interesting thoughts. As we advance in years, we really grow happier, if we live intelligently.

* * * * *

The unused talent now going to waste among persons who think they are on the shelf could win world peace, mitigate racial tensions, help economically less advanced people and give new hope to life throughout the world.

* * * * *

We should cease fighting age as if it were a foe. Memories of past experiences may be even sweeter than these experiences were in reality.

* * * * *

Character is always associated with something old and takes time to grow, like the beautiful facial lines on an older person, lines that are the steady imprint of man's evolving character.

* * * * *

To me, old age is always fifteen years older than I am.

--Bernard Beruch

* * * * *

The brain is like a muscle. The more you use it, the more it develops. That's the opinion of leading scientists who studied the relationship of mental ability to aging. In other words, a seventy-five year old who has been exercising his brain is more likely to be mentally sharp and alert than a fifty-five year old whose brain has been half asleep since he got out of school.

* * * * *

Nobody grows old merely by living a number of years; people grow old by deserting their ideals. Years wrinkle the skin, but giving up enthusiasm wrinkles the soul. Worry, doubt, self-distrust, fear and despair -- these are the long years that bow the head and turn the growing spirit back to dust. You are as young as your faith, and as old as your doubts; as young as your self-confidence, as old as your fears; as young as your hope, as old as your despair.

* * * * *

Grow old along with me!
The best is yet to be,
The last of life, for which the first was made:

Our times are in His hand
Who saith, "A whole I planned,"
Youth shows but half; trust God; see all, nor be afraid!

* * * * *

Are you fully aware
Your youth get up has been spent?
That your get and go
Has go up and went?

But you shouldn't mind
When you think with a grin
Of all the nice places
Your get up has been.

* * * * *

I'm Fine

There is nothing whatever the matter with me.
I'm just as healthy as I can be.
I have arthritis in back and knees.
And when I talk, I talk with a wheeze.
My pulse is weak; my blood is thin,
But I'm awfully well for the shape I'm in.

My teeth eventually had to come out.
And my diet I hate to think about.
I'm overweight and I can't get thin,
My appetite is sure to win.
But I'm awfully well for the shape I'm in.

Arch supports I have for my feet
Or I wouldn't be able to go on the street
Sleep is denied me night after night
And every morning I'm a sight;
My memory is failing, my head's in a spin,
But I'm awfully well for the shape I'm in.

The moral is this as the tale we unfold,
That for all those who are growing old
It's better to say "I'm fine," with a grin,
Than to let folks know the shape you're in.

--Author Unknown

* * * * *

It Is Later Than You Think

Everything is farther than it used to be. It is twice as far from my house to the station now, and they've added a hill that I've just noticed. The train leaves sooner too, but I've given up running for them because they are faster than they used to be.

You can't believe the time tables anymore, and why ask the conductor? I'll bet I ask him a dozen times if the next stop is where I get off, and he always says it isn't. I gather up my packages anyway, just so I won't go by the right stop. Once in awhile I make doubly sure by getting off at the station ahead.

Seems to me they are making staircases steeper than in the old days. The rises are higher, and there are more of them, because I've noticed it's harder to make them two at a time. It's all one can do to make them one at a time.

Have you noticed the small print they are using lately? Newspapers are getting farther and farther away when I hold them, and I have to squint to make out the news. Now it's ridiculous to suggest that a person of my age needs glasses, but it's the only way I can find out what's going on without someone reading to me, and that isn't much help because everyone seems to speak in such a low voice that I can scarcely hear them.

Times sure are changing. The barber doesn't hold a mirror behind me when he finishes so I can see the back of my head. The material in my clothes, I notice, shrinks in certain places (you know, around the waist or in the seat). Shoe laces are so short they are almost impossible to reach.

Even the weather is changing. It's getting colder in the winter and the summers are hotter than in the old days. Snow is much heavier when I attempt to shovel it, and rain is so much wetter, that I have to wear rubbers. I guess the way they make windows now makes drafts more severe.

People are changing too. For one thing, they are younger than they used to be when I was their age. On the other hand, people my age are so much older than I am. I realize that my generation is approaching middle age, but there's no reason for my classmates tottering into senility.

I ran into my roommate the other night and he had changed so much I didn't recognize him. "You've put on a little weight, Bob," I said. "It's this modern food." Bob replied. "It seems to be so much more fattening."

I got to thinking about poor old Bob this morning while shaving. Stopping a moment, I looked at my own reflection in the mirror. Seems like they don't make the same kind of glass for mirrors anymore.

* * * * *

Staying Young

I've something to say to you older folks, and you young folks listen too,
For what I'm about to say, will some day apply to you.

I know that some of you older folks are happily retired,
And have no ties to bind you, and work is no longer required.

So you're sitting around in idleness, each day becomes a bore,
You're beginning to start thinking, there's nothing worth living for.

You'd like to be in some business, but think it's too late to begin,
Well, I'll tell you about a business, that all of you can be in.

Be in the business of staying young, make staying young a career,
Don't live in the past; plan a future: look forward to each added year.

Don't sit around and sigh, and let the world pass you by,
Get with it, and stay with it, all you have to do is to try.

Be willing to forget yourself, for at least once in awhile,
Place yourself second, and cause someone else to smile.

Kindness pays a thousand fold, this fact is more than true,
Try doing a favor here and there, and it will work for you.

Be willing to admit mistakes, humility is always grand,
The humble people are the ones that need a helping hand,

Be willing to work for what is right however rough the way,
For in the end the righteous always have the final say.

This life can be wonderful, tender and thrilling,
You can always find happiness, that is if you're willing.

There's a place for you in this world, work that needs to be done,
So make up your mind you're not too old to try to help someone.

I've been in the business of staying young since I hit the fifty mark,
And it's a wonderful business, in which all of us can embark,

It gives you that happy feeling of starting your life anew,
But like any other business, it requires time and attention too!

So be in the business of staying young, and the heights of joy you will reach,
Make staying young your new career, and practice what you preach.

Age can be a frightening thing, if you let yourself fear it...
You can't help being up in years, but needn't be down in spirit.

Take pride in your appearance, always look up to par,
It's a way of making others forget just how old you are.

I know I'm not indestructible, time is taking it's toll,
But I have a goal to reach, and I know I'm not too old.

So get busy and be useful each day of your life on this earth
With your talents and your efforts, find a way to prove your worth.

And be grateful that you're living in a world of youth today,
And you, too, can be youthful, if you think and live that way.

Always be serene and gentle: if in this life things don't go your way,
Turn your left cheek, and be happy, to the unkind words that people say.

God has given us all a cross to bear, but first he measured us and found,
That when we reach the portals, He will exchange our cross for a crown.

It's there we'll meet our loved ones that have gone on before,
It's there we'll wear the robes of white, and dwell forevermore.

So let us live from day to day, while here upon this earth,
To do someone a golden deed, and our duty let us not shirk.

God will keep us strong and healthy, if in His hands we place our life,
We're living in a world that needs us, though it's filled with envy, sin and strife.

Let's help make it a better place, so all can plainly see,
That each hour we spend here, is part of our eternity.

--Author Unknown

* * * * *

AMERICA

It seems a little ridiculous now, but this country was originally founded as a protest against taxation.

* * * * *

God, Give Us Men!

God, give us men! A time like this demands
Strong minds, great hearts, true faith and ready hands;
Men whom the lust of office does not kill;
Men whom the spoils of office cannot buy;
Men who possess opinions and a will;
Men who have honor; men who will not lie;
Men who can stand before a demagogue
And damn his treacherous flatteries without winking!
Tall men, sun-crowned, who live above the fog
In public duty and in private thinking;
For while they rabble, with their thumb-worn creeds,
Their large professions and their little deeds,
Mingle in selfish strife, lo! Freedom weeps,
Wrong rules the land and waiting Justice sleeps.

--Josiah Gilbert Holland

* * * * *

I Am An American

I am an American. Listen to my words. Listen well, for my country is a strong country, and my message is a strong message. I am an American, and I speak for Democracy, and the dignity of the individual...

I am an American, and my ancestors have bequeathed to me: the laughter of a small boy as he watches a circus clown's antics, delicious coldness of the first bite of peppermint ice cream on the 4th of July, the little tenseness of a baseball crowd as the umpire calls "Batter Up!": These and many other things they fought for and left for me...

I am an American, and in my churches and homes everyone worships God in his own way: the young Jewish boy saying: "Hear, O Israel, the Lord is One," the Protestant boy singing: "A mighty Fortress is our God": each one believing and praying as he must, and all joining in the universal prayer: "Our Father who art in Heaven," with the voice in the soul of every human being that cries out to be free. I am an American, I believe that America has answered that voice...

Show me now a country greater than my country, a people happier than my people. I speak for Democracy and the dignity of the individual.

--Elizabeth Ellen Evans

* * * * *

Why I Am An American

I am an American because I believe in a government of laws and not of man, and in a national allegiance to high principle and lofty ideals instead of to a personal sovereign.

I am an American because I believe in a government with three distinct, separate branches, each mutually independent of the other, with no power of delegation or appropriations of rights or powers by any one to or from any other.

I am an American because I believe that government 'must derive its just powers from the consent of the governed.'

I am an American because I believe in the greatest possible measure of self government, and because I believe in a federal system of government which keeps local affairs in the hands of local governments.

I am an American because I believe in a bill of rights which places matters affecting "life, liberty, and the pursuit of happiness" and specifically the right of freedom of conscience and worship, the right of free speech and free press, the right peaceably to assembly and petition government, and the right to gain and hold property without molestation except by due process of law.

I am an American because under our form of government the people of the United States have made a progress never before made by any other people in the world in an equal time during the whole period of recorded history.

I am an American because standards of life and of living of the entire American people are far beyond those enjoyed by any other people in any other part of the world, either now or at any other time, which is a living testimony and evidence of the kindly beneficence of our free institution.

I am an American because I firmly and earnestly believe that the Constitution is an inspired document designed by our maker to set up a government which would make sure and secure the rights set forth in the Bill of Rights, and particularly the right of freedom of conscience and worship.

I am an American because I believe that the destiny of America is to be the abiding place of liberty and free institutions, and that its own practice and enjoyment of these blessings shall be to the world a beacon light which shall radiate its influence by peaceful means to the uttermost parts of the world, to the uplifting of all humanity.

--J. Reuben Clark
Congressional Record,
June 11, 1940

* * * * *

Creed

I am an American:
That's the way we put it,
Simply, without any swagger, without any brag,
In those four plain words.
We speak them softly, just to ourselves.
We roll them on the tongue, touching every syllable, getting the feel of them, the enduring flavor.
We speak them humbly, thankfully, reverently:
I am an American.

They are more than words, really,
They are the sum of the lives of a vast multitude of men and women and wide-eyed children.
They are a manifesto to mankind; speak those four words anywhere in the world -- yes, anywhere -- and those who hear will recognize their meaning.
They are a pledge. A pledge that stems from a document which says: "When in the course of human events," and goes on from there.
A pledge to those who dreamed that dream before it was set to paper, to those who have lived it since, and died for it.
Listen, and you can hear the voices echoing through them, words that sprang white-hot from bloody lips, scornful lips, lips a-tremble with human pity:

Laughing words, June-warm words, words cold as January ice:
You can hear the slow cadences of a gaunt and weary man at Gettysburg, dedicating not a cemetery, but a nation.
But they aren't words any longer; they're a way of life, a pattern of living.
They are a pattern of life as lived by a free people, freedom that has its roots in rights and obligations:
The right to hope, to dream, to pray; the obligation to serve.
These are some of the meanings of those four words, meanings we don't often stop to tally up or even list.
Only in the stillness of a moonless night, or in the thin dawn of a new day, when our world is close about us, do they rise up in our memories and stir in our sentient hearts.

They're plain words, those four. Simple words.
You could write them on your thumbnail, if you chose,
Or you could sweep them all across the sky, horizon to horizon.
But you needn't. You needn't do any of those things,
For those words are graven in the hearts of 210,000,000 people,
They are familiar to 210,000,000 tongues, every sound and every syllable,
But when we speak them we speak them softly, proudly, gratefully:
I am an American.

--Hal Borland

* * * * *

The Price They Paid

Have you ever wondered what happened to those men who signed the Declaration of Independence?

Five signers were captured by the British as traitors, and tortured before they died. Twelve had their homes ransacked and burned. Two lost their sons in the Revolutionary Army, another had two sons captured. Nine of the fifty-six fought and died from wounds or the hardships of the Revolutionary War.

What kind of men were they? Twenty-four were lawyers and jurists. Eleven were merchants, nine were farmers and large plantation owners, men of means, well-educated. But they signed the Declaration of Independence knowing full well that the penalty would be death if they were captured.

They signed and they pledged their lives, their fortunes, and their sacred honor.

Carter Braxton of Virginia, a wealthy planter and trader, saw his ships swept from the seas by the British navy. He sold his home and properties to pay his debts, and died in rags.

Thomas McKean was so hounded by the British that he was forced to move his family almost constantly. He served in the Congress without pay, and his family was kept in hiding. His possessions were taken from him, and poverty was his reward.

Vandals or soldiers or both, looted the properties of Ellery, Clymer, Hall, Walton, Gwinnett, Heyward, Ruttledge, and Middleton.

At the Battle of Yorktown, Thomas Nelson Jr., noted that the British General Cornwallis, had taken over the Nelson home for his headquarters. The owner quietly urged General George Washington to open fire, which was done. The home was destroyed, and Nelson died bankrupt.

Francis Lewis had his home and properties destroyed. The enemy jailed his wife, and she died within a few months.

John Hart was driven from his wife's bedside as she was dying. Their thirteen children fled for their lives. His fields and his grist mill were laid waste. For more than a year he lived in forests and caves, returning home after the war to find his wife dead, his children vanished. A few weeks later he died from exhaustion and a broken heart.

Norris and Livingston suffered a similar fate.

Such were the stories and sacrifices of the American Revolution. These were not wild-eyed, rabble rousing ruffians. These were soft-spoken men of means and education. They had security, but they valued liberty more. Standing tall, straight, and unwavering, they pledged: "For the support of this declaration, with a firm reliance on the protection of the Divine Providence, we mutually pledge to each other, our lives, our fortunes, and our sacred honor." They gave us an independent America. Can we keep it?

* * * * *

The Amazing American

The amazing American whips enemy nations, and then gives them the shirt off his back. He yells for speed laws that will stop fast driving, but won't buy a car if it won't do a hundred and twenty.

The amazing American gets scared half to death if we vote one billion dollars for education, but he's cool as the center seed of a cucumber about spending three billion dollars a year for smoking tobacco.

He gripes about the high prices of the things he has to buy. He gripes about the low prices of the things he has to sell. He knows the lineup of every baseball team in the American and National leagues, but doesn't know half the words in "The Star Spangled Banner."

An American will get mad at his wife for not running their home with the efficiency of a hotel and mad at a hotel for not being homelike.

He'll spend half a day looking for vitamin pills to make him live longer, then drive ninety miles an hour on slick pavement to make up for the time he lost.

The amazing American will complain about his wife's cooking. Yet, on a camping trip, he'll eat half fried potatoes, burnt fish and coffee made with gritty creek water in a rusty bucket and think it's wonderful.

The amazing American will work hard on a farm so he can move to town so he can make more money so he can move back to the farm.

In his office he likes to talk about baseball, football, fishing. Out at the game or on the creek bank, he talks business.

He is the only guy in the world who will pay 50 cents to park his car while he eats a 25 cent sandwich.

An American likes to cuss his government but he will fight any foreigner who does. He has more food to eat than anybody and more diet fads to keep him from eating it. His is the most civilized, most Christianized nation on earth, but he dares not deliver a payroll without an armored car.

In America we have more experts on marriage than any country in the world and more divorces.

The amazing American allows enemies of his country to hide behind the constitution while they seek to set fire to it. He's likely to fight them in Vietnam and tolerate them in Cuba.

He would not steal money from his neighbor but he'll pay tax collectors to steal it for him.

He irrigates desert to make farmland, then puts the extra acres in a soil bank. He spends 280 million dollars this year on tranquillizers and an equal sum on pep pills.

He tosses beer cans out the car window, drops gum wrappers in the gutter, plants auto graveyards along the highways, hides a mountain or meadow with a billboard selling laxatives, then stands up at his civic club meeting and, with a lump in his throat, sings "America, the Beautiful."

Yet, for all of that the amazing American is still a pretty nice guy.

Despite all that he is not, because of all that he is, calling anybody "a real American" is still the highest compliment you can pay.

--Anonymous

* * * * *

BIBLE

A young lady bought and read a book. Laying it aside, she made the mental notation that it was the dullest book she ever read. Not long after that she met a young man, and in the course of time friendship ripened into love. One night she said, "I have a book home in my library which was written by a man with a name just exactly like yours. Isn't that a coincidence?" "I think not," he replied, "for the simple reason that I wrote the book."

That night after she returned home, the young woman took the book from the shelf and read it from the beginning to the end. This time she found it to be the most fascinating book she's ever read. The secret? She knew and loved the author.

It is the same with the Scriptures.

* * * * *

"Mother, I've found an old dusty thing
High on the shelf -- just look!"
"Why, that's a Bible, Tommy dear;
Be careful -- that's God's book."
"Then, Mother, before we lose it,
We'd better send it back to God,
For you know we never use it."

* * * * *

BOYS

The best time to tackle a small problem is before he grows up.

* * * * *

Many a boy is the kind of kid his mother would not want him to play with.

* * * * *

There's that about small sons that quite unpins a mother's poise; for even when they're quiet, she can hear them <u>thinking</u> noise.

* * * * *

Description of a BOY

Got any boys around the house? Giving you any trouble...little trouble like noise and confusion and things like that? Then listen...I think you'll like this:

"After a male baby has grown out of long clothes and triangles and has acquired freckles...and so much dirt that relatives don't care to kiss it between meals...it becomes a boy."

"A boy is nature's answer to the false belief that there is no such thing as perpetual motion. A boy can run like a deer...eat like a pig...swim like a fish...climb like a squirrel...bellow like a bull...or act like a jackass... according to climatic conditions."

"The world is so full of boys that it's impossible to touch off a firecracker... strike up a band...or pitch a ball without collecting a thousand of them. Boys are not ornamental...they're useful...if it were not for boys, newspapers would go undelivered and un-read...and a hundred thousand picture shows would go bankrupt."

"A boy is a natural spectator. He watches parades...fires...fights...football games...automobiles and planes with equal fervor...However, he will not watch a clock."

"A boy is a piece of skin stretched over an appetite. He eats only when he's awake. Boys imitate their dads, in spite of all efforts to teach them good manners. Boys are not popular...except with parents...but they do have many fine qualities. You can absolutely rely on a boy...if you know what to rely on."

"Boys are very durable. A boy...if not washed too often...and kept in a cool place after every accident will survive broken bones...hornets nests... swimming holes...and five helpings of pie."

"Boys love to trade things. They'll trade fish-hooks...marbles...broken knives for anything that is priceless and worthless."

"When he grows up he'll trade puppy love...energy...warts...bashfulness... and a cast-iron stomach for a bay window...pride...ambition...pretense... and a bald head. And then will immediately begin to say, 'Boys aren't like they used to be in the good old days'."

--Frank Hemingway

* * * * *

CHARACTER

Inner Peace

Today I haven't moved the world
With any new inventions:
I've built no towering monument,
Attracted no attention.
I've organized no government
No armies have defeated:
No stay of fortune made
Have I this day repeated.
But all this day, praise be to God,
My thoughts have I succeeded
In keeping pure as morning dew...
No ill have I conceded.
And so, tonight, my mind is calm
As yonder verdant pastures,
And worry, fear, and human strife,
This day are not my masters.

* * * * *

Promise Yourself

To be strong that nothing can disturb your peace of mind.
To talk health, happiness and prosperity to every person you meet.
To make all your friends feel that there is something in them. To look on the sunny side of everything and make your optimism come true.
To think only of the best, to work only for the best, and to expect only the best.
To be just as enthusiastic about the success of others as you are about your own.
To forget the mistakes of the past and press on to greater achievements of the future.
To wear a cheerful countenance at all times and give every living creature a smile.
To give so much time to the improvement of yourself that you have no time to criticize others.
To be too large for worry, too noble for anger, too strong for fear,
And too happy to permit the presence of trouble.

To think well of yourself and to proclaim this fact
to the world, not in loud words, but in great
deeds.
To live in the faith that the world is on your side
so long as you are true to the best that is
in you.
I PROMISE MYSELF.

* * * * *

You Tell On Yourself

You tell on yourself
By the friends you seek,
By the every manner in which you speak;
By the way you employ your leisure time,
By the use you make of a dollar or dime.

You tell what you are
By the things you wear,
By the spirit by which your burdens you bear;
By the kind of things at which you laugh,
By the records you play on the phonograph.

You can tell what you are
By the way you talk,
By the manner in which you bear defeat;
By so simple a thing as what you eat,

By the books you choose from a well-filled shelf.
In these ways and more, you tell on yourself.
So there is really not a particle of sense
In your efforts to keep up your false pretense.

* * * * *

Your Mind's Garden

What seed have you sown in your garden of mind?
What thoughts have you sent into space?
Remember they yield you a harvest in kind
A life you henceforth must face.

For you are the sower, you choose your own seed
You fashion your future each day
Your garden is fertile, producing with speed
The fruit of each thought tucked away.

So if you wish happiness, health and peace
Then choose well each seed as you sow
Your future is shaped by the thoughts you release
Each hour, each day as you go.

--Elizabeth B. Waddell

* * * * *

"He that conquereth himself is greater than he that taketh a city."

--Proverbs

* * * * *

You can't build a reputation on what you are going to do.

* * * * *

Character is the sum of all choices.

* * * * *

There are three requirements necessary to the establishment of resolute, enduring character: a faith to live by, a self you can live with, and a purpose to live for.

* * * * *

Choose the reputation you want, then live up to it.

* * * * *

Personality is what people think we are. Character is what we know we are.

* * * * *

When you want strength, get it out of your heart, not out of your head.

* * * * *

When God measures a man, he puts the tape around the heart instead of the head.

* * * * *

It takes a lifetime to build a good reputation, but you can lose it in a minute.

--Will Rogers

* * * * *

With each honor, there is an equal responsibility.

* * * * *

I pray thee, O God, that I may be beautiful within.

--Socrates

* * * * *

This is the final test of a gentleman -- his respect for those who can be of no possible service to him.

--Phelps

* * * * *

Let no pleasure tempt thee, no profit allure thee, no ambition corrupt thee, to do anything which thou knowest to be evil; so shalt thou always live jollily; for a good conscience is a continual Christmas.

--Ben Franklin

* * * * *

Men show their character in nothing more clearly than by what they think laughable.

--Goethe

* * * * *

Remember this: the mind is a storehouse and you are the keeper. Why let the ugly and bad crowd out the good and beauty.

* * * * *

Mothers are the first professors in the school of character.

--Hugh B. Brown

* * * * *

Character

"Character is the aim of true education; and science, history, and literature are but means used to accomplish this desired end. Character is not the result of chance, but of continuous right thinking and right acting."

--David O. McKay

* * * * *

Character

Men may be divided almost any way we please, but I have found the most useful distinction to be made between those who devote their lives to conjugating the verb "to be", and those who spend their lives conjugating the verb "to have".

--Sydney J. Harris

* * * * *

Your greatness is measured by your kindness,
Your education and intellect by your modesty,
Your ignorance is betrayed by your suspicions
and prejudices,
Your real caliber is measured by the consideration
you have for others.

* * * * *

I would be true, for there are those who trust me;
I would be pure, for there are those that care;
I would be strong, for there is much to suffer;
I would be brave, for these is much to dare;
I would be a friend to all -- the foe, the friendless;
I would be giving, and forget the gift;
I would be humble, for I know my weakness;
I would look up and laugh, and love, and lift.

* * * * *

If you would really know men, study them:

When angry.
When in love.
When eating (alone and unobserved, as they believe)
When writing.

When in trouble.
When joyful and triumphant.
When downcast and defeated.
When facing catastrophies of a hazardous nature.
When trying to make a "good impression" on others.
When informed of anothers misfortune.
When informed of anothers good fortune.
When losing in any sort of game or sport.
When winning at a sport.
When alone, in meditative moods.

--Napoleon Hill

* * * * *

Two Temples

A Builder builded a temple.
He wrought it with grace and skill;
Pillars and groins and arches
All fashioned to work his will.
Men said, as they saw its beauty,
"It shall never know decay;
Great is the skill, O Builder!
Thy fame shall endure for aye."

A Mother builded a temple
With loving and infinite care,
Planning each arch with patience,
Laying each stone with prayer.
None praised her unceasing efforts,
None knew of her wondrous plan,
For the temple the Mother builded
Was unseen by the eyes of man.

Gone is the Builder's temple,
Crumpled into the dust;
Low lies each stately pillar,
Food for consuming rust.
But the temple the Mother builded
Will last while the ages roll,
For that beautiful unseen temple
Was a child's immortal soul.

--Hattie Rose Hall

* * * * *

You Never Can Tell

You never can tell when you send a word
Like an arrow shot from a bow
By an archer blind, be it cruel or kind,
Just where it may chance to go.
It may pierce the breast of your dearest friend,
Tipped with its poison or balm,
To a stranger's heart in life's great mart
It may carry its pain or its calm.

You never can tell when you do an act
Just what the result will be,
But with every deed you are sowing a seed,
Though the harvest you may not see.
Each kindly act is an acorn dropped
In God's productive soil;
You may not know, but the tree shall grow
With shelter for those who toil.

You never can tell what your thoughts will do
In bringing you hate or love,
For thoughts are things, and their airy wings
Are swifter than carrier doves.
They follow the law of the universe --
Each thing must create its kind,
And they speed o'er the track to bring you back
Whatever went out from your mind.

--Ella Wheeler Wilcox

* * * * *

Personal Philosophy

"It is our daily duty to consider that in all circumstances of life, pleasurable, painful or otherwise, the conduct of every human being affects more or less, the happiness of others especially of those in the same house; and that as life is made up, for the most part, not of great occasions, but of small everyday moments, it is the giving to those moments there greatest amount of peace, pleasantness and security, that contributes the most to human good.

Be peaceable.
Be cheerful.
Be true.

--Leith Hunt

* * * * *

Discouragement

A Chinese legend describes how the Father of Sin decided to have a sale and dispose of all the tools he owned to anyone who would pay his price.

The implements were laid out in a row for inspection. Among them were tools labeled: Malice; Hatred; Envy; Jealousy; and Deceit. Every one had a price tag on it. Apart from the others lay a harmless looking wedge-shaped tool, very worn from use, that was priced a great deal higher than any of the rest.

One of the buyers asked the Devil what it was. "That," he said, "is discouragement, and it's in fine shape."

"But why have you priced it so high?"

"Because it's more useful than any of the others. I can pry open and get inside a man's conscience with that wedge when I couldn't get near him with any other. And, believe me, once I get inside I can use that man to whatever suits me best. Of course, you'll notice it's a little worn; that's because I use it with nearly everybody, for very few of you mortals know that it belongs to me."

However the price was so high that this particular tool was never sold.

The Devil still owns it and is still using it today.

* * * * *

As A Man Soweth

We must not hope to be mowers,
And to gather the ripe gold ears,
Unless we have first been sowers
And watered the furrows with tears.

It is not just as we take it,
This mystical world of ours,
Life's field will yield as we make it
A harvest of thorns or flowers.

--Johann Wolfgang von Goethe

* * * * *

CHASTITY

Don't get affectionate just because it's late at night.

* * * * *

A mind engrossed in sex is good for little else.

* * * * *

Girls, the flower by the roadside that catches the dust of every traveller is not the one to be admired, and is seldom if ever plucked; but the one blooming way up on the hillside, protected by a perpendicular cliff is the flower with the virgin perfume, and the one the boys will almost risk his life to possess.

--David O. McKay

* * * * *

The Plea

Why does it have to be like this?
Why do boys just have to kiss?
No matter the face, no matter the name,
Alone with a girl they're all the same.
And every time as it gets dark
His first impulse is to park.
Maybe he likes the lipstick taste,
Or maybe he has some time to waste;
But time like air, is warm and free
Whenever a boy's on a necking spree.
And when the wrestling match is done
You wonder who has really won.
A swell hair-do is all but shot;
Your lipstick's gone and smeared alot.
In the dark he looks so queer
With lipstick smeared from ear to ear.
I'd like just once to meet a boy
Whose company I could enjoy;
A boy who would inspire respect
Simply because he didn't neck.

--by a girl

* * * * *

Answer To The Plea

The answer, girls, is simply this,
It's you who want to make us kiss.
You spend your coin for a new hair-do,
To win a date you simply stew.
You turn on us your warmest glance,
You pose and flirt and look so sweet,
Dry ice would melt beneath your feet.
With luscious lips and painted nails
You trap us unsuspecting males.
And so we fall, and like it too
Just like you planned for us to do.
But if a boy won't kiss and neck
You say, "Oh well, what the heck.
He's mama's little lambie pie --
You can't get thrills from such a guy."
So girls don't start to cuss us boys
To make us stop, turn off your poise.
The boys you go with neck with you
Simply because you want them to.

--by a boy

* * * * *

Chastity

(Innocence vs. Purity)

It's easy enough to be virtuous
When nothing tempts you to stray
When without and within, no voice of sin
Is luring your soul away
But it's only a negative virtue
Until it's tried by fire
And the soul that is worth the blessings of earth
Is the soul that resists desire.

* * * * *

Chastity

(Sin vs. Purity)

The story is told that some shepherds once saw an eagle soar out from a crag. It flew majestically far up into the day but by and by became unstead and began to waiver in its flight. At length one wing dropped and then the other, and the poor bird fell swiftly to the ground. The shepherds sought the fallen bird and found that a little serpent had fastened itself upon it while it was resting upon the crag. The eagle did not know the serpent was there, but it crawled through the feathers and while the proud monarch was sweeping through the air, its fangs were thrust into the eagle's flesh, and he came reeling into the dust. This could be the story of many a life. Some secret sin has been eating its way into the heart and at last a proud life lies soiled and dishonored in the dust.

* * * * *

There is a beauty every girl has -- a gift from God, as pure as the sunlight, and as sacred as life. It is a beauty all men love, a virtue that wins all men's souls. That beauty is chastity. Chastity without skin beauty may enkindle the soul; skin beauty without chastity can kindle only the eye. Chastity enshrined in the mold of true womanhood will hold true love eternally.

--David O. McKay

* * * * *

A beautiful, modest, chaste woman is creation's masterpiece. When in addition to these virtues a woman possesses as guiding stars in her life righteousness and godliness and an irresistible impulse and desire to make others happy, no one will question if she be classed among those who are truly great.

--David O. McKay

* * * * *

CHRIST

God so loved the world that He did not send a committee.

--Churchill

* * * * *

I have now disposed of all my property to my family. There is one thing more I wish I could give them, and that is the Christian religion. If they had that, and I had not given them one shilling, they would be rich; and if they had not that, and I had given them all the world, they would be poor.

--Patrick Henry

* * * * *

A cathedral without windows, a face without eyes, a field without flowers, an alphabet without vowels, a continent without rivers, a night without stars, and a sky without the sun -- these would not be so sad as a world without the Bible, or a soul without Jesus Christ.

--James L. Gordon

* * * * *

In Nazareth, the narrow road,
That tires the feet and steals the breath,
Passes the place where once abode
The Carpenter of Nazareth.

And up and down the dusty way
The village folk would often went;
And on the bench, beside Him, lay
Their broken things for Him to mend.

The maiden with the doll she broke,
The woman with the broken chair,
The man with broken plough, or yoke,
Said, "Can you mend it carpenter?"

And each received the thing he sought,
In yoke, or plow, or chair or doll;
The broken thing which each had brought
Returned again a perfect whole.

So, up the hill the long years through,
With heavy step and wistful eye,
The burdened souls their way pursue,
Uttering each the plaintive cry;

"O Carpenter of Nazareth,
This heart, that's broken past repair,
This life, that's shattered nigh to death,
Oh, can you mend them Carpenter?"

And by His kind and ready hand,
His own sweet life is woven through
Our broken lives, until they stand
A new creation -- "All things new."

The shattered idols of my heart,
Desire, ambition, hope and faith,
Mould Thou into the perfect part,
O Carpenter of Nazareth!"

--George Blair

* * * * *

This Stranger of Galilee

In fancy I stood on the shore one day
Of a beautiful murmuring sea,
I saw the great crowds as they thronged the way
Of the stranger of Galilee.

I saw how the man who was blind from birth
In a moment was made to see;
The lame were made whole by the matchless skill
Of the stranger of Galilee.

His look of compassion, His words of Love,
Shall never forgotten be,
When sin-sick and helpless He saw me there,
This stranger of Galilee.

I heard Him speak peace to the angry waves
Of that turbulent, raging sea,
And lo, at His words are the waters stilled,
This stranger of Galilee.

A peaceful, a quiet, a holy calm
Now and ever abides with me;
He holdeth my life in His mighty hands,
This stranger of Galilee.

Come ye who are driven and tempest tossed
And His gracious salvation see;
He will quiet life's storms with His peace be still.
This stranger of Galilee.

Then He bids me to go and the story tell
What He ever to you will be,
If only you'll let Him with you abide,
This stranger of Galilee.

Oh, my friend, won't you love Him forever
So gracious and tender is He,
Accept Him today as your Savior,
This stranger of Galilee.

* * * * *

Does Jesus Live At Your House

Does Jesus live at your house?
I heard a child once ask.
Her little brow was furrowed,
As she struggled with a task.

He used to live at our house,
With mama and daddy too.
But now He has gone away somewhere
I don't know what to do.

For daddy is not the same today,
And mama laughs no more.
They never bother much with me,
They say I'm just a bore.

But it didn't seem to be that way,
With Jesus in our house.
For every night my daddy came
When all my curls were combed.

And helped me say my bedtime prayers,
And mama helped me too.
And then they smiled and tucked me in
And now they never do.

Could you tell me where Jesus is?
For everything seems black.
We want Him in our home again,
We want Him to come back.

And when He comes we'll keep Him
For we truly need Him so.
If Jesus lives at your house,
Oh, don't ever let Him go.

The child then turned and left me,
While I pursued my way
And thought of many home fires
That could be bright today.

Does Jesus live at your house?
How much those words portend.
Yes, on that question's answer
Our hopes, our all, depends.

* * * * *

Unawares

They say the Master is coming
To honor the town today,
And none can tell at whose house or home
The Master will choose to stay.
And I thought while my heart beat wildly,
What if He should come to mine?
How would I strive to entertain
And honor this Guest Divine?

And straight I turned to toiling,
To make my house more neat;
I swept and polished and garnished,
And decked it with blossoms sweet,
I was troubled for fear the Master
Might come ere my task was done,
And hastened and worked the faster
And watched the hurrying sun.

But right in the midst of my duties
A woman came to my door;
She had come to tell me her sorrows,
And my comfort and aid implore.

And I said, "I cannot listen,
Nor help you any today;
I have greater things to attend to,"
And the pleader turned away.

But soon there came another --
A cripple, thin, pale, and gray --
And said, "O, let me stop and rest
Awhile in your home, I pray.
I have traveled far since morning,
I am hungry, and faint, and weak
My heart is full of misery,
And comfort and help I seek!"

And I said, "I am grieved and sorry
But I cannot help you today;
I look for the great and noble guest."
And the cripple went away.
The day wore onward swiftly
And my task was nearly done,
And a prayer was ever in my heart,
That the Master to me might come.

And I thought I would spring to meet him,
And serve him with utmost care,
When a little child stood by me
With a face so sweet and fair --
Sweet, but with marks of tear drops
And his clothes were tattered and old;
A finger was bruised and bleeding,
And his little bare feet were cold.

And I said, "I'm sorry for you,
You are sorely in need of care;
But I cannot stop to give it,
You must hasten on elsewhere."
And at the words a shadow
Swept o'er his blue-veined brow --
"Someone will feed and clothe you, dear,
But I am too busy now."

At last the day was ended
And my toil was over and done
My house was swept and garnished,
And I watched, but no footsteps sounded,
No one e're passed at the gate,
No one entered my cottage door,
I could only pause and wait.

I waited until night had deepened,
And the Master had not come;
"He has entered some other door," I cried,
"And gladdened some other home,
My labor has been for nothing."
And I bowed my head and I wept.
My heart was sore with longing,
Yet in spite of all I slept.

Then the Master stood before me.
His face was grave and fair;
"Three times today I came to your door,
And craved your pity and care;
Three times you sent me onward,
Unhelped and uncomforted,
And the blessings you might have had are lost,
And your chance to serve had fled."

"Oh, Lord, dear Lord, forgive me
How could I know it was Thee?"
My very soul was shamed and bowed
In the depths of humility.
And he said, "The sin is pardoned
But the blessing is lost to thee;
For comforting not the least of mine,
You have failed to comfort me."

* * * * *

No Hands But Ours

Shortly after the culmination of the Second World War, a devastated city in England began its heartbreaking and wearying work of restoration. In the old city square had stood a large statue of Jesus Christ, with His hands outspread in an attitude of invitation. On the pedestal were carved the words, "Come unto me."

In the process of the restoration of the statue, with the aid of master artists and sculptors, the figure eventually was reassembled, except for the hands, of which no fragments could be discovered anywhere in the surrounding rubble. Someone made the suggestion that the artists, since the former hands could not be found, would have to fashion new hands.

Later came a public protest, couched in the words, "No, leave Him without hands!" So today, in the public square of that English city, the restored statue of Christ stands without hands, and on its base are carved the words, "Christ has no hands but ours!"

* * * * *

What It Means To Know Christ

A man passed away and was resurrected and waiting in a room to be interviewed. Another man was ahead of him. The door opened, the man entered, the door closed. The man on the outside could hear the conversation on the other side of the door. The interviewer began: I want you to tell me what you know about Jesus Christ.

Well, He was born of a virgin in Bethlehem; He lived thirty-three years, spending the last three in His ministry organizing His church, choosing His apostles to direct it, giving the gospel to direct our lives.

The interviewer stopped him and said: Yes, yes, that's all true, but I want you to tell me what you know about Jesus Christ.

Well, He was tortured and crucified that we might have eternal life. Three days later He was resurrected that we might return to Heavenly Father.

Yes, yes, that is true, but I want you to tell me what you know about Jesus Christ. The man, a little perplexed, again began: Well, He restored the Gospel in its fulness to the earth through Joseph Smith, reorganized His Church, gave us temples wherein we might do work to save our dead. He gave us family prayer and family home evening where we might unite with our families. He gave us the Priesthood to heal the sick and personal ordinances for our salvation and exaltation.

The interviewer again stopped him and said: All of what you have said to me is true. The man was then invited to leave the room. After he left the door opened and the second man entered. As he approached the interviewer he fell upon his knees and cried, "My Lord, My God."

--Author unknown

* * * * *

Testimony Of A Scientist

"I was almost a devout atheist, I did not believe that God was any more than a conglomeration of everyone's mind put together, and the good that was there, that was God as far as I was concerned. As for the real, all-powerful God existing and loving us all, with power over everything, I did not believe that.

Then one day I had an experience that really set me thinking. I was in a large pathological laboratory where we were attempting to find the wave length of the brain. We found a channel of wave lengths, and that channel has a mach room in it wherein the different wave lengths of each individual's brain are further separated in identity more clearly than are the finger prints of each individual's hand. This is a point we should remember: God can actually keep in heaven a record of our thoughts as individuals just as the FBI can keep a record of our finger prints in Washington, D.C.

We wanted to make an experiment to discover what took place in the brain at the moment of transition from life to death. We chose first a lady whose family had sent her to a mental institution but who had been discharged.

The doctors could find nothing wrong with her other than the fact she had cancer of the brain. This affected the balance of her body only. As far as her alertness of mind was concerned and in every other way, she was exceptionally brilliant. We knew she was on the verge of death and she was informed, in this research hospital, that she was going to die.

We arranged a tiny pick-up in her room to ascertain what would take place in the transition of her brain from life to death. We also put a very small microphone, about the size of a shilling, in the room so that we could hear what she said, if she had anything to say.

Five of us hardened scientists -- perhaps I was the hardest of the group -- were in an adjoining room with our instruments prepared to register and record what transpired. Our device had a needle pointing to "0" in the center of the scale. To the right the scale was calibrated to 500 points positive, to the left the scale was calibrated to 500 points negative. We previously had recorded on this identical instrument the power used by a fifty-kilowatt broadcasting station in sending a message around the world. The needle then registered 9 points of the positive side.

As the last moments of this woman's life arrived, she began to pray and praise the Lord. She asked the Lord to be merciful unto those who had despitefully used her, then she reaffirmed her faith in God, telling Him she knew He was the only power, and the only living power. He always had been and always would be. She praised God and thanked Him for His power and for her knowledge of His reality. She told Him how much she loved Him.

We scientists had been so engrossed with this woman's prayer that we had forgotten our experiment. We looked at each other and saw tears streaming down scientific faces.

Suddenly we heard a clicking sound on our forgotten instrument. We looked and the needle was registering a positive 500, desperately trying to go higher only to bounce against the 500 positive post in its attempt!

By actual instrumentation we had recorded that the brain of a woman alone and dying in communication with God had registered more than 55 times the power used by a fifty-kilowatt broadcasting station sending a message around the world.

After this we decided to try a case very unlike the first one. We chose a man lying in the research hospital stricken with a deadly social disease. His brain had become atrophied to the very point of death. He was practically a maniac.

After we had set up our instruments, we arranged for one of the nurses to antagonize the man. Through her wiles, she attracted his interest in her, and then suddenly told him she did not want to have anything more to do with him. He began to verbally abuse her, and the needle began to register on the negative side. Then he cursed her and took the name of God in vain. The needle then clicked back and forth against the 500 negative post.

By actual instrumentation we had registered what happened to the brain when that brain broke one of God's Ten Commandments, "Thou shalt not take the name of the Lord thy God in vain."

We had established by instrumentation the positive power of God and the negative power of the adversary. We had found that beneficial truth is positive, and non-beneficial things covered by the "Thou shalt nots" of the Ten Commandments are negative.

If we scientists can record these things, I believe with all my heart that the Lord God can keep a record of our thoughts."

--Dr. W. Jerome Stowell

* * * * *

CHRISTMAS

Christmas, my child, is love in action. Every time we love, every time we give, it's Christmas.

--Dale Evans Rogers

* * * * *

He who lives for himself will have small troubles; but they will seem to
him great.
He who lives for others will have great troubles; but they will seem to
him small.
That is the spirit called Christmas.

--E. Paul Hovey

* * * * *

The best thing to give at Christmas is forgiveness to your enemy; to an opponent, tolerance; to a friend, your heart; to your child, a good example; to a father, defference; to your mother, conduct that will make her proud of you; to yourself, respect; to all men, charity.

--Balfour

* * * * *

Many years ago a little girl, who was wondering about the existence of Santa Claus, wrote this letter to the New York Sun:

Dear Editor:

I am 8 years old. Some of my friends say there is no Santa Claus. Papa says if you see it in the Sun, it is so. Please tell me the truth, is there a Santa Claus?

Virginia O'Hanlow

Dear Virginia:

Your little friends are wrong.

They have been affected by the skepticism of a skeptical age. They do not believe except what they see. They think that nothing can be which is not comprehensible by their minds. All minds, Virginia, whether they be men's or children's are little.

In this great universe of ours, man is a mere insect, an ant, in his intellect, as compared with the boundless world about him, as measured by the intelligence capable of grasping the whole of truth and knowledge.

Yes, Virginia, there is a Santa Claus. He exists as certainly as love and generosity and devotion exist, and you know that they abound and give to your life its highest beauty and joy. Alas! How dreary would be the world if there were no Santa Claus! It would be as dreary as if there were no Virginias. There would be no childlike faith then, no poetry, no romance, to make tolerable this existence. We should have no enjoyment, except in sense and sight. The eternal light with which childhood fills the world would be extinguished.

Not believe in Santa Claus! You might as well not believe in Fairies! You might get your papa to hire men to watch in chimneys on Christmas evening to catch Santa Claus, but even if they did not see Santa Claus coming down, what would that prove? Nobody sees Santa Claus, but that is no sign that there is no Santa Claus. The most real things in the world are those that neither children nor men can see.

Did you ever see Fairies dancing on the lawn? Of course not, but that's no proof that they are not there. Nobody can conceive or imagine all the wonders there are unseen and unseeable in the world.

You may tear apart the baby's rattle and see what makes the noise inside, but there is a veil covering the unseen world which not the strongest man, nor even the united strength of all the strongest men that ever lived, could tear apart. Only faith, fancy, poetry, love, romance, can push aside that curtain and view and picture the supernal beauty and glory beyond.

Is it real? Ah, Virginia, in all this world there is nothing else real and abiding.

No Santa Claus?
Thank God, he lives and he lives forever. A thousand years from now, Virginia, nay, ten times ten thousand years from now, he will continue to make glad the heart of childhood.

Charles Dana
Editor

* * * * *

God Bless It

"I have always thought of Christmas time, when it has come around, as a good time: a kind, forgiving, charitable, pleasant time; the only time I know of, in the long calendar of the year when men and women seem by one consent to open their shut-up hearts freely, and to think of people below them as if they really were fellow-passengers, and not another race of creatures bound on other journeys. And, therefore, though it has never put a scrap of gold or silver in my pocket, I believe that it has done me good, and will do me good and I say, God Bless It!"

--Charles Dickens

* * * * *

A Christmas Prayer

Let us pray that strength and courage be abundant and given to all who work for a world of reason and understand; that the good that lies in every man's heart may day by day be magnified; that men will come to see more clearly not that which divides them, but that which unites them, that each hour may bring us closer to a final victory, not of nation over nation, but of man over his own evils and weaknesses; that the true spirit of the Christmas Season -- its joy, its beauty, its hope, and above all its abiding faith -- may live among us; that the blessings of peace be ours -- the peace to build and grow, to live in harmony and sympathy with others, and to plan for the future with confidence.

* * * * *

Keeping Christmas

There is a better thing than the observance of Christmas Day, and that is keeping Christmas.
Are you willing to forget what you have done for other people and to remember what other people have done for you?
To ignore what the world owes you, and to think what you owe the world?
To admit that the only good reason for your existence is not what you are going to get out of life, but what you are going to give to life?
Are you willing to stoop down and consider the needs and desire of little children?
To remember the weakness and loneliness of people who are growing old?
To stop asking how much your friends like you, and ask yourself whether you love them enough?
To try to understand what those who live in the same house with you really want, without waiting for them to tell you?
To make a grave for your ugly thoughts and a garden for your kindly feelings, with the gate open?
Are you willing to do these things even for a day?
Then you can keep Christmas.
Are you willing to believe that love is the strongest thing in the world -- stronger than hate, stronger than death -- and that the blessed Life which began in Bethlehem nineteen hundred years ago is the image and brightness

of Eternal Love?
Then you can keep Christmas.

--Henry van Dyke

* * * * *

A Different Kind of Shopping List for Christmas

One package of cooperation: This is a basic ingredient in every successful venture.

One pound of mixed nuggets of wisdom and inspiration: The shelf life of these nuggets is very short so serve fresh while still on your mind.

One bottle of enthusiasm: May be sprinkled liberally on everything you do, but it is astonishing what even a few drops can do.

One box of compromise pills: At first, these may seem like bitter pills to swallow, but they contain a magic catalyst that results in improved human relations.

One large economy carton of patience: Keep a good supply on hand -- a most useful item, and, during the holiday season, it's so easy to run short at the most inconvenient times.

A matching pair of bookends marked "Appreciation" and "Gratitude." No matter how these are used or to whom they are given, they are always welcome.

One spool of tact and understanding: Good for mending hurt feelings and patching up injured egos. Much better than Elmer's glue. Maybe you'd better get two spools while you're at it.

One do it yourself humility-hat set: This fully equipped kit has everything you need. The little humility-hat comes in all sizes and shapes. Be sure to select one size smaller than you usually wear because that's just what you need. Kit also includes one South African head shrinking device made in Japan -- guaranteed to keep little minds from getting puffed up. This is one gift you may wish to wrap for yourself. You'll be proud you did!

A gallon jug of common sense: May be combined with so many other things and in so many different ways. Can also be used as a substitute when other ingredients are not available. This is a must on your shopping list. Costs only a few cents. All stores have a large supply because most people don't keep much on hand.

One warm and comfy blanket of love: Contains no synthetic fibers. The material is actually made from natural, long lasting fibers according to an ancient pattern first used in Bethlehem and Nazareth, and then perfected along the Jordan River and up the winding road to Calvary. Even the smallest size can be wrapped around all your friends and relatives, especially at Christmas time. Because of the way it is woven, it warms the heart even before the hands. It can be used in emergencies to wipe away tears, cares and sorrows. No couple can afford to be without one, particularly on birthdays, anniversaries, and Valentine's Day. If worn constantly, it will last forever.

* * * * *

A Brother Like That

A friend of mine named Paul received a new automobile from his brother as a pre-Christmas present. On Christmas Eve, when Paul came out of his office, a street urchin was walking around the shiny new car, admiring it.

"Is this your car, Mister?" he asked.

Paul nodded, "My brother gave it to me for Christmas."

The boy looked astounded. "You mean your brother gave it to you, and didn't cost you anything? Gosh I wish..."

He hesitated, and Paul knew what he was going to wish. He was going to wish he had a brother like that. But what the lad said jarred Paul all the way down to his heels.

"I wish," the boy went on, "that I could be a brother like that."

Paul looked at the boy in astonishment, then impulsively he added, "Would you like to ride in my automobile?"

"Oh, yes, I'd love that!"

After a short ride the urchin turned, and with his eyes aglow said, "Mister, would you mind driving in front of my house?"

Paul smiled a little. He thought he knew what the lad wanted. He wanted to show his neighbors that he could ride home in a big automobile. But Paul was wrong again.

"Will you stop right where those steps are?" the boy asked. He ran up the steps. Then in a little while, Paul heard him coming back, but he was not coming fast. He was carrying his little polio-crippled brother. He sat down on the bottom step, then sort of squeezed up right against him and pointed to the car.

"There she is, Buddy, just like I told you upstairs. His brother gave it to him for Christmas, and it didn't cost him a cent, and someday I'm gonna give you one just like it; then you can see for yourself all the pretty things in the Christmas windows that I've been trying to tell you about."

Paul got out and lifted the little lad into the front seat of his car. The shining-eyed older brother climbed in beside him and the three of them began a memorable holiday ride.

That Christmas eve, Paul learned what Jesus meant when He said, "IT IS MORE BLESSED TO GIVE..."

* * * * *

The Man Who Missed Christmas

It was Christmas Eve; and, as usual, George Mason was the last to leave the office. He walked over to a massive safe, spun the dials, swung the heavy door open. Making sure the door would not close behind him, he stepped inside.

A square of white cardboard was taped just above the topmost row of strongboxes. On the card a few words were written. George Mason stared at those words, remembering...

Exactly one year ago he had entered this self-same vault. And then, behind his back, slowly, noiselessly, the ponderous door swung shut. He was trapped -- entombed in the sudden and terrifying dark.

He hurled himself at the unyielding door, his hoarse cry sounding like an explosion. Through his mind flashed all the stories he had heard of men found suffocated in time vaults. No time clock controlled this mechanism; the safe would remain locked until it was opened from the outside. Tomorrow morning.

Then realization hit him. No one would come tomorrow -- tomorrow was Christmas.

Once more he flung himself at the door, shouting wildly, until he sank on his knees exhausted. Silence came, high-pitched, singing silence that seemed deafening. More than thirty-six hours would pass before anyone came -- thirty-six hours in a steel box three feet wide, eight feet long, seven feet high. Would the oxygen last? Perspiring and breathing heavily, he felt his way around the floor. Then, in the far right-hand corner, just above the floor, he found a small, circular opening. Quickly he thrust his finger into it and felt, faint but unmistakable, a cool current of air.

The tension release was so sudden that he burst into tears. But at last he sat up. Surely he would not have to stay trapped for the full thirty-six hours. Somebody would miss him. But who? He was unmarried and lived alone. The maid who cleaned his apartment was just a servant; he had always treated her as such. He had been invited to spend Christmas Eve with his brother's family; but children got on his nerves and expected presents.

A friend had asked him to go to a home for elderly people on Christmas Day and play the piano -- George Mason was a good musician. But he had made some excuse or other; he had intended to sit at home, listening to some new recordings he was giving himself.

George Mason dug his nails into the palms of his hands until the pain balanced the misery in his mind. Nobody would come and let him out, nobody, nobody, nobody...

Miserably the whole of Christmas Day went by, and the succeeding night.

On the morning after Christmas the head clerk came into the office at the usual time, opened the safe, then went on into his private office.

No one saw George Mason stagger out into the corridor, run to the water cooler, and drink great gulps of water. No one paid any attention to him as he left and took a taxi home.

Then he shaved, changed his wrinkled clothes, ate breakfast and returned to his office where his employees greeted him casually.

That day he met several acquaintances and talked to his own brother. Grimly, inexorably, the truth closed in on George Mason. He had vanished from human society during the great festival of brotherhood; no one had missed him at all.

Reluctantly, George Mason began to think about the true meaning of Christmas. Was it possible that he had been blind all these years with selfishness, indifference, pride? Was not giving, after all, the essence of Christmas because it marked the time God gave His son to the world?

All through the year that followed, with little hesitant deeds of kindness with small, unnoticed acts of unselfishness, George Mason tried to prepare himself...

Now, once more, it was Christmas Eve.

Slowly he backed out of the safe, closed it. He touched its grim steel face lightly, almost affectionately, and left the office.

There he goes now in his black overcoat and hat, the same George Mason as a year ago. Or is it? He walks a few blocks, then flags a taxi, anxious not to be late. His nephews are expecting him to help them trim the tree. Afterwards, he is taking his brother and his sister-in-law to a Christmas play. Why is he so happy? Why does this jostling against others, laden as he is with bundles, exhilarate and delight him?

Perhaps the card has something to do with it, the card he taped inside his office safe last New Year's Day. On the card is written, in George Mason's own hand:

"TO LOVE PEOPLE, TO BE INDISPENSABLE SOMEWHERE, THAT IS THE PURPOSE OF LIFE. THAT IS THE SECRET OF HAPPINESS."

--J. Edgar Park

* * * * *

The Sixth Word

Just a week before Christmas, I had a visitor. This is how it happened. I had just finished the household chores for the night and was preparing to go to bed when I heard a noise in the front of the house. I opened the door of the front room, and to my surprise, Santa Claus himself stepped out from behind the Christmas tree. He placed his fingers over his mouth so I would not cry out.

"What are you doing..." I started to ask, but the words choked up in my throat as I saw he had tears in his eyes. His usual jolly manner was gone -- gone was the eager, boisterous soul we all know.

He then answered me with a simple statement of "teach the children." I was puzzled. What did he mean? He anticipated my question and with one quick movement brought forth a miniature toy bag from behind the tree. As I stood there bewildered, Santa said again, "Teach the children. Teach them the old meaning of Christmas -- the meanings that Christmas nowadays has forgotten."

I started to say, "How can I..." when Santa reached into the toy bag and pulled out a brilliant shiny star.

"Teach the children the star was the heavenly sign of promise long ages ago. God promised a savior for the world and the star was a sign of the fulfillment of that promise. The countless shining stars at night -- one for each man -- now show the burning hope of all mankind." Santa gently laid the star upon the fireplace mantle and drew forth from the bag a glittering red Christmas tree ornament.

"Teach the children red is the first color of Christmas. It was first used by the faithful people to remind them of the blood which was shed for all the people by the Savior. Christ gave His life and shed His blood that every man might have God's gift of Eternal Life. Red is deep, intense, vivid -- it is the greatest color of all. It is the symbol of the gift of God."

"Teach the children," he said as he dislodged a small Christmas tree from the depths of the toy bag. He placed it before the mantle and gently hung the red ornament on it. The deep green of the fir tree was a perfect background for the ornament. Here was the second color of Christmas.

"The pure green color of the stately fir tree remains green all year round," he said. "This depicts the everlasting hope of mankind. Green is the youthful, hopeful, abundant color of nature. All the needles point heavenward -- symbols of Man's returning thoughts toward heaven. The great green tree has been man's best friend. It has sheltered him, warmed him, made beauty for him." Suddenly, I heard a soft tinkling sound.

"Teach the children that as the lost sheep are found by the sound of the bell, it should ring for man to return to the fold -- it means guidance and return. It further signifies that all are precious in the eyes of the Lord. As the soft sound of the bell faded into the night, Santa drew forth a candle. He placed it on the mantle and the soft glow from its tiny flame cast a glow about the darkened room. Odd shapes in shadows slowly danced and weaved upon the walls.

"Teach the children," whispered Santa, "that the candle shows man's thanks for the star of long ago. Its small light is the mirror of starlight. At first, candles were placed on the trees -- they were like many glowing stars shining against the dark green. The colored lights have now taken over in remembrance."

Santa turned the small Christmas tree lights on and picked up a gift from under the tree. He pointed to the large bow and said, "A bow is placed on a present to remind us of the spirit of the brotherhood of man. We should remember that the bow is tied as men should be tied, all of us together, with the bonds of good will toward each other. Good will forever is the message of the bow."

Santa slung his bag over his shoulder and began to reach for the candy cane placed high on the tree. He unfastened it and reached out toward me with it.

"Teach the children that the candy cane represents the shepherd's crook. The crook on the staff helps bring back the strayed sheep to the flock. The candy cane represents the helping hand we should show at Christmas time. The candy cane is the symbol that we are our brothers' keepers."

As Santa looked about the room, a feeling of satisfaction shone in his face. He read wonderment in my eyes, and I am sure he sensed admiration for this night.

He reached into his bag and brought forth a large holly wreath. He placed it on the door and said, "Please teach the children the wreath symbolizes the eternal nature of love; it never ceases, stops, or ends. It is one continuous round of affection. The wreath does double duty. It is made of many things and in many colors. It should remind us of all the things of Christmas. Please teach the children."

* * * * *

Little Lost Angel

Long ago, on that first Christmas Eve, when the angels came out from Heaven to bring their tidings of great joy, there was a very little angel who slipped out with them. She was so little she did not sing very well, and, to tell the truth, she didn't quite understand what the angels were singing.

"Glory to God in the highest, and on earth peace, good will toward men." -- Yes, she knew about that, but what was it the beautiful big angel alone was singing?

"For unto you is born this day, in the city of David, a Saviour...Ye shall find the babe wrapped in swaddling clothes, lying in a manger."

The little angel didn't know what swaddling clothes were. And what -- oh, what -- was a manger?

Wondering, she floated down to the grassy field below her to wait until the angels finished singing and could take her back to Heaven. And in the field, huddled close together, she found the sheep that the shepherds had forgotten. They were so soft, so warm, so quiet that the little angel lay down among them and fell asleep.

When she woke up, it was very still. The big angels had gone back into Heaven, and the shepherds were hurrying to find the new baby about whom the angels had sung.

"I'm glad the big star is there," said the little angel. "But I wish the big angels had waited for me. I had better try and find them. I'm sure I can't find my way back to Heaven without them."

She straightened the crown upon her golden head and picked up her little harp which had fallen to one side. Then, gently spreading her wings, she went out onto the roadside.

"Why, there is one of the angels now," she cried and hurried to him.

But it wasn't an angel she found -- only a man, a man walking by himself, his head hung down so that he did not see even the great star.

The little angel looked at him. "Why don't you sing?" she asked.

"Sing! Why should I sing? What is there to sing about?" growled the man.

"It makes you happy to sing," laughed the little angel. She ran her fingers across the harp she was carrying and sang softly a little song. "There, isn't that pretty?"

"Very, very pretty," said the man, looking at her at last.

"Here, you take it -- then you can sing," said the little one, putting the harp into his hands. "And, please, will you tell me if the angels went this way?"

"Angels? Angels?"

"Didn't you see them?" asked the little one. "Oh, see! Isn't that one of them just beyond us?"

She flew on to look, but alas, again it was a stranger to whom she came -- a woman this time. Her clothes were rich and gay but her face was hard and sullen, and she spoke roughly to the little angel.

"Go away! Go away! I'm no fit person for a child to be seen with."

"Is it because you've lost your crown?" asked the angel anxiously. "Because if you have, you may have mine. And, please, could you tell me which way the angels went?"

"Angels?" said the woman in a startled voice.

She held the crown in her hands, and as she looked at it, long-lost tears ran down her face.

"What is this that is happening to me?" she whispered.

But the little angel had gone -- more quickly now that she had no harp to carry, no crown upon her head. So fast did she go that she almost fell upon a little boy sitting by the roadside and crying as though his heart would break.

"What is that strange sound you are making, little one?" asked the angel.

"I'm crying," the little boy told her. "I wanted to see the King -- the new King who is to be in Bethlehem tonight. But they have all gone away and left me. I'm lame, you see, so I can't walk fast, and by the time I get there, the King will be gone."

"A King!" said the angel. "I thought it was a baby."

"They said he was a King," said the little boy and he began to cry again.

"Take my wings," said the angel. "You can't walk very well so it is you who should have them."

She fastened her wings carefully to his shoulders. They were soft, fluttery things that caught the low night breezes and bore the boy forward in a gentle, rapturous motion.

"Thank you, oh, thank you," he called back, but the little angel scarcely heard him. She was trying to walk without her wings. She had not known it would be so difficult. She kept falling to the ground, and her tender feet were cut and bruised by the stones in the roadway.

"But the big star is there," she thought, as she went slowly along. "And see, a light! Is it Heaven at last?"

But it was not a light from Heaven she saw -- only candles from a home nearby.

The angel knocked timidly and stood waiting -- a little thing with pleading eyes and tangled golden hair.

A woman opened the door, then stood staring at the little angel, unable to believe what she saw.

"Peter," she whispered back into the room. "Peter, come! Do you see what I see? Oh, is it a miracle because we have prayed so long? Is this a child sent to us at last?"

She put out her hands and drew the lost angel to her. She bathed the soiled and bleeding feet and combed the tangled hair. Then she held her close and sang a low song of great joy, and the little angel closed her eyes and dreamed that she was in Heaven.

When she awoke it was morning. She had found not Heaven, but a new home and a mother and father.

They so loved her that she almost forgot she had been a little angel. She ran about the fields while the man Peter tended his sheep, and she helped the woman Dorcas make the bread and sweep the floor. She played in the meadows and vineyards with the other children, and they loved her because she was so gentle and sweet.

Many years passed, and Peter and Dorcas at last grew old and passed away. But the lost angel stayed in their home alone. Now it was she who tended the sheep and gathered the grapes and made the bread. She was friendly to all who came to her door. Many travelers knocked there and always found a welcome, food, and rest. They told her about the lands through which they had come and of the people they had met or of whom they had heard.

Many of their stories were of the great ones in the world. They told her of a poet who sang his way straight into the hearts of men. They told of a great-hearted woman who spent her life helping the poor and sinful. They told her of a leader of the people -- lame, it is true, but inspired and beloved.

And the angel heard them with a smile. She knew that the poet was the man to whom she had given her harp, that the great-hearted woman was the one who wore her crown, and that the leader of the people was the boy who had taken her wings.

--Janet Field Heath

* * * * *

Unexpected Christmas

We were well over half way to our farm in East Texas when the storm broke. Lightning flashed, thunder crashed and a tree fell with a great ripping noise. When the rain poured in such a flood that we could not see the road, my husband drove off on to what seemed to be a bit of clearing deep in the piney woods.

As we waited I sensed we would not get to the farm that night to celebrate Christmas Eve with our family. We were sitting there, miserable and dejected, when I heard a knocking on my window. A man with a lantern stood there beckoning us to follow him. My husband and I splashed after him up the path to his house.

A woman with a lamp in her hand stood in the doorway of an old house; a boy of about twelve and a little girl stood beside her. We went in soaked and dripping, and the family moved aside in order that we might have the warmth of the fire. With the volubility of city people, my husband and I began to talk, explaining our plans. And with the quietness of people who live in the silence of the woods, they listened.

"The bridge on Caney Creek is out. You are welcome to spend the night with us," the man said. And though we told them we thought it was an imposition, especially on Christmas Eve, they insisted. After we had visited a while longer, the man got up and took the Bible from the mantle. "It's our custom to read the story from St. Luke on Christmas Eve," he said, and without another word he began:

"And she brought forth her firstborn Son, and wrapped Him in swaddling clothes, and laid Him in a manger..."

The children sat up eagerly, their eyes bright in anticipation, while their father read on: "And there were in the same country shepherds abiding in the field, keeping watch over their flocks by night." I looked at his strong face. He could have been one of them.

When he finished reading and closed the Bible, the little children knelt by their chairs. The mother and father were kneeling, and without any conscious will of my own I found myself joining them. Then I saw my husband, without any embarrassment at all, kneel also.

When we arose, I looked around the room. There were no bright-wrapped packages or cards, only a small, unadorned holly tree on the mantle. Yet the spirit of Christmas was never more real to me.

The little boy broke the silence. "We always feed the cattle at 12 o'clock on Christmas Eve. Come with us."

The barn was warm and fragrant with the smell of hay and dried corn. A cow and a horse greeted us, and there was a goat with a tiny, woolly kid that came up to be petted. This is like the stable where the Baby was born, I thought. Here is the manger, and the gentle animals keep watch.

When we returned to the house there was an air of festivity and the serving of juice and fruitcake. Later, we bedded down on a mattress made of corn shucks. As I turned into a comfortable position, they rustled under me and sent up a faint fragrance exactly like that in the barn. My heart said, "You are sleeping in the stable like the Christ Child did."

As I drifted into a profound sleep, I knew that the light coming through the old pine shutters was the Star shining on that quiet house.

The family all walked down the path to the car with us the next morning. I was so filled with the Spirit of Christmas they had given me that I could find no words. Suddenly I thought of the gifts in the back seat of our car for our family.

I began to hand them out. My husband's gray woolen socks went to the man. The red sweater I had bought for my sister went to the mother. I gave away two boxes of candy, the white mittens and the leather gloves while my husband nodded approval.

And when I was breathless from reaching in and out of the car and the family stood there loaded with the gaiety of Christmas packages, the mother spoke for all of them. "We thank you," she said simply. And then she said, "Wait."

She hurried up the path to the house and came back with a quilt folded across her arms. It was beautifully handmade; the pattern was the Star of Bethlehem. I looked up at the tall beautiful pines because my throat hurt and I could not speak. It was indeed Christmas.

Every Christmas Eve since then, I sleep under that quilt, the Star of Bethlehem, and in memory I visit the stable and smell again the corn shucks, and the meaning of Christmas abides with me once more.

--Marguerite Nixon

* * * * *

The 'Little Ole' Donkey That Had Little To Say

It was the night before Christmas when all the beasts came together from the farthest places of the earth to talk. The first voice to be heard was the deep, rich bass of the lion. "I speak," he said, "as the king of beasts." And truly he looked a king with his beautiful thick mane and his tawny rippling muscles. "I won't repeat my good deeds. I shall not again tonight repeat the shining stories of the days when the Romans loved me. I shall not recall the story of the one man, Daniel, who defied me in my own den -- a story humbling to me -- which I have often told you to prove I am not proud. I shall say nothing of my stealthy fury that makes the whole continent tremble at the very sound of my name..."

"Then I shall speak," -- and by the trumpet sound, the beasts knew the elephant spoke. "I am the biggest beast on earth. My size and my strength awe nations. Yet I can walk so softly and lightly that no ear can hear my coming. Isn't that something to be proud of? And I don't believe any of you can flip a tremendous teak log over your shoulder as handily as I can. That takes power. Yes, and who else here has been a beast of war? Who else has crossed the Alps? You know how very high the Alps are! I and my strong brothers helped the famous General Hannibal and his soldiers over them in one of his great campaigns. And Hannibal's in history books all over the world."

A strange, whispering voice broke in: "You know me, the giraffe. Usually I stay silent, but I hope you'll remember I'm the tallest and can look down on you. But please don't think I am bragging because I'm up here above you. I eat from the tops of trees. Nobody else here can do that. Besides, being the tallest, I can run faster than most..."

"Let me interrupt." It was the leopard's voice. "You'd have to move pretty fast to outrun certain striped and spotted cousins of mine who hold most of the speed records. Right, cousins?" The tiger nodded his head and the cheetah, fastest of all, smiled.

The camel, till now, had been chewing his cud and watching with sad eyes. He cleared his throat and his voice rasped out: "I am neither handsome nor fleet. I have some trouble keeping clean. But I have the right to feel as proud as anyone here. I helped build the pyramids of Egypt! Have any of you ever tackled a job that big? I am also the only animal in the world that can have two humps on his back. I am used to going many days without water, across scorching sands that would burn the feet off most of you within hours. My friends, the camel counts, and I have a right to feel happy."

For a long while after the camel's speech, there was silence. Then the llama coughed and said: "I am by nature modest. One thing, however -- I, have had much experience crossing mountains. You have heard of the Andes, my home, and the war work I've done."

Others spoke too. The goose honked, "I layed a golden egg once. Who else has done that?" The turtle said, "I'm the slowest. It's better. When you go fast, you go round in circles." The fox said: "I am the slyest, the trickiest, and probably the brainiest of you all." The zebra said: "For confusion, I'm best. Am I black with white stripes or white with black?" The grizzly bear said: "Who that is as heavy as I can climb a tree as well?" And the polar bear said: "Can anybody but me swim with icebergs or catch fish with a paw?"

All this time a little grey beast stood listening. Finally, the other animals looked his way. There wasn't much he could do but speak. "I am a donkey," he began, in a voice so hoarse and low that the beasts leaned forward to hear. "I can't run fast or go days without water. I couldn't swim a stroke among icebergs. I've never climbed a tree. Nobody is afraid of me."

Lower and lower sank the little donkey's voice. His ears drooped, and his head was bowed. The other beasts could hardly hear him. Suddenly he raised his head. His eyes looked far away in time and space and there was a strange glow around him. "Only one thing I have ever done has stuck in my mind. It happened a long, long time ago...on the way to Egypt in the dark of night. I carried a mother who carried a King."

--C. Ralph Bennett

* * * * *

The Christmas Story

Jesus Christ, the Savior and the Son of God, appeared this Christmas season for a moment among the people of the world. Oh, of course, this was not the coming in which He will appear according to his promise at the end of time in all His heavenly glory, and which will be sudden "as lightning flashing from east to west." No, He visited the modern world briefly as if to catch the real spirit of man in his enlightened age. He came softly and unobserved, and appropriately, He came during the Christmas season. The multi-colored lights and trappings, the green boughs of the Yule tree, the hasty greeting of the season, and the nervous movements of crowds flowing from store to store, all signified the approach of Christmas-tide.

Perhaps the trace of a wry smile lightened His features as He thought of all this feverish activity. Truly, what was man celebrating and to what purpose? Supposedly they reveled in and paid homage to His birth. It mattered not so much that the time of celebration was altered from the actual event. What did matter was the spirit and intent engendered by the occasion. To determine the depth and direction of this spirit and intent was the purpose of His visit.

He moved silently in our midst with a gentle countenance and a smile of infinite compassion. The sun of love burning in His heart; light and power shining from His eyes. Yet, to nearly all, He is unrecognized -- but not totally so. An old man, blind from childhood, passing in the throng, touched His garments and perceived His being.

"O, Lord, heal me and I shall see," the old man cried.

And as it were, scales fell from his eyes and the blind man saw.

A child of the street, not too long from His heavenly presence, felt His influence and placed her tiny hand in His. This brief encounter with its silent exchange of knowing confidence and guileless love was reminiscent of similar occasions so long ago.

The blind man and the child shared for a brief moment what the entire world sought but was too busy to recognize.

He passed on through the madding throng, absorbing the moods of the occasion. A young couple stood in front of the music store. They were arguing rather heatedly over their financial status. These two, who were tenderly endeared to one another less than an hour ago, were now in real danger of losing that sweet feeling.

"Oh, my children," thought the Saviour. "As if the true spirit of love was measured by the cost or size of a trinket."

He recalled the story told of another couple -- the cutting of her hair to provide a watch chain -- and the sale of his watch to provide matching combs for her hair. Would that all lovers could feel this same spirit toward each other.

He passed by the unhappy opponents, fleetingly touching each in turn. Her lowered eyes, jeweled with tears, raised to meet those of her mate.

"I do love you."

"And I, you," he replied.

The young voices of a quartet emenated from the music store. The words: "All I want for Christmas is to keep the things I have."

The Saviour, seeking sanctuary from the milling shoppers, made His way into a building and became a spectator, with others, of the traditional first grade portrayal of His birth. Emerson School had enacted the nativity story each year since its founding. This year the presentation had proved like all the rest, a test for teachers to get the correct reactions from six-year-old shepherds and wise men. One problem had been particularly persistent. The little boy with the round face and the very tender heart had been asked to play the part of the inn keeper. Each practice, when the time came for him to deny the saintly Mary and the quiet Joseph a place to sleep, he would develop a quivering lip and finally break into tears. He was just not able to turn them away. Finally, the teacher in charge felt that an understanding had been reached. She had carefully explained to the weeping inn keeper that it wasn't really his fault that the inn was full. It was just completely sold out and there was nothing he could do about it. This explanation seemed to restore the necessary emotional balance and the nativity was presented. The crucial moment arrived when the inn keeper had to do this imperative duty.

"There is no...,"

A quivering lip.

"...room."

A sob, a pause, and then a half smile.

"But won't you come in for a drink of water?"

There was little wonder in the Saviour's heart as to why little children made up the bulk of His kingdom.

The department store was large and stocked to overflowing with nearly every conceivable device and need of man. The Christ made his way through the mountains of merchandise that paled the remembrances of the Phoenician bazaars and trading ships of long ago. A knot of people in one corner of the store attracted His attention. A flaxen bearded man with a red suit and black boots sat on a chair at the head of a long line of children and parents. Santa Claus looked tired and Jesus felt a distinct kinship to him, for He understood how tiring a day of requests could be.

Two little girls -- one six and the other about three -- made their way forward and essenced themselves on each knee of the bewhiskered union man. The usual pattern of question and answer followed.

"And what do you want Santa to bring you this Christmas?"

Instead of really listening to the replies, Santa was noticing the poor material and roughly patched clothing of the two. Stringy hair and pinched faces surrounded bright and expectant eyes.

"And have you been good little girls?"

Again, he failed to hear. Their stockings had long ago lost their elasticity and their shoes had disintegrated under the relentless wear given them.

Santa gave each eager pair of hands the plastic bank the store had provided for each child as a memento of the occasion. But he couldn't seem to let the experience end here. He reached into his pocket and drew forth nine coins and proceeded to place them alternately in each bank. The intense childish eyes grew wide with excitement, and Santa saw what joy even his small offering was bringing. Each coin had been received with such ecstacy that he wished each one could have been a hundred in number.

Each child had four coins in her possession and a moment of decision had arrived -- what to do with the ninth?

Santa asked, "And who should I give this last one to?"

The older and more precocious spoke with little hesitation.

"Give it to my little sister."

The Saviour saw the mist of emotion cloud the eyes of Santa Claus as he placed a kiss on two cheeks.

The Redeemer left as He had come, quietly and unobserved. He had seen and felt some of the good and the bad of the world. But He left with a confidence that right would prevail. The jarring and contending of governments seemed to be offset by the inherent good will emanating from man to man. It is true that the excessive commercial drive and intent of the Christmas season reminded Him somewhat of the money changers in a past time, but the spirit of "giving" was everywhere prevalent and dominated the commercialism found in some quarters. He noticed, too, that often the true meaning of Christmas was submerged under fable and folly. And yet, the underlying strength of the real story permeated all the other and influenced it for good.

—E. Widtsoe Shumway

* * * * *

Dear Admiral McDonald:

This letter is a year late. Nevertheless, it is important that you receive it. Eighteen people have asked me to be sure to write to you.

Last year, at Christmas time, my wife, three boys and I were in France, on our way from Paris to Nice. For five wretched days everything had gone wrong. Our hotels were 'tourist traps;' our rented car broke down; we were irritable and restless. On Christmas Eve, when we checked into a hotel in Nice, there was no Christmas spirit in our hearts. It was cold and raining when we went out to eat. We found a drab little cafe, shoddily decorated for the holiday.

Only five tables in the restaurant were occupied. There were two German couples, two French families and an American sailor by himself. In the corner a piano player listlessly strummed away. I was too stubborn, too tired and miserable to leave. I looked around and noticed that the other customers were eating in stony silence. The only person who seemed happy was the American sailor; He was writing a letter, smiling to himself. My wife ordered our meal in French. The waiter brought us the wrong thing. I scolded my wife, she began to cry, and the boys defended her. Then on my left, at the table of one French family, the father slapped one of his children for some minor fault; the boy cried. On our right, the German wife berated her husband.

All of us were suddenly interrupted by an unpleasant blast of cold air. Through the door came an old French flower woman. She wore a dripping, tattered overcoat, and shuffled in on wet, run-down shoes. Carrying her basket of roses she went from table to table. "Flowers?" No one bought any, and wearily she sat at a table between the sailor and us. To the waiter she said:

"Bowl of soup. I haven't sold a flower the whole afternoon." To the piano player she said hoarsely: "Can you imagine, Joseph, ordering only a bowl of soup on Christmas Eve!"

Joseph pointed to his empty tipping plate. The young sailor finished his meal, and got up to leave. Putting on his coat, he walked over to the flower woman's table. "Happy Christmas," he said smiling, and picking out two roses he said: "How much are these?" "Two francs, Monsieur." Pressing one of the flowers into the letter he had written, he handed the woman a 20-franc note. "I'll have to get some change, Monsieur." she said. "No ma'am," said the sailor, kissing the ancient cheek. "This is my Christmas present to you." Straightening up, he came to our table, holding the other rose in front of him. "Sir," he said to me, "may I present this to your beautiful daughter?" In one quick motion he gave the rose to my wife, wished us a Merry Christmas and departed. Everyone had stopped eating. Everyone had been watching the sailor. Everyone was sitting in thoughtful silence.

A few seconds later, Christmas exploded through the restaurant like a bomb. The old flower woman jumped up waving her 20-franc note. Hobbling out into the middle of the room she did a jig, shouting to the piano player: "Joseph, my Christmas present -- you shall have a feast too." With sudden enthusiasm the piano player began to play "Good King Wenceslas," beating the keys with magic hands, nodding his head to the rhythm. My wife waved her rose in time to the music. She was radiant, looking twenty years younger. The tears had left her eyes. She began to sing and our three sons joined in, bellowing loudly. The Germans jumped on the chairs and began singing. The waiter embraced the flower woman. Waving their arms, they sang in French. The French man who had slapped the boy beat a rhythm with his fork against a bottle and the lad climbed on his lap. The owner of the restaurant started the First Noel, and we all joined in, half of us crying as we sang. People crowded in from the street until many were standing. The walls shook as hands and feet kept time to the rousing Yuletide carols.

A few hours before eighteen people had been spending a miserable evening in a shoddy restaurant. It ended up being their happiest Christmas Eve ever. This, Admiral McDonald, is what I'm writing you about. As top man in the navy you should know about the very special gift that the U.S. Navy gave to my family, and to me and to other people in that French restaurant. Because your young sailor had Christmas spirit in his soul, he released the love and joy that had been smothered within us. He gave us Christmas.

Thank you sir, very much.

* * * * *

DEATH

Suicide is only a change of scenery. You can't get rid of you.

* * * * *

Found on an old grave stone:

"Pause, stranger, when you pass me by
As you are now, so once was I
As I am now, so you will be
So prepare for death and follow me."

A tourist put this at the bottom:

"To follow you, I'm not content
Until I know which way you went."

* * * * *

Death

He dreamed that he was lying in the room he really was in, but that he was quite well and unwounded. Many various, indifferent, and insignificant people appeared before him. He talked to them and discussed something trivial. They were preparing to go away somewhere. Prince Andrew dimly realized that all this was trivial and that he had more important cares, but he continued to speak, surprising them by empty witticisms. Gradually, unnoticed, all these persons began to disappear and a single question, that of the closed door, superseded all else. He rose and went to the door to bolt and lock it. Everything depended on whether he was, or was not, in time to lock it. He went, and tried to hurry, but his legs refused to move and he knew he would not be in time to lock the door though he painfully strained all his powers. He was seized by an agonizing fear. And that fear was the fear of death. It stood behind the door. But just when he was clumsily creeping toward the door, that dreadful something on the other side was already pressing against it and forcing its way in. Something not human -- death -- was breaking in through that door, and had to be kept out. He seized the door, making a final effort to hold it back -- to lock it was no longer possible -- but his efforts were weak and clumsy and the door, pushed from behind by that terror, opened and closed again.

Once again IT pushed from outside. His last super-human efforts were vain and both halves of the door noiselessly opened. IT entered, and it was DEATH, and Prince Andrew died.

But at the instant he died, Prince Andrew remembered that he was asleep, and at the very instant he died, having made an effort, he awoke.

"Yes, it was death! I died -- and woke up. Yes, death is an awakening!" And all at once it grew light in his soul and the veil that had till then concealed the unknown was lifted from his spiritual vision. He felt as if powers till then confined within him had been liberated, and that strange lightness did not again leave him.

* * * * *

Tommy's Prayer

In a dark and dismal alley,
Where the sunshine never came,
Dwelt a little lad named Tommy;
Sickly, delicate, and lame.
He had never yet been healthy,
Since the day that he was born;
Dragging out his weak existence,
Well nigh shoeless and forelorn.

It was just five years ago,
Since his drunken mother dropped him;
And the babe was crippled so.
He had never known the comfort
Of a mother's tender care.
But her cruel blows and curses
Made his grief still worse to bear.

There he lay within the cellar
From the morning till the night,
Starved, neglected, cursed, ill-treated;
Naught to make his dull life bright.
Not a single friend to love him,
Not a single thing to love,
For he knew not of a Savior;
Or a heaven up above.

'Twas a quiet summer evening,
And the alley, too, was still;
Tommy's little heart was sinking
And he felt so lonely, till,
Floating up the quiet alley
Wafted inward from the street
Came the sound of someone singing,
Singing -- oh, so clear and sweet.

Quietly did Tommy listen
As the singer nearer came;
Oh, that he could see the singer,
How he wished he wasn't lame.
So he called and shouted loudly
Till the singer heard the sound,
And on noting whence it issued
Soon the little cripple found.

'Twas a maiden, rough and rugged,
Hair uncombed and naked feet,
All her garments torn and ragged,
Her appearance far from near;
"So you called me," said the maiden,
"Wonder what you want with me?

Most folks call me "Singing Jessie".
What may your name chance to be?"
"My name's Tommy; I'm a cripple,
And I want to hear you sing;
For it makes me feel so happy.
Sing me something, anything."
Jessie laughed and answered, smiling,
"I can't stay here very long,
But I'll sing a song to please you,
Which I call the glory song."

Then she sang to him of heaven.
Pearly gates, and streets of gold;
Where the happy angel children
Are not starved or nipped with cold;
But where happiness and gladness
Never can decrease nor end,
And where kind and loving Jesus
Is their sovereign and their friend.

Oh! How Tommy's eyes did glisten
As he drank in every word,
As it fell from Singing Jessie;
Was it true what he had heard?
And, so anxiously he asked her,
"Is there really such a place?"
And a tear began to trickle
Down his pale little face.

"Tommy, you're a little heathen.
Why, it's up beyond the sky.
And if you will love your Savior,
You will go there when you die."
Then said Tommy, "Tell me, Jessie,
How can I the Savior love
When I'm down here in this cellar,
And He's up in heaven above?"

So the little ragged maiden,
Who had heard at Sunday School
All about the way to Heaven
And the Christian Golden Rule,
Taught the little crippled Tommy
How to love, and how to pray;
Sang a song to him of Jesus,
Kissed his cheek and went away.

Tommy lay within the cellar,
Which had grown so dark and cold,
Thinking of the little children
In the streets of shining gold.
But he hated not the darkness
Of that bleak and chilly room,
For the joy of Tommy's bosom
Could despise the darkest gloom.

"Oh! If I could only see Him,"
Thought the cripple as he lay;
"Jessie said that Jesus listens.
So he put his hands together,
And he closed his little eyes,
And in accents weak yet earnest
Sent his message to the skies.

"Gentle Jesus, please forgive me,
For I never knew before,
That you cared for crippled children
That are weak and very poor;
But I never heard of heaven
Till that Jessie came today,
And she told me all about it,
So I want to try to pray.

"You can see me, can't you, Jesus?
Jessie told me that you could,
And I almost must believe it,
For it seems so kind and good;

And she told me if I love you,
I should see you when I die,
In that bright and happy heaven,
That is up beyond the sky.

"Lord, I'm only just a cripple
And of no use here below;
For I hear my mother whisper,
She'd be glad if I would go;
And I'm cold and hungry sometimes,
And I feel so lonely, too;
Can't you take me, gentle Jesus,
Up to heaven along with you?

"Oh! I'd be so good and patient,
And I'd never cry or fret,
And your kindness to me, Jesus,
I would surely not forget;
I would love you all I knew of
And would never make a noise;
Can't you find me just a corner
Where I'd watch the other boys?

"Oh! I think you'll do it, Jesus,
Something seems to tell me so,
For I feel so glad and happy
And I do so want to go;
How I do so long to see you,
You and all the children bright;
"Come and fetch me, won't you, Jesus,
Come and fetch me home tonight?"

Tommy ceased his supplication,
He had told his soul's desire;
And he waited for the answer
Till his head began to tire;
Then he turned toward the corner
And he cuddled in a heap,
And he closed his eyes so gently,
And was quickly fast asleep.

Oh! I wish that every scoffer
Could have seen that childish face
As he lay there in the cellar,
In that damp and noisom place;

For his countenance was shining
Like an angel fair and bright,
And it seemed to fill the cellar
With a holy, heavenly light.

He had only heard of Jesus
From a ragged, singing girl;
He might well have wondered, pondered,
Till his brain began to whirl;
But he took it as she told it,
And believed it then and there,
Simply trusting in the Savior,
And His kind and Loving care.

In the morning when the mother
Came to wake her crippled boy,
She discovered that his features
Wore a look of sweetest joy;
She then shook him somewhat roughly,
But the crippled face was cold.
He had gone to join the children
In the streets of shining gold.

Tommy's prayer had soon been answered,
And the Angel Death had come
To remove him from the cellar
To his bright and heavenly home;
Where sweet comfort, joy, and gladness
Never can decrease nor end,
And where Jesus reigns eternal,
As his sovereign and his Friend.

* * * * *

The Death of a Son

There was not even a 48-hour warning between the first x-rays of Kelden's knee and the surgery which amputated his leg. When his physician-father took him for x-rays Sunday afternoon instead of waiting until Monday, I should have suspected something was very wrong. But I didn't. Kelden had suffered a sharp pain in his knee when he moved quickly, but that didn't seem anything to cause concern. I remember standing in the warm California sun that afternoon watering some ivy grown scrawny from lack of attention and thinking how peaceful was the hour -- vowing not to fret so over the small, irritating inconveniences that accompany a new move with four small children. The year in California promised to be a peaceful interlude between the completion of my husband's medical training and his beginning a private practice. But the peace was flown minutes later when father and son returned home.

A strange growth had appeared on the x-rays, and the doctors felt a biopsy should be done immediately to determine if the growth was what it appeared to be -- an osteogenic sarconia (cancer of the bone) -- a condition rarely found in children. The survival rate, even with a high amputation of the leg to prevent spreading, was not more than five percent.

I never considered that he might die. The thought that our beautiful five-year-old boy might lose his leg before his life had really begun held a terror my mind could not go beyond. We reacted that evening as our parents, themselves reared in Mormon homes, had reacted in times of illness and trouble. We first called in the elders of our church holding the authority to administer to the sick. We ourselves fearfully knelt in prayer -- and we called our parents and family to ask for their prayers and support. Because the community was new to us, we were not acquainted with the church members, but the bishop and his counselor came in response to our pleas. How can I express, as we knelt while the elders prayed, our desperate hope for an assurance from our Father that the doctors were wrong, that their fears were unfounded, and that our son would be found without disease after all. As we rose to our feet, the bishop extended his hand to us with the words we so longed to hear.

"I have never had a stronger feeling that all is well. I feel certain that when this child is examined tomorrow, everything will be right with him."

Kelden was admitted to the hospital the next afternoon for surgery the following morning. In the months that followed I learned to accept and even treasure many things -- among them were "last moments" -- moments precious because they would never be again, moments filled with words and actions that had to be recorded within the heart clearly enough to last for a lifetime of remembering. But on that August afternoon as Kelden and I shopped for a new book to read in the hospital, I still rejected the thought that never again would my son and I walk hand in hand. Nor could I treasure the moment when I tucked him in his hospital bed for the night and gave a final caress to the strong little leg.

I had not yet learned.

Both my father and father-in-law are spiritual men. My husband and I lean heavily upon their judgment. That evening after we returned home from the hospital, my father called. During his prayers that afternoon, he had received a profound feeling of reassurance that all would be well with his grandson. Later that evening my husband's father called, again expressing his feelings of peace regarding our son.

But still we feared, my husband and I.

Kelden's father knew better than anyone else close to the little boy, that the chances of a benign growth were practically non-existent. And so he, too, placed his hopes in a power greater than medical science. He fasted and prayed throughout the day and night for wisdom to make a decision -- and for a miracle. When he returned to bed in the hour before dawn after walking over and over again the streets of our neighborhood, I whispered. "What if the growth is malignant? Are we going to let them amputate? Wouldn't it be a lack of faith in the healing power of the Lord to amputate his leg?"

My husband lay a reassuring hand over mine. "Don't worry about that. As I walked home after my prayers tonight, I felt suddenly at peace and certain that all will be well."

The next morning we watched while someone rushed by on his way to the lab with tissue from Kelden's knee. "Now -- please, please don't let it be true!" Our combined energy was spent in this silent plea with God. I remembered Kelden's excitement at watching a "mixed-up television show" the doctor had promised the anesthesia would bring, and how irrestible he had been during his final examination before surgery. He had joked with the doctor, and hopped gaily from one foot to the other when he was pronounced a very healthy young man.

Then, suddenly, the waiting was over, and I knew that what I had feared in my heart was real -- the bone was infected with cancer, and the leg had to come off at once if the disease were to be stopped.

"Five minutes," the surgeon said. "I'll give you five minutes to decide. It must be done now."

"No," I insisted. "We still believe in miracles."

Why had everyone been so certain this would not be? Had we deceived ourselves? Now there was no time to think -- to prepare.

"Of course, amputate." This from the father who was also a doctor. "We have no choice but to try." And so the leg came off.

The cry "If I had only known" must have been uttered millions of times by as many lips. All the unrelenting uncertainty of mind about the decision to amputate that little leg was in truth irrelevant. If I had only known the ending of this story from its beginning, what suffering I could have saved myself and those about me. Because as it happened, that decision had no influence on the destiny of the child.

Eventually he awakened, and his questions had to be answered. His first words were, "Mommy, why don't you give me a drink of water?" Those unexpected but familiar, petulant words sounded with joy in my heart. My child had lost a leg, yet he was still my Kelly; as incredible as it seemed to me then, he was still the same impatient, determined, immeasurably dear little boy as ever he had been. At that moment I understood that we had not been deceived. All was going to be right with our son. What was the loss of a leg when he was alive and the world still before him to conquer. With his own special gifts of nature, it would be easier for him than most.

"Mommy, my leg hurts."

Oh how fervently I prayed for the words to explain and comfort.

"I know, Kelly. The leg was sick, and because we didn't want it to make the rest of you sick, the doctor had to take it off. But it's all right, son, because in a few weeks we'll get you another one -- one that can walk and run and even jump. And until then, I will be your legs. We'll go together wherever you want to go."

"Mommy, did you want them to cut if off?"

"Oh, yes, son. You're not going to be sick now. It's all right!"

He didn't cry, but he wasn't fooled. A single tear rolled down his cheek. "Can I still drive an airplane?"

And then -- "Where did they put it? They didn't use a hatchet, did they?"

His recovery from the amputation was immediate. In three days he was home and climbing to the top of the terraced lawn in back of our house, swinging with his brothers and flying his new airplane. There were times when he seemed almost gay, and times when he was silent and reflective. Although he learned to use crutches, he preferred to hop, climb, and scoot with his own remaining limbs. Hours were spent in the fitting of an artificial leg. He knew the frustration and excitement of learning to walk again, and the heartbreaking realization that the new leg would never be really the same as the old one. He insisted upon reality, and refused to even make-believe about anything he knew required two real legs. At first he was hurt and cried when his neighborhood chums tired of swinging in our yard beside him and ran into the neighboring yards to play, leaving him behind to call tearfully after them. But he learned very soon to be independent.

It was late one afternoon just four weeks after the surgery that his father came home looking bewildered and peculiarly over-tired. He seemed discouraged, I thought, but it was far more than encouragement he needed. The very pillars of his life -- his belief in a God and his own ability to communicate and receive direction from such a God -- had been toppled.

He had just come from a consultation with the radiologists, where I had taken Kelden earlier in the day for a check-up. Routine x-rays had unbelievably shown an identical tumor in the remaining leg! Our child was going to die unless some miracle intervened, and how could we expect a miracle from a God who had deceived us -- who had sent a feeling of well-being and peace to all who had prayed in the child's behalf. My husband was consumed with self-accusation -- with a feeling that he had hypnotized himself into believing what he wanted to believe. It seems naive, especially for persons knowledgeable about the medical significance of this disease, but neither my husband nor I had ever considered that Kelden might die, not since the first strong feeling of reassurance we had received in answer to our prayers.

And now he was definitely not all right. We considered for a few endless hours a high amputation of the remaining leg which would leave our son a cripple and give only a slight chance for his life. May we never know again the despair and loneliness of those hours when we believed we lived upon this earth without a supreme, interested Father to give purpose and plan to existence. It was not until we knew a little boy's trust in death and its awakening, his dignity while facing pain, that we understood the truth of the promise given us by our Father: All is well with your son. He lives forever.

There was no need to amputate the other leg -- further tests showed it was too late. And so we knew, barring a miracle, that he must die. The weeks remaining would surely be slow. And somehow, he knew, too. We drew the courage to face them from our son.

The pale, misshapen little figure lying against the white sheets, and the unused artificial leg standing in one corner of the room, spoke his story to all who entered. His flesh had withered quickly away, and the huge tumors which had crushed the bones in his shoulders rendered his arms and hands useless. Two-thirds of his abdomen was filled with bone tumor, and the skin was drawn so tightly over his face that the eyelids would no longer close. Only his eyes and lips moved. The slightest movement of the bed caused him intense pain. It had been only four months since that day he had hopped so gaily from one foot to the other. But though his beautiful body was being devoured, his mind and spirit seemed to soar. In the beginning he was very possessive of the gifts which came continually to the house for him, and was irritable because of the pain. He had been particularly so with the x-ray staff at the hospital where he received daily super-voltage therapy for pain in the remaining knee, and so his father and I were surprised when he asked, as we carried him into the hospital for his last treatment, "Do you think I make George sad? He loves me, and I'm not very nice to him. I haven't much longer to make him happy, have I?"

During a card-playing session the evening before, Kelly had looked up pleadingly at his father and asked, "What happens when you die, Daddy?" and his father had answered, "Why, you go back to live with your Heavenly Father, son." But this wasn't enough. The child knew that he would soon have to leave us, and he needed to know what would become of him. The usual childhood answers would not do. This was the first of many sessions between father and son. I don't know exactly what was said during those hours but I know that both father and son grew in courage and peace of mind. I know that Kelden was concerned with Christ's crucifixion and atonement. "How much was the hurt?" he asked. "Who helped him be so brave? Do you know if He cried?"

"If Christ still had the nail holes, will I have just one leg?"

At first he had been restless with the long prayers that we offered over him, but later on when the bishop came to see him he asked, "Would you like to say a prayer for me, Bishop?" And when we were alone, he confided, "The bishop likes to say prayers, you know. It makes him happy."

Due to the devotion of his doctor who called on him daily, we were able to keep Kelden at home with us. In spite of his illness and the continuous doses of medication, he remained lucid and eager to learn. And he prayed -- always before each injection of pain medication. He eventually needed as many as twelve a day. "Daddy," he asked, "Don't give the shot until I pray. Please hold my hands tight, Mother." And then --

"Father in Heaven:
Please help me to be brave.
Help me to stand the hurt,
And help Daddy to give a good shot.
In Jesus' name,
Amen."

Then, with little clenched fists and gritted teeth, he would call, "Okay, Dad."

Although he was not afraid of death, he clung stubbornly to his life. He said to his older brother, "Maybe I'll die, and maybe I won't." He hated terribly to leave us, more than he minded the pain, it seemed. "Mommy," he would plead, "When I go to heaven, can't you come too?"

It was few days before Christmas that Kelly suggested a ride in the car to see the lights and pick out a Christmas tree. His doctors had insisted several times that he could not last more than a few hours, but time and again he rallied, each time to increased pain, leaving his doctors at a loss to discover the source of his strength. He had received a dollar bill in the mail that morning and was delighted at the prospect of treating the family to hamburgers. We slid him gently onto a small mattress and carried it to the back of the station wagon. He winced with every movement but never cried out. "Five hamburgers," he called out in a clear voice at the hamburger stand, "And one french fry. We'll have to share it." He wanted everything as usual on this day. I helped him take a bite from the hamburger he had saved for himself. "No more today, Mother," he whispered. "Let's save it. Maybe I'll finish it tomorrow in heaven."

The next morning, Kelden's pain had become intense. "I'll try to be brave while you're putting that under me," he promised as I tried to change the sheet. But the pain was too great, and his father was not home. "I guess you'll have to give me the shot, Mom." And I began with trembling fingers, but because there was no flesh left in which to inject the needle, I tried again and again, actually bending the needle, but without success. "Oh, Kelly," I cried, "I can't do it! I can't!" Then my five-year-old son whispered to me, "Mommy, look at me. You can do it. If I say you can do it, you can do it." And I did.

Late that afternoon, after the tree had been trimmed at the foot of his bed, he died. His spirit struggled to free itself from that wasted body, and he was gone.

Oh, how empty was that room. I wrapped what was left of his little body tenderly in a blanket and held it close in my rocking chair as I had yearned so long to do. He could feel the pain no longer. And when at last I gave him up to the mortician, he received the body with tears on his cheeks.

That body had grown in four months from a child to a wasted old man. And his spirit had grown large enough to fill all of our hearts and lives with faith and expectation until we meet again.

--Carola C. Hansen

* * * * *

DETERMINATION

Nothing ever built arose to touch the skies unless some man dreamed that it should, some man believed that it could, and some man willed that it must.

--Charles F. Kettering

* * * * *

Remember: Everyone who got where he is had to begin from where he was.

--Jim Carlson

* * * * *

What is now proved was once only imagined.

* * * * *

Man is like a postage stamp. He may get licked, depressed, stuck in a corner, and sent from post to post, but he will always succeed and arrive in the right place if only he will stick to it.

* * * * *

"I am only one, but I am one...
I cannot do everything, but I can do something.
And what I can do, that I ought to do:
And what I ought to do,
By the grace of God, I shall do..."

* * * * *

Twelve Guideposts for Living

I will do more than belong -- I will participate.
I will do more than care -- I will help.
I will do more than believe -- I will practice.
I will do more than be fair -- I will be kind.
I will do more than forgive -- I will forget.
I will do more than dream -- I will work.
I will do more than teach -- I will inspire.
I will do more than earn -- I will enrich.
I will do more than give -- I will serve.

I will do more than live -- I will grow.
I will do more than be friendly -- I will be a friend.
I will do more than be a citizen -- I will be a patriot.

* * * * *

I Challenge You Not To Be Good...To Be Best

Good is
the enemy of best;
and the thing that most do not realize
is that
it is not much harder to achieve the second
than the first.
Rather
it is a question of which you expect of
yourself;
and of your ability to see adversity
not as a roadblock
but as a challenge of great interest.

Desire
is the whole point.
And what your mind sees when it looks
through the sights
of your goals
is where your effort will strike.

--Paul H. Dunn

* * * * *

You Can Win

How do you tackle your work each day?
Do you grapple the task that comes your way
    With a confident, easy mind?
Do you start to toil with a sense of dread
    Or feel that you're going to do it?

You can do as much as you think you can.
    But you'll never accomplish more.
If you're afraid of yourself, young man,
    There's little for you in store.

For failure comes from the inside first.
    It's there, if we only knew it.

And you can win, though you face the worst,
If you feel that you're going to do it.

--Edgar A. Guest

* * * * *

Concentration

In one of the laboratories in Washington there is a great sun glass that measures three feet across. It is like the "burning glasses" we use to treasure when we were boys, only much larger. This great glass gathers the rays of the sun that strike its flat surface and focuses them in a single point in space a few feet below. That single spot is hotter than a blow torch. It will melt through a steel plate as easily as a red-hot needle burns through paper. This terrific heat -- it cannot be measured, for it melts all instruments -- is just three feet of ordinary sunshine concentrated on a single point. Scattered, these rays are hardly felt, perhaps just pleasantly warm; concentrated, they melt adamant. The same principle applies to human endeavor. Scattered, a man's energies do not amount to much. Once they are focused on the task at hand, seemingly tremendous difficulties melt like snow on a hot stone. Get the habit of concentrating when you start to do a thing: throw on all the steam you have and focus every energy on the task at hand. Remember that three feet of sunshine concentrated will burn through anything.

* * * * *

Eternity Is Now

The little time we spend on earth
Is only just a wink.
Compared to all eternity
It's hardly time to think.
Three score and ten is all we have
And some of us have less.
To grow so much, to learn so much
To find true happiness.

There is no time for us to waste.
We have so much to do.
The days and years march by so fast
Even hours are to few.
"We'll prove them now herewith," He said
When placing us below,
"To see if they'll do what is right
And in every wisdom grow."

Now is the time, this is the place,
Eternity is here.
We must unto our Father's plan
Consistently adhere.
This life is real, its meaning great
And we must not forget
Our place in all eternity
We now are helping set.

Let's look ahead, yet live today
As if it were our last.
Today is ours, tomorrow hence,
And yesterday is past
So in our every effort,
Let our eyes be on a star
With eternal light to guide us
To the Majesty afar.

* * * * *

No one in our small Utah town knew where the Countess had come from; her careful precise English indicated that she was not a native American. From the size of her house and staff we knew that she must be wealthy, but she never entertained and she made it clear that when she was at home she was completely inaccessible. Only when she stepped outdoors did she become at all a public figure and then chiefly to the small fry of the town, who lived in awe of her.

The Countess always carried a cane, not only for support, but as a means of chastising any youngster she thought needed disciplining. And at one time or another most of the youngsters in our neighborhood seemed to display that need. By running fast and staying alert I had managed to keep out of her reach. But one day when I was about thirteen, as I was shortcutting through her hedge, she got close enough to rap my head with the stick.

"Young man, I want to talk to you," she said. I was expecting a lecture on the evils of trespassing, but as she looked at me, half smiling, she seemed to change her mind.

"Don't you live in that green house with the yellow trees in the next block?"

"Yes, Ma'am."

"Do you take care of your lawn? Water it? Clip it? Mow it?

"Yes, Ma'am."

"Good, I've lost my gardener. Be at my house Thursday morning at seven, and don't tell me you have something else to do; I've seen you slouching on Thursdays."

When the Countess gave an order, it was carried out. I didn't dare not come on Thursday. I went over the whole lawn three times with a mower before she was satisfied, and then she had me down on all fours looking for weeds until my knees were as green as the grass. She finally called me up to the porch.

"Well, young man, how much do you want for your day's work?"

"I don't know. Fifty cents maybe."

"Is that what you figure you're worth?"

"Yes'm. About that."

"Very well, here's the fifty cents you say you're worth, and here's the dollar and a half that I earned for you by pushing you. Now I'm going to tell you something about how you and I are going to work together. There are as many ways to mow a lawn as there are people, and they may be worth anywhere from a penny to five dollars. Let's say that a three dollar job would be just about what you have done today, except that you would do it all by yourself. A four dollar job would be so perfect that you'd have to be something of a fool to spend that much time on a lawn. A five dollar lawn is -- well, it's impossible so we'll forget about that. Now then, each week I'm going to pay you according to your own evaluation of your work."

I left with my two dollars, richer than I remembered being in my whole life, and determined that I would get four dollars out of her the next time. But I failed to reach even the three dollar mark. My will began to falter the second time around her yard.

"Two dollars again, eh? That kind of job puts you right on the edge of being dismissed young man."

"Yes'm, but I'll do better next week."

And somehow I did. The last time around the lawn I was exhausted, but I found I could spur myself on. In the exhilaration of that new feeling, I had no hesitation in asking the Countess for three dollars.

Each Thursday for the next few weeks, I became more acquainted with her lawn, places where the ground was a little high or a little low, places where it needed to be clipped short or left long on the edges to make a more satisfying curve along the garden. Then I became more aware of just what a four dollar lawn would consist of. And each week I would resolve to do just that kind of job. But by the time I had my three or three and one-half dollar mark I was too tired to remember even having had the ambition to go beyond that point.

"You look like a good consistent $3.50 man," she would say as she handed me the money.

"I guess so," I would say, too happy at the sight of the money to remember that I had shot for something higher.

"Well, don't feel too bad," she would comfort me. "After all, there are only a handful of people in the world who could do a four dollar job."

And her words were a comfort to me at first, but then, without my noticing too much what was happening, her comfort became an irritant that made me resolve to do that four dollar job, even if it killed me. In the fever of my resolve I could see myself expiring on her lawn, with the Countess leaning over me, handing me the four dollars with a tear in her eye, begging my forgiveness for having ever thought I couldn't do it.

It was in the middle of such a fever, on Thursday night when I was trying to forget the day's defeat and get some sleep, that the truth really hit me -- so hard that I sat upright, half choking in my excitement. It was the five dollar job I had to do, not the four dollar one! I had to do the job that no one could do because it was impossible.

I was well acquainted with the difficulties ahead. I had the problem, for example, of doing something about the worm mounds in the lawn. The Countess might not even have noticed them yet, they were so small; but in my bare feet I knew about them and had to do something about them. And I could go on trimming the garden edges with shears, but I knew that a five dollar lawn demanded that I line up each edge exactly with a yard stick and then trim it precisely with the edger. And there were other problems that only I and my bare feet knew about.

I started the next Thursday by ironing out the worm mounds with a heavy roller. After two hours of that I was ready to give up for the day. Nine o'clock in the morning and my will was already gone. It was only by accident that I discovered how to regain it. Sitting under a walnut tree for a few minutes after finishing the rolling, I surveyed my job. The lawn looked so good, and felt so good under my feet, I was anxious to get on with the job.

I followed this renewal secret for the rest of the day, reviewing a few minutes every hour or so to regain my perspective. Between reviews I mowed four times, two times lengthwise, and two times across, until the lawn looked like a green velvet checkerboard. Then I dug around every tree, crumbling the big clods and smoothing the soil with my hands, then finished with the edger, meticulously lining up each stroke so the effect would be perfectly symmetrical. And I carefully trimmed the grass between the flagstones of the front walk. The shears wore my fingers raw, but the walk never looked better.

Finally about eight o'clock that evening it was all completed. I was so proud I didn't even feel tired when I went up to the door.

"Well, what is it today?" she asked.

"Five dollars," I said, trying for a little calm and sophistication.

"Five dollars? You mean four dollars don't you? I told you that a five dollar lawn job was impossible."

"Oh, no, it isn't. I just did it."

"Well, young man, the first five dollar lawn in history certainly deserves some looking around."

We walked about the lawn together in the light of the evening, and even I was overcome by the impossibility of what I had done.

"Young man," she said putting her hand on my shoulder, "What on earth made you do such a crazy wonderful thing?"

I didn't know why, but even if I had, I could not have explained it in the excitement of hearing that I had done it.

"I think I know," she continued, "how you felt when this idea first came into your head, this idea of caring for a lawn that I told you was impossible to accomplish. It made you very happy when it first came, then a little frightened, am I right?"

She could see she was right by the startled look on my face.

"I know how you felt, because the same thing happens to almost everyone. They feel this sudden burst in them of wanting to do some great thing. They feel a wonderful happiness. But then it passes because they have said, 'No, I can't do it. It's impossible.' Whenever something in you says, 'It's impossible,' remember to take a careful look and see if it isn't really God asking you to grow an inch, or a foot, or a mile that you may come to a fuller life."

Since that time some twenty-five years ago, when I have felt myself at an end with nothing before me, suddenly with the appearance of the word "impossible"

I have experienced with the unexpected life, the leap inside me, and know that the only possible way lay right through the very middle of impossible.

* * * * *

This happened a long, long time ago. I never see a man limp without thinking of that day. The sky wept. No rift of brighter colour broke the drabness of it. I thought the universe wept. That was my outlook. The very times were in misery. Men were out of work. I was one of them.

I had slept the night before on the cold, cement floor of the city's jail. I slept as a tired dog sleeps, a dog worn out with a fruitless chase. All of the night before, I had walked, walked, walked -- my pride keeping me from this place. And so the day had found me walking aimlessly, looking only for food, shelter and work. This could not last forever, so that night I had stumbled down the low, narrow hallway to the jail, and been let into a barred cell with a hundred others. And there I had lain as one dead, on the cold, hard floor.

But it is the day that followed that night in the jail that you shall hear. For that was the day of my life. It was then that I found "THAT SOMETHING."

My feet were very tired. My soul wept with the sky. I stood, as in a wilderness alone, on the corner of a great thoroughfare in a great city. And then a man stopped by my side. He was of my height and build. I caught a glimpse of his face. I thought that this man might have been myself, if -- but my present need drove out reflections. And so I laid my hand on his arm.

"I am hungry," I said simply.

He turned slowly and looked at me. First his gaze took in every detail of the outer man from my water soaked cap to my poor cracked shoes. And then, through my eyes, he seemed to search my soul. I stood there abashed. I laugh when I think of that now. But then -- it was different.

"Well," he said presently, "suppose you are fed. What then?"

I shifted my weight from one tired foot to the other. "I'd try to get a job somewhere," I muttered after a moment.

"You'd try?" he asked.

"Yes, try," I answered, "although there is little chance. Nobody wants men now. I'll try, sir. But I don't care for that now, it's food I want. I'm hungry. Can you help me?"

"No," he answered, a note of pity in his voice. "I cannot help you. No man can."

"But you could feed me," I said, with some petulance in my voice.

"It's not food that you need!"

"What then?" I asked.

"THAT SOMETHING!" was his reply.

A man joined him. They began talking of matters of mutual interest. I was shuffling away through the drizzling rain, when he called me back, and handed me his card.

"Man, go find 'That Something'" he said. "And when you've found it, come to me."

"Come to you for what?" I asked.

"To thank me," was his answer, and he and his friend passed on.

I believe in miracles. There used to be such things. Man has been taught to work the miracles of today. He's given them another name. But they are miracles just the same.

There are two words that stuck in my mind. "THAT SOMETHING!"

I fell to wondering. I turned into a pool room, and found a seat. I sat there thinking. The balls on the tables before me clicked nickels away from men who could ill afford the pleasures of the place. I sat there a long, long time. There was nowhere else to go. Ahead of me I saw another night in jail. Yet the day seemed longer than the night. It was warm in there. The hum of voices, the regular click, click, click of the ivory, the occasional thumping of cue on marble floor -- all this in time developed into a dull chorus of monotony and I fell asleep.

I believe in God. I believe in miracles. I believe in visions as well. But it is only natural that I should have dreamed of "THAT SOMETHING" -- so perhaps it was neither miracle nor vision. You will think it a foolish dream. Yet it changed my life. That's reason enough for the telling. You may laugh at it scornfully. Then my dream will do you no good. You may see in it what I saw. <u>Then</u> you will take your place with the masters of men.

There were once two men who went out to find gold. Each found what he sought. The one threw what he found back into the muddy stream. The other recognized the gold for what it was. The one was a failure. The other a success. It is so in life.

And this was my dream:

I dreamed that I awoke! That is the most wonderful part of the dream. For in my dream, I realized that I had been asleep. A long, long sleep, from the very beginning of things. And I saw myself, there in the pool room, asleep. Then I saw myself start, my eyes opened and I dreamed that I saw.

"What waked me?" I asked in my dream.

"You waked yourself," answered a voice nearby.

I turned about, but no one was near. "Who are you?" I asked.

"I am 'THAT SOMETHING,'" came the reply.

"But where are you?"

"I am hidden in your soul."

For some moments I thought over what was said. "How," I stammered then, "how did you get there?"

"I was born there."

"Why have I not known you were there before?"

"No man knows it," answered the voice, "until he awakes."

"No man?" I asked. "Are you in other men's souls as well?"

"There is 'THAT SOMETHING' in every man's soul, which can move the mountains or dry the seas."

"Then," said I, "you must be Faith!"

"Yes," came the answer. "I am Faith, but I am more than Faith. I am that which makes men face the fires of Hell, and win."

"Then," said I, "you must be Confidence as well."

"I am more than Confidence. I am that which makes the babbling brooks lift worlds upon their wavelets."

"You are Power," I cried.

"I am more than Power," answered the voice. "I am that which makes the wretched failure lift himself and rule the world."

"You are Ambition, I know you now," I cried.

"Yes," answered the voice, "I am all you say, Faith, Confidence, Power, Ambition and more. For greater than all is 'THAT SOMETHING.' I am that which every man must find in his soul, or else he will be but a clutterer of the earth on which he lives."

"But how can man find you?"

"Even as you are finding me now," came the answer. "First you must awake, then seek, and when you have found, you must learn to control..."

"Control what?" I asked, confused.

"THAT SOMETHING," came the reply. "Borrow it from your soul and baptize your life with it. Anoint your eyes, that you may see; anoint your ears that you may hear; anoint your heart that you may BE!"

"But tell me," I cried frantically, for the voice was trailing off to almost nothing. "How can I do this? How? How?"

"This is the secret," came the voice to me as the whisper of a gentle breeze of springtime, "the talisman of success, which writes upon your memory in letters of fire."

"Yes! Yes! What is this talisman?"

"These words: I WILL."

And then I awoke with a start. A man was shaking me roughly.

"Clean out of here," he was saying. "We ain't running no free rooming house for bums. If you want to sleep, take a sleeper, but get out of here."

"I will," I answered unthinkingly, as I turned towards the door of the place.

"I WILL."

My words brought the dream back to me vividly. I stood in the doorway, peering out into the rain. A boy with a dozen bundles stopped near me to shift his load.

"I'll help you, son," I said, and I laughed gladly as I took half his load and started with him down the street.

"Gee mister," he said, "dat's pretty square of you, all right. How far you going this way?"

"Where are you taking these things?" I asked. He told me. "Why that's right where I'm going," I answered, in mock surprise. And so we hurried on our way. It was then the clouds overhead began to break. Before we had gone half way, the sun peeped out, and the boy by my side laughed with the pure delight of it. "By golly, mister, she's going to be some handsome day tomorrow, ain't it?"

"I will," I answered absently.

He looked up at me, startled at my answer, started to ask a question, thought better of it, and giving me another queer look, trudged on in silence. When he had delivered his packages, he turned back towards the thoroughfare, and, as I followed, he asked me, with the innocent impertinence of boyhood:

"Say mister, where do you work?"

"Why, I'm working for you right now. It's good to work, don't you think?"

"But ain't you got no steady job?"

"Yes," I answered firmly. "I WILL."

Again he cast at me his queer look, and quickened his pace. We went together to the store at which he worked. It was the largest in the city. We hurried through a doorway at the rear, and I found myself in a large room. A man stepped up to me and asked what I wanted.

"I have come here to work."

"What department?" he asked. "Who sent you?"

There were many men in there packing boxes. Before I could answer his question, someone called him and he hurried away. I took off my coat, and hung it on a nail near the door where the other men had hung theirs. I started to work, following the example of those near me. A half hour later, the man who first accosted me, passed.

"Oh," he said, as he paused behind me, "so they put you at it while I was gone, did they?"

"I'm doing my best, sir," I answered as I drove a nail home with a bang. And so I worked until six o'clock and the sun was very bright outside. When the six o'clock bell rang the men began filing by the clock.

"What about the clock?" I asked the man in charge.

"Didn't they give you a number?"

"No."

Then I told him my name, he gave me a number and I punched out.

The boy was waiting for me at the door. "How'd you get the job?" he asked curiously.

"Why, that was secured for me before I showed up there," I answered.

"Who got it for you?" he asked.

"THAT SOMETHING," was my answer.

"Aw," he answered, "quit your stringing me. How'd you get in. I seen a dozen men trying to get in on that work this morning, and they all got turned down."

"But," I explained with a smile, "they had never found 'THAT SOMETHING.'"

He again favoured me with the queer look. "Say, where do you live?" he asked finally.

"I am going to find a place now," I answered.

"Well, say," he cried, "my maw keeps a boarding house, and it's all right too. Why don't you come up to my place?"

There was but one other boarder. He was a professor of a number of ology branches at a nearby denominational college. He was a little man, with unreasonable hair on his face, and very little on his head. He wore thick glasses perched on a beaked nose. His eyes were small and black like shoe buttons. He watched me covertly as I ate. When the meal was finished, he invited me to sit with him in his room.

"I hope you don't think me prying," he said, when we were seated, "but I have been trying to figure you out."

"Yes?"

"Yes," he reiterated, "and I have come to the conclusion that you are a student of sociology."

I laughed.

"Bobby tells us you are packing boxes down at his store."

I nodded assent.

"Then," he said triumphantly, "of course, it is for the study of the conditions of the working masses that you are among down there."

"Yes," I admitted, "I am very much interested in conditions of the masses right now."

"Then you can help me," he cried. "I am writing a series of papers on that very subject. Will you answer me this please. What is it that keeps the under-dog down; what is it that the upper ten possess that the under ten thousand do not have?"

"Why, it's 'THAT SOMETHING,'" I answered.

"What do you mean? Education? Environment?"

Before my mind was flashed the picture of my boyhood. I saw my home. I remembered the tender care of my parents, the love of a mother, the guiding hand of a father. I saw myself in college, at the head of my class. I remembered that day when I was given a sheet of parchment and was told that I was a Master of Arts. And then, in the twinkling of an eye, the scene changed, and I saw that awful room, with a hundred men lying around me on the cold, hard floor.

"No," I answered, thoughtfully. "It is neither of those things. 'THAT SOMETHING' is different entirely. I don't just know what it is myself now, but I am going to find it, pin it down and then I will tell you more about it." And as I looked into his face, I noticed the same puzzled expression as the boy had worn. And so, by mutual consent, the subject was changed and we talked of trivial things.

And for a week or more I packed boxes and drove nails. I was a good packer. I made 'THAT SOMETHING' work with me all the time. One day, I noticed the shipping clerk had ahead of him more than he could handle. There were men in the department idle. They could do nothing until he checked up to them. I laid down my hammer and walked over to where he stood.

"I am to help you this afternoon," I said simply.

He looked up with a start. "Oh," he exclaimed. Then: "Well, that's good. I'm glad they have sense enough to give me somebody to help out at last." He handed me a bunch of papers, and made room for me at the desk. The superintendent of the department was out of the room at the time. Presently he returned and glanced at me curiously.

"So, they've got you helping out Dickey?" he asked.

I shrugged my shoulders without looking up, and continued figuring. When I left the room that night, the superintendent of the department joined me.

"Say," he said, as we turned up the street. "I never did just get on to how you were put in there. What's the idea? Working through to learn the business?"

"Yes," I answered with confidence. "Just that. I am to learn every detail of it."

"Well, I thought something of the kind. Which one of 'em are you kin to?"

"I do not think it wise to discuss that at this time," was my answer.

"Oh sure," he hastened to say. "I don't mean to be inquisitive. Anything I can do to help you, let me know," and then he left me.

The shipping clerk was a bright, young fellow. I liked him, and he liked me. One day, shortly after I had received my first raise in wages, he came to me with a problem. That night I stayed down with him and we worked it out together. We soon got in the habit of staying down one night of every week, and working over his systems. He lacked originality. I helped him. He had been doing things just like the fellow before him had done them. The business had been growing rapidly, practically doubled. We worked out an improved system. We drew up forms. We planned out in every detail.

One day, he carried our plans to the Man in Authority. There came up a question that the shipping clerk did not quite understand. And so they sent for me. I was well dressed at the time. Nothing flashy, nothing loud, but well clothed. That had been my first investment. My approach was far different from that of the snivelling beggar who had asked the man on the street corner for food.

The Man in Authority looked at me in surprise. "Who are you?"

I handed him my card. These cards were my second investment.

He thumbed it a moment in silence. "You are packing boxes?" he asked in surprise.

"I am in the packing room -- temporarily." And then we went over the shipping clerk's plans in detail.

"I think they're all right," said the Man in Authority finally. "I'll have these forms sent to the printer in the morning."

As we turned to leave the office, he called me back. "How long have you been in the packing rooms?"

"Sixty-three days," I answered.

"You've been there long enough. There is nothing more for you to learn there, is there?"

"No."

He studied me for a while in silence. "Funny neither of 'em has ever said anything about you to me," he said at length speaking half to himself. "I suppose the Old Man's idea was for you to work out your own salvation. Is that it?"

"In a way," I replied. "What any man accomplishes must eventually come from 'THAT SOMETHING' within him."

He pondered this for a moment. Then he scrawled a few words on a piece of paper. "Hand that to Perkins in the Auditing Department tomorrow morning, and we'll see how you show up there."

I thanked him and turned to leave the room.

"And say," calling me back the second time. "Better forget about my having said anything about your relations with the Old Man. After all, you see, it's none of my business."

"Certainly," I answered, and left the room.

Three months later, I left Bob's mother's boarding house. It hurt me to do this. She had been almost a mother to me. There was a home life about the place that I had learned to love. Even a little hairless ology professor and his fanciful theories had become dear to me. The 'THAT SOMETHING' demanded that I move on. And so I moved up the hill. I arranged for a small suite of rooms at a quiet family hotel. It was at the suggestion of the Man in Authority that I choose this hotel. It was where he lived. And so we became at first acquaintances. Then friends. He urged that I join his club. I made friends of the right sort there. All of these things were investments. And never once did the Man in Authority mention the fact that I was "learning the business."

And so a year rolled 'round. It was the time Perkins took his vacation. I was given his place until he returned. One day the Old Man came into the office. He looked at me keenly. Directly the Man in Authority also came in. The Old Man called him aside. I overheard a portion of their conversation.

"Who's the man at Perkins' desk?" the Old Man asked. The Man in Authority mentioned my name.

"Funny I never heard of him before," said the Old Man. The Man in Authority gasped. And the rest was spoken in guarded tones, and I heard no word further.

That night, the Man in Authority came into my sitting room. "Say," he began, "you've certainly got me looped or something of the sort. I have been figuring you out all along as a ward or a long lost cousin of the Old Man's. Now, today he comes in and jumps on me about putting you in this place of responsibility without first knowing all about you. Of course, I know you're all right," he added kindly. "But by Jupiter, I'm placed in a deucedly unholy kind of a light anyway."

"What's all the trouble?" I asked. "My work going wrong?"

"I should say not," he exclaimed with enthusiasm, "but that's aside from the question. What's got me going is how the dickens you did it. How you got to hold the most responsible job in the works without anybody knowing just what you really are. Tell me about yourself, will you?"

"Well," I began in a sing-song voice. "I was born of poor honest parents, in a quaint little hamlet of Virginia, where the rising sun..."

"Oh, drat the history and the rising sun. Tell me who you are kin to, or who is backing you up. It's the pull that counts these days. Who gave you your start with the company?"

I leaned back in my leather Morris chair. Memory brought back the picture of that drab day, of just a year before. And that brought to mind the card that had been given me. I had not thought of it before until that minute. I arose and went to the closet where hung the very suit I had worn on that eventful day. I had kept it as a souvenir of my awakening. And as I had hoped, the card was in a pocket of the shabby vest. For the first time, I read the name engraved thereon.

Matthew Morrison Randolph
Bonds

I handed it to the Man in Authority. He read it with wondering eyes. Now, Randolph was the silent partner of the business. Impossible coincidence? You may think so. I know men who believe success is impossible. And to them, success IS impossible. And so, perhaps, you believe this impossible. But I tell you it as it happened.

"Funny Randolph never mentioned your name to the Old Man," the Man in Authority was saying. "Anyway, I wish I'd known this when he was talking about you today."

"I'm glad you didn't," I answered with a short laugh.

"Why?" he asked, puzzled.

"Go there to the phone and call up Randolph. I think he will tell you why."

"But --" he began.

"Go on and call him up. I want you to," I insisted.

In a moment, Randolph was on the line.

"Ask him," I insisted. The Man in Authority did so.

I watched the expressions changing on his face.

"You...say...you...never...heard...of...the...man," gasped the Man in Authority. "Why, he's holding down the most responsible job on the place."

"Better let me talk to Mr. Randolph," I interrupted. His hand was trembling as he surrendered the phone. "Mr. Randolph," I said. "I know you do not remember my name, for I am quite sure you have never heard it. You may, however, remember one miserable day, one year ago, when a beggar asked you for food."

"Well, go on," came a crisp voice over the phone.

"You may also remember telling that beggar that it was not food he needed. You told that man that it was 'THAT SOMETHING.' I have learned to use it, and I want to thank you for having shown me the way. When may I have the opportunity of telling you about it?"

An hour later, the story you have just heard was told to a strange trio: the man in Authority, the Professor of ologies and Matthew Morrison Randolph. From time to time, as I told the tale, Randolph nodded his head in approval, and I noticed a strange light begin to glow in the little professor's eyes. When I had finished, we sat for a long time in silence, broken at last by Randolph, who said:

"And now tell me just what you think 'THAT SOMETHING' really is."

I shook my head in dismay. "You folks know as much as I do about it," I answered. "But of this one thing I am convinced, through and through. It is real POWER, as truly as the electric current. It is the power of the inner man, the fuel of the soul machine. It is the one thing necessary. We are all of us born much alike. We come into the world all animals of a type. All of us have senses, equally developed. And then we begin to live, animals all. Until we wake 'THAT SOMETHING' of the soul, we live as a horse lives. We bear on our muscle those that have found 'THAT SOMETHING.' And we bear them on up the mountain, to take their places among the masters of men.

'THAT SOMETHING' lies dormant in every soul until aroused. With many, it sleeps until the last great sleep. Sometimes it does not wake until man stands tottering on the border of the grave. Sometimes it is found by the child, playing by its mother's knee. Some men have sneered, and called it luck. Luck is but the fleeting smile of Fortune. 'THAT SOMETHING' is an awful force. A man's success depends alone on 'THAT SOMETHING,' 'THAT SOMETHING' OF HIS SOUL.

Abraham Lincoln found it when a lad. It warmed the cold floor on which he lay and studied. It added light to the flickering glow of the wood fire, that he might see to read. It spurred him on, and on, and on.

'THAT SOMETHING' is the highway to her home. It made of a puny Corsican the Ruler of the World! It made of a thin chested bookkeeper the money king of a great country! It made of Edison the greatest man of his age! It made Carnegie! It made Woodrow Wilson! It made Roosevelt! It can make YOU! And it is NOW IN YOUR SOUL! Awake it -- NOW! 'THAT SOMETHING.'"

Again the silence followed. I watched the Professor of many ologies. I saw the kindled fires in his eyes gradually die out. He shook his head wearily.

"No, it can't be done, it can't be done," he murmured. "I have drunk deeply of the cup of life, and I am now drinking of the dregs. The cup is filled but once, and when it's gone, there's nothing left but the dregs of old age and poverty."

"You fool," cried Randolph, leaning forward and shaking the little man roughly. "You almost had 'THAT SOMETHING' in your power, and now you sing it back to sleep with your silly song of pessimism. It's the false philosophy that such as you sing, which has kept men in the ruts of their own digging for centuries past. Wake man, wake! Wake 'THAT SOMETHING' in your power, within your own soul.

The two men sat looking deeply into each other's eyes. It was the little man who broke the silence. "Thank you, Randolph," said he quietly. "You are right. I WILL!"

Then Randolph turned to me. "Man, write that story you've told us. Write it so that every man may read. Send that message out into the world. If men will read that story: read and re-read, until it is written on their memories, if men will believe the message you bring, and then if they will but awake 'THAT SOMETHING' within their souls that now lies asleep -- I say if you can make men do this, you will have done more for mankind than any man or thousand men have done in many, many years. Write it, man, write it word for words as you have told it here, so every man may read. Write it, man, write it!"

And so it has been written.

And you who have read it through, I pray that you may read it every word again and again, and 'THAT SOMETHING' of your souls may have been aroused, and you have taken your places among the Rulers of the World.

THE END
WHICH IS THE BEGINNING

* * * * *

ENDURANCE

That which we persist in doing becomes easy to do.
Not that the nature of the thing has changed, but the ability to do has increased.

* * * * *

You can eat an elephant, if you just eat him a bite at a time.

* * * * *

Limitations are self-imposed. No one ever fails without self-consent.

* * * * *

All things are difficult before they are easy.

* * * * *

No one ever collapsed under the burdens of a single day. It is when the burdens of tomorrow are added to it that it becomes unbearable. Live one day at a time.

* * * * *

The will to persevere is often the difference between failure and success.

--David Sarnoff

* * * * *

From one of the company mills, Charles M. Schwab, the personal steel magante, once telegraphed his immediate superior, Andrew Carnegie:

"All records broken yesterday"

Instead of a congratulatory message, back came the soul-searching reply:

"But what have you done today?"

* * * * *

A little more persistence, a little more effort, and what seemed hopeless failure may turn to glorious success. There is no failure except in no longer trying. There is no defeat except from within, no really insurmountable barrier save our own inherent weakness of purpose.

--Hubbard

* * * * *

Endurance

Little Jane, just out of bed one morning, was crying as though her heart would break. Her mother came hurrying to ask, "Jane, what in the world is the matter?" Sobbing, she answered, "I was just thinking. I'll have to put on my clothes every day as long as I live."

* * * * *

Judgment

You call me master and obey me not.
You call me light and seek me not.
You call me way and walk me not.
You call me life and desire me not.
You call me wise and follow me not.
You call me fair and love me not.
You call me rich and ask me not.
You call me eternal and seek me not.
You call me gracious and trust me not.
You call me mighty and honor me not.
You call me just and fear me not.
If I condemn you -- blame me not.

* * * * *

Achievement

It took Michelangelo twelve years -- one brush stroke at a time -- to paint his Biblical scenes in the Sistine Chapel. It took Brahms twenty years -- one note at a time -- to compose his First Symphony. It took Edmund Hillary and Tenzing Norgay eighty days -- one step at a time -- to climb the 29,000 feet of Mount Everest. Word by word, brush stroke by brush stroke, note by note, step by step, problem by problem, prayer by prayer -- this is the secret of achievement.

* * * * *

Stick to your task,
Till it sticks to you.
Beginners are many
But enders are few.
Honor, power, place and praise,
Will come in the time of him who stays.

Stick to your task,
Till it sticks to you.
Bend at it, sweat at it, smile at it too.
For out of the bend, the sweat and the smile,
Will come life's victories after a while.

* * * * *

Playing The Game

Whatever the game, and whatever the odds,
The winning is all up to you;
For it isn't the score, and it isn't the prize,
That counts when the playing is through!
In the great game of Life, it's the purpose to win,
And the courage to fight to the end,
That determines for you what degree of success
Will be scored to your credit, my friend.
The best you can do may not be quite enough
To defeat your opponents today;
But you never can lose, and you never can fail,
If you "put all you've got" in your play;
And the greatest reward that you efforts can bring,
Is the fact that you stood to the test --
That you played a clean game, and you fought a good fight,
And you always were doing your best!

--Steward Warnerite

* * * * *

Persistence

In 1831 he failed in business. A year later he was defeated for a seat in the legislature. A year after that he failed in business again. Finally, in 1834, he was elected to the Legislature only to suffer a nervous breakdown two months later. Then in the next ten years before he was elected to Congress, he was defeated in an election for Speaker, Elector, Land Officer and Congressman. Once elected to Congress in 1846 he was defeated for re-election in 1848. In 1855, he failed to gain a seat in the senate, and in 1856 he was defeated for Vice President. Again in 1858 he failed to be elected a Senator. But, finally, in 1860 he was elected President! Yes, he was Abraham Lincoln.

* * * * *

"Nothing in the world can take the place of persistency and concentration on one thing at a time. Talent will not; nothing is more common than unsuccessful men with talent. Genius will not; un-rewarded genius is a proverb. Education will not; the world is full of educated derelicts. Persistence and determination alone are omnipotent. The watchword "Hand On" has solved and always will solve problems of the human race."

--Calvin Coolidge

* * * * *

The Journey

I started on a journey, not many years ago,
Just where the road would lead me, I really
did not know.
I left my Father's house that day; I was anxious
yet afraid.
I knew that I must leave him, for the plans had
now been made.
So I took myself a body and started on my way,
Down the road of Eternity and hoped I would not
stray.
At first the road was very clear, I walked along
with ease.
It wasn't going to be so hard. My Father would
be pleased.
Then I saw the path of pleasure, it looked so
nice and gay,
It wouldn't hurt to stop awhile, because I need
not stay.
There were paths in all directions, it was very
hard to choose.
"Why not try them all?" I thought, "I surely
could not lose."
I saw the path of evil that's laid out for the
weak.
I simply couldn't pass it by without a little
peek.
And then the path of worldly gain, it looked like
such high style.
I simply had to linger on for just a little while.
By now I was so weary I surely needed rest,
So I took the path of discouragement, to see if
it were best.
I rested there for a while, but found no peace
of mind.

And so I started on again to see what I could find.
And as I walked along one day, I was as weary
    as could be.
I wondered why it was so hard, I simply could
    not see.
I thought of all the steps I took and all the
    paths I'd tried,
And wondered why it was so hard to find the
    path to God.
Then suddenly I realized that the road was
    straight and fine,
And all those little side trips were just a
    waste of time.

* * * * *

I Would Be Worthy

I thank thee, Lord, that thou hast called me "son,"
And fired my soul with the astounding thought
That there is something of thee in me.
May the prophecy of this relationship --
    Impel me to be worthy.

I am grateful for a covenant birth;
For noble parents and an ancestry who beckon me
To heights beyond my grasp, but still attainable
If with stamina and effort I cultivate their seed --
    And prove that I am worthy.

I am grateful for a companion on this Eternal Quest,
Whose roots and birth and vision match my own;
Whose never-failing faith and loyalty have furnished light in darkness,
    Inspire me to be worthy.

I am grateful for the cleansing power of parenthood,
With its self-denial and sacrifice -- prerequisites to filial and parent love:
For each child entrusted to our care, I humbly thank thee;
If I would associate with them eternally,
    I know I must be worthy.

I am grateful for the one who was recalled in youth,
For his love and loyalty and sacrifice.
May the memory of his clean and manly life keep resolute the hope
That I may renew companionship with him -- and thee;
    For this I would be worthy.

I am grateful for the children of my children.
And, in anticipation, for others yet to be.
Keep alive, I pray, within my bosom, a sense of obligation unto them.
To pass a name unsullied as it came. To become an honored sire.
O make me worthy!

I am grateful for the lifting power of the gospel of thy Son;
For the knowledge thou hast given me of its beauty, truth and worth.
To attain its promised glory, may I to the end endure,
And then, forgiven, let charity tip the scales and allow me
To be considered worthy.

--Hugh B. Brown

* * * * *

Give Thanks for the Hard Things In Life

There are those who give thanks for the pleasures
And comforts which come to their door;
But repine at the trials and hardships,
And complain that their burdens are sore.

There are souls who accept all the bounties
Bestowed by One gracious and just:
But lament if the road is o'ershadowed
Or obscured by the storm and the dust.

Shall we then, accept only the good things,
The ones which are easy to bear:
And revile at the fate which requires us
To remove from the path thorn and snare?

Not alone for the easy and pleasant
Should our praise and thanksgiving ascend;
For the Father in sending us trials.
But proves He's more truly our friend.

Not to each comes the same kind of troubles.
Yet hardships we surely must bear
If we are to prove our true mettle.
And pure gold is always too rare.

So let us give thanks for the heartaches,
For the briar-strewn way and the tear;
They are stepping-stones higher and farther,
They are helping us grow year by year.

And instead of lamenting and grieving
When difficult things come our way.
Let us fasten our armour the closer
And cheerfully, calmly obey.

Thank God for the beauty of labor;
The glory which follows the strife;
For the strength which is born of our weakness --
Thank God for the hard things in life!

--Nancy Smith Lowe

* * * * *

ESPECIALLY FOR MORMONS

Fasting

Fast day means many different things to different people, but I had never heard this one before. Just after testimony meeting was over, someone said, "Well, let's go home and celebrate the feast of the fast over."

* * * * *

Church Work

Who is this stranger, Mother dear?
Ain't he funny, ain't he queer?
Hush my child, don't ramble so.
He's your father, don't you know?
He's my father? No such thing!
Father passed away last spring.
No, he did not die, dear chick,
Your father joined the bishopric.
Now he meets and meets and meets.
He has no time for sleep or eat.
He at funerals must preside,
He must kiss the pretty bride,
There are meetings every day,
Welfare, Priesthood and MIA,
Sunday School and picture show,
Or what have you, he must go.
Kiss him darling, he won't bite.
Let us treat this stranger right.

* * * * *

Candles of Light

Candles of Light, traveling by twos,
Visiting each house, chasing the blues,
Teaching the Gospel, spreading their light,
Shining examples of lives that are right.

Unselfishness and kindness kindle the flame,
Friendship's the wax that cradles the same,
The Gospel's the wick that runs it's way through.
Leaving it's message, old yet new.

Candles of Light traveling this way,
Can lighten the load of a dreary day,
Or cast the shadows from the darkest night
And make all earth seem more bright.

Yes, visiting teachers are candles of light,
Spreading their rays o'er all in their sight,
Rays of smiles and hope and cheer
May they shine eternally, year after year.

--Elsie Jones

* * * * *

"If"
For Relief Society Visiting Teachers

IF you can love each woman that you visit,
Because she is a mother of a home;

IF you can find in each a lovely virtue --
Then finding it -- be sure to pass it on;

IF you can disregard the littered parlor
Or dirty dishes that you're sure to find;

But take your message to the one who lives there
And make her feel you're friendly, wise and kind.

IF you can sympathize where there is sorrow,
Can calm the troubled waters where there's strife;

IF you can make her know that her tomorrows
Hold more than just the struggles of this life;

IF you can help wherever help is needed,
Can share with her her joys, as well as tears;

IF you can leave one thought or inspiration
For her to carry with her through the years.

IF she can confide in you when she's troubled,
And know that you, her confidence will keep;

IF you can help a tired or weary Mother
To make a bed, or rock a child to sleep;

IF you can do these things, and all the others
That I am sure are there for you to do,

Yours is a mission not unlike the Master's
And blessings will be given unto you.

* * * * *

A Letter From The Devil

Bottomless Pit
Brimstone Avenue
Hell

Dear Members:

I visited the Relief Society meeting last Tuesday and I was overjoyed that so many of you had not come. I heard the lesson which was not well prepared and the visiting teachers reported they had made few visits or contacts with the members the past week. That made my heart leap for joy.

I was thrilled last Sunday when I visited your Sunday School and saw such a small number present. I saw so many families hurrying away to go on picnics and outings and I knew that they would not return for Sacrament Meeting because they would be too tired when they got back home. I always tremble when they attend Sacrament Meeting because there they get their soul fed and some will give their hearts to the Lord and will not listen to my counsel. It is always helpful to me when the members dodge their responsibilities.

Then, too, I laughed with joy when I saw so many of you fail to pay your tithing and fast offerings. I like to see you make your Bishops squirm and worry about finances. It takes away from them the time they could be using to win souls for the Lord.

The Primary is the one I like to watch best. They are young and if I can get them now, I may be able to keep them. If you don't go to MIA, then the President will become discouraged and that is one of my best tools. I use it more than any of the others. When the sisters stay away from Relief Society, I know I'm getting results. This way they don't set the proper example, and they don't become good mothers -- this way I can get the children to listen to me.

Remember your TV shows and how comfortable it is at home. Please stay away from all these meetings. It makes my work much more pleasant. Hope to have you all with me soon.

The all-wise deceiver,

Lucifer

* * * * *

Your Good Name

A number of years ago I was seriously ill. In fact, I think everyone gave me up but my wife. With my family I went to St. George, Utah, to see if it would improve my health. We went as far as we could by train, and then continued the journey in a wagon, in the bottom of which a bed had been made for me.

In St. George we arranged for a tent for my health and comfort, with a built-in floor raised about a foot above the ground, and we could roll up the south side of the tent to make the sunshine and fresh air available. I became so weak as to be scarcely able to move. It was a slow and exhausting effort for me even to turn over in bed.

One day, under these conditions, I lost consciousness of my surroundings and thought I had passed to the Other Side. I found myself standing with my back to a large and beautiful lake, facing a great forest of trees. There was no one in sight, and there was no boat upon the lake or any other visible means to indicate how I might have arrived there. I realized, or seemed to realize, that I had finished my work in mortality and had gone home. I began to look around, to see if I could not find someone. There was no evidence of anyone's living there, just those great, beautiful trees in front of me and the wonderful lake behind me.

I began to explore, and soon I found a trail through the woods which seemed to have been used very little, and which was almost obscured by grass. I followed this trail, and after I had walked for some time and had traveled a considerable distance through the forest, I saw a man coming towards me. I became aware that he was a very large man, and I hurried my steps to reach him, because I recognized him as my grandfather. In mortality he weighed over three hundred pounds, so you may know he was a large man. I remember how happy I was to see him coming. I had been given his name and had always been proud of it.

When Grandfather came within a few feet of me, he stopped. His stopping was an invitation for me to stop. Then -- and this I would like the boys and girls and young people never to forget -- he looked at me very earnestly and said:

"I would like to know what you have done with my name."

Everything I had ever done passed before me as though it were a flying picture on a screen -- everything I had done. Quickly this vivid retrospect came down to the very time I was standing there. My whole life had passed before me. I smiled and looked at my grandfather and said:

"I have never done anything with your name of which you need be ashamed."

He stepped forward and took me in his arms, and as he did so, I became conscious again of my earthly surroundings. My pillow was as wet as though water had been poured on it -- wet with tears of gratitude that I could answer unashamed.

I have thought of this many times, and I want to tell you that I have been trying, more than ever since that time, to take care of that name. So I want to say to the boys and girls, to the young men and women, to the youth of the Church and of all the world; Honor your fathers and your mothers. Honor the names that you bear, because some day you will have the privilege and the obligation of reporting to them (and to your Father in Heaven) what you have done with their name.

--George Albert Smith

* * * * *

The Necessity of Having the Holy Ghost

I am pleased to meet with so many of our friends this morning, and I feel desirous to talk to you upon a principle that I very seldom dwell upon before the congregations of the Saints. I have had my mind somewhat exercised of late on various things, perhaps for purposes known to the Lord better than myself, though they are principles we are all more or less acquainted with.

One of the Apostles said to me years ago, "Brother Woodruff, I have prayed for a long time for the Lord to send the administration of an angel to me. I have had a great desire for this, but I have never had my prayers answered." I said to him that if he were to pray a thousand years to the God of Israel for that gift it would not be granted unless the Lord had a motive in sending an angel to him. I told him that the Lord never did nor never will send an angel to anybody merely to gratify the desire of the individual to see an angel. I said to him that these were my views. The Lord had sent angels to men from the creation of the world, at different times, but always with a message or with something to perform that could not be performed without. I rehearsed to him different times when angels appeared to men. Of course, I referred to the last days an angel would fly in the midst of heaven, having the everlasting Gospel to preach to them that dwelt on the earth. The reason it required an angel to do this work was the Gospel and the Priesthood had been taken from among men. Hence, God had to restore it again.

Now, I have always said, and I want to say it to you, that the Holy Ghost is what every Saint of God needs. It is far more important that a man should have that gift than he should have the ministration of an angel, unless it is necessary for an angel to teach him something that he has not been taught.

I am going to refer to some of my own experiences with regard to the ministration of angels and that operation of the Holy Ghost. I have never prayed for the visitation of an angel, but I have had the ministration of an angel several times in my life.

One visitation I received in Kentucky, at the house of A. O. Smoot's mother, while on my first mission. I went through Jackson County into Arkansas Territory, and from Little Rock waded the Mississippi swamp 180 miles to get across into Tennessee. I arrived in Henry County, Tennessee, on the west at the same time that David Patten and Warren Parrish landed in that region on the north. We met and labored together for a while and built up some churches there. I then held the office of a Priest. I traveled thousands of miles and preached the Gospel as a Priest, and, as I have said to congregations before, the Lord sustained me and made manifest His power in the defense of my life as much while I held that office as He has done while I have held the office as an Apostle. The Lord sustains any man that holds a portion of the priesthood, whether he is a Priest, an Elder, a Seventy, or an Apostle if he magnifies his calling and does his duty.

I will give you an instance of the Lord's protecting care over me while I was a Priest. I had this experience while in Arkansas with my companion who was an Elder. There was a man in the country who with his wife, and five sons had been in Jackson County. His wife died there. The old gentleman was in the faith apparently when he left there. He was driven out the same as the rest of the Saints were, and some of his sons were shipped with hickory gads in the persecution there. I knew he was in this Arkansas county, and I felt anxious to go and see him, as he was the only Latter-day Saint that we knew anything about in that region. The night before I got there I had a peculiar dream. I dreamed that an angel appeared to us and pointed out a certain path that we must follow, and that the blessings of God would attend us in following that path. As we went along this path, we came to a log cabin with a wall on each side ten or fifteen feet high. This road led right through that building. When I went to the door and opened it, it was full of serpents. My companion said he was not going into that room for anything or anybody. "Well," says I, "I am, or I'll die trying. The Lord told us to follow that path, and I am going to walk in it, unless I am stopped by some power that I know not of." I stepped into the door. Those serpents all arose up ready to jump on me and there was a very large one in the middle of the floor that made a pass at me. It appeared to me as though I would be destroyed, but when the serpent reached near to me it dropped dead, and they turned black and burst open, after which they took fire and burned up, and both of us went through safely. The morning after, we arrived at this man's house; his name was Akeman. It was Sunday morning, and we went into the house; Mr. Akeman and his daughter were at breakfast. His sons were settled in cabins around him. We sat down, but there seemed to be a peculiar spirit in the place. I finally stepped up to the mantelpiece on which I saw a Book of Mormon. I picked it up and said, "Brother Akeman, you've got a very good book here." He said, "It's a book that came from hell." I then began to understand a little of what lay before us. He had apostatized. He cursed everything and everybody -- Joseph Smith, Lyman Wight, the Apostles, and a good many whom he also named. He was very angry. I inquired about his sons. He said they were settled around him there. Well, we took up our valises and left. I looked up one of his sons, the youngest, I believe, and the only one that was in the faith, and he was like a drowning man; but my praying with him he got the Spirit of the Lord in him, and we had a pretty good time with him. We told him of our experience at his father's, and I said we were desirous to have some meetings there if we could. He said he did not know; his father had apostatized and was at war against everything that was Mormon. He told us, however, where an old gentleman lived close by to whom he had loaned a Book of Mormon. He was an aged man and his wife was an aged woman. Their name was Hubbard. We went to see them and they were very glad to receive us. In the morning my companion said he was going to leave the place. Of course, he was an Elder and I was only a Priest, and we generally suppose that the lesser should obey the greater; but I said to him, calling him by name, "You are not going to leave here, nor I either; we shall both of us stay here till I see the fulfillment of my dream. It is here, and I am going to stay and see it, and you will too." It is not natural for me to take a stand of that kind, but I felt led to do it upon that occasion. We stopped there three weeks and cleared land for father Hubbard, while he fed and housed us. Three times while we were there I was warned of the Lord to go and warn this Mr. Akeman. The last warning I received from the Lord was on Saturday night of the third week. I went up to his house which was about three-quarters of a mile distant, and when I got there his daughter stood in the doorway. I walked in and saluted him. He was walking the room, but did not say anything to me. I told him the Lord had sent me to pay him a visit. Then he made some exclamation that was rather profane. I sat down and commenced warning him. I told him that he had apostatized from the Gospel of Christ; he had had the Priesthood and he was pursuing a course that would send him to destruction, and the judgments of God would overtake him. Well, he raged like a demon. That is about all I said to him. I certainly did not stay long, but I delivered my message. When I left the house he followed me, and when he came to where I was he fell dead at my feet as though he had been struck with a thunderbolt from heaven. He was a very large man and he turned as black as an African and his skin seemed almost to burst open. The next day I attended his funeral. But had raised a mob and had sent for them to come and drive us out of the country or hang us, and they had sent warning to us to leave. The consequence was there were some fifteen or twenty deaths during my stay there. Many were taken with what was called pleurisy. Doctors came in and opened a vein, and they died in five minutes. One of these men sent for me, and I went and saw him. Two men were holding him. He said to me, "I wish you would cut open my side; I have a pain here and it is skin deep. You can cut it out and save my life." I looked at him, but did not say anything to him. I said to myself, "If your eyes were open, you would see the angel of death standing by your side." He died while I was there. After this my partner left me and I went alone to Memphis, Tennessee, and met with Brothers Patten and Parrish.

After laboring in that part for a length of time, I received a letter from Joseph Smith and Oliver Cowdery, in which they requested me to stay in that country and take charge of the churches that we had built there. The Prophet promised me many things and said I should lose no blessings by tarrying in that country and doing as he wished me and letting the other brethren go and get their endowments. I was then at the house of Brother Abraham O. Smoot's mother. I received this about sundown. I went into a little room where there was a sofa to pray alone. I felt full of joy and rejoicing at the promises God had made to me through the Prophet. While I was upon my knees praying, my room was filled with light. I looked and a messenger stood by my side. I arose and this personage told me he had come to instruct me. He presented before me a panorama. He told me he wanted me to see with my eyes and understand with my mind what was coming to pass in the earth before the coming of the Son of Man. He commenced with what the revelations say about the sun being turned to darkness, and moon to blood, and the stars falling from the heaven. Those things were all presented to me one after another, as they will be, I suppose, when they are manifest before the coming of the Son of Man. Then he showed me the resurrection, of the dead -- what is termed the first and second resurrection. In the first resurrection I saw no graves nor anyone raised from the grave. I saw legions of celestial beings, man and woman, who had received the Gospel all clothed in white robes. If the form they were presented to me, they had already been raised from the grave. After this he showed me what is termed the second resurrection. Vast fields of graves were before me, and the Spirit of God rested upon the earth like a shower of gentle rain, and when that fell upon the graves they were opened, and immense host of human beings came forth. They were just as diversified in their dress as we are here, or as they were laid down. This personage taught me with regard to these things. Among other things he showed me, there were seven lions like burning brass placed in the heavens. I asked the messenger what they were for. He said they were representative of the different dispensations of the Gospel of Christ to men and they would all be seen in the heavens among the signs that would be shown. After this passed by me, he disappeared. Now if I had been a painter, I could have drawn everything that I was able to see. It made an impression upon me that has never left me from that day to this. The next day we had a meeting in the academy. Brother Smoot and some others went with me; but I was a lost man. I hardly knew where I was so enveloped was I in that which I had seen.

I refer to this as one of the visitations that was given me in my boyhood, so to speak, in the Gospel. I was a Priest at the time. Of course, there was a motive in the personage visiting me and teaching me those principles. He knew a great deal better than I did what lay before me in life. It was doubtless sent to me for the purpose of strengthening me and giving me encouragement in my labors.

The other instance I want to refer to is what I spoke about at the recent General Conference. I need not dwell particularly upon this now; but I had a motive in laying it before the people on that occasion. The history of Brother Kimball's operations with these evil spirits in England is before the Church. And while on this point, I want to correct a mistake that I made in referring to this matter at our General Conference. I said Brother Kimball rebuked those evil spirits from Brother Hyde, when in fact, it was Brother Kimball who was afflicted with those evil spirits and Brother Hyde administered to him. As this is a matter of history, I wish to state it correctly, and therefore make this explanation. When Brother Kimball, Brother George A. Smith and myself went to London, we encountered these evil spirits. They sought to destroy us. The very first house that was opened to us was filled with devils. They had gathered there for our destruction so that we should not plant the Gospel in that great city. Brother Kimball went to Manchester on some business, and left Brother George A. Smith and myself there. One night we sat up till eleven o'clock, talking Mormonism, and then we went to bed. We had only must laid down when these spirits rested upon us, and we were in a very fair way of losing our lives. It was as if a strong man had me by the throat, trying to choke me to death. In the midst of this a spirit told me to pray. I did so, and while praying, the door opened, the room was filled with light and three messengers came in. Who they were I know not. They came and laid their hands upon us, and rebuked those powers, and thereby saved our lives. Not only so, but by the power they held they rebuked the whole army of devils that were in that great city, and bound them so that they have never troubled any elder from that day to this.

Now these messengers were sent to us because it was necessary. We would have lost our lives if somebody had not delivered us. We needed help, and we could not get it anywhere else.

This is all I want to say with regard to the administration of angels to myself. This apostle that I refer to told me he had prayed and prayed for the administration of angels. Well, if it had been necessary to save his life, as it was in my case, he would have had the administration of angels. But, he had access to the gift of the Holy Ghost, as all of us have. And that, brethren and sisters, is what I want to talk to you about.

One morning, while we were at Winter Quarters, Brother Brigham Young said to me and the brethren that he had had a visitation the night previous from Joseph Smith. I asked him what he said to him. He replied that Joseph had told him to tell the people to labor to obtain the Spirit of God; that they needed that to sustain them and to give them power to go through their work in the earth.

Now I will give you a little of my experience in this line. Joseph Smith visited me a great deal after his death, and taught me many important principles. The last time he came was while I was in a storm at sea. I was going on my last mission to preside in England. My companions were Brother Leonard W. Hardy, Brother Milton Homes, Brother Dan Jones and another brother and my wife and two other women. We had been traveling three days and nights in a heavy gale and were being driven backwards. Finally I asked my companions to come into the cabin with me, and I told them to pray that the Lord would change the wind. I had no fears of being lost; but I did not like the idea of being driven back to New York, as I wanted to go on my journey. We all offered the same prayer, both men and women; and then we got through and we stepped on to the deck and in less than a minute it was as though a muslin handkerchief out and it would not have moved it. The night following this, Joseph and Hyrum visited me, and the Prophet laid before me a great many things. Among other things he told me to get the spirit of God; that all of us needed it. He also told me what the Twelve Apostles would be called to go through on the earth before the coming of the Son of Man, and what the reward of their labors would be; but all that was taken from me for some reason. Nevertheless, I know it was most glorious, although much would be required at our hands.

Joseph Smith continued visiting myself and others up to a certain time, and then it stopped. The last time I saw him was in heaven. In the night vision I saw him at the door of the temple of heaven. He came and spoke to me. He said he could not stop to talk with me because he was in a hurry. The next man I met was Father Smith; he could not talk with me because he was in a hurry. I met half a dozen brethren who had held high positions on earth and none of them could stop to talk with me because they were in a hurry. I was much astonished. By and by I saw the Prophet again, and I got the privilege to ask him a question. "Now," I said,"I want to know why you are in a hurry. I have been in a hurry. I have been in a hurry all through my life but I expected my hurry would be over when I got into the (celestial) kingdom of heaven, if I ever did." Joseph said, "I will tell you, Brother Woodruff, every dispensation that has had the Priesthood on the earth and has gone into the celestial kingdom has had a certain amount of work to do to prepare to go to the earth with the Savior when He goes to reign on the earth. Each dispensation has had ample time to do this work. We have not. We are the last dispensation, and so much work has to be done and we need to be in a hurry in order to accomplish it." Of course, that was satisfactory with me, but it was a new doctrine to me.

Brigham Young also visited me after his death. One occasion he and Brother Heber C. Kimball came in a splendid chariot, and fine white horses, and accompanied me to a conference that I was going to attend. When I got there I asked Brother Brigham if he would take charge of the conference. "No," he said, "I have done my work here. I have come to see what you are doing and what you are teaching the people." And he told me what Joseph Smith had taught him in Winter Quarters, to teach the people to get the Spirit of God. He said, "I want you to teach the people to get the Spirit of God. You cannot build up the Kingdom of God without that."

That is what I want to say to the brethren and sisters here today. Every man and woman in this Church should labor to get that Spirit. We are surrounded by those evil spirits that are at war against God and against everything looking to the building up of the Kingdom of God and we need this Holy Spirit to enable us to overcome those influences. I have had the Holy Ghost in my travels. Every man has that has gone out into the vineyard and labored faithfully for the cause of God. I have referred to the administration of angels to myself. What did those angels do? One of them taught me some things relating to the signs that should preceed the coming of the Son of Man. Others came and saved my life. What then? They turned and left me. But how is it with the Holy Ghost? The Holy Ghost does not leave me if I do my duty. It does not leave any man who does his duty. John Taylor was told on the occasion to labor to get the spirit of God, and to follow its dictation, and it would become a principle of revelation within him. God has blessed me with that, and everything I have done since I have been in this Church has been done upon that principle. The Spirit of God has told me what to do, and I have had to follow that.

In the time of the apostasy in Kirtland, Joseph Smith hardly knew when he met a man, unless the Spirit of God revealed it to him, whether he was a friend or foe. Most of the leading men were fighting him. Right in the midst of that darkness the Spirit of God said to me, "You choose a partner and go straight to Fox Islands." Well, I knew no more what was on Fox Islands than what was on Kolob. But the Lord told me to go, and I went. I chose Jonathan H. Hale, and he went with me. We cast out some devils there, preached the Gospel and performed some miracles. I crossed Lake Ontario and went into Connecticut, where my father lived. I had not seen one of my relatives from the time I embraced the Gospel. I preached the Gospel, there, and baptized my father, my stepmother and sister, and uncles and aunts, and organized a branch there. Every member of that branch was a relative of mine, excepting one, and he was a Methodist class leader who boarded at my father's house. This was all promised to me by old Father Smith when he blessed me. I got to Fox Islands and did a good work there. Through the blessings of God I brought nearly a hundred from there up to Zion, at the time the Saints were driven out of Missouri into Illinois.

So it has been all through my life. If I have undertaken to do anything, and the Lord has wanted to do something else, He has had to tell me. When we were sent to England, we were sent by revelation. I went into the Staffershire potteries with Brother Alfred Codon. We were doing a splendid work, baptising almost every night, and I thought it was the finest mission I ever was on. I went into the town over-flowing. The spirit of the Lord came upon me and said that that was the last meeting I should be with them. After the meeting, they asked me where I was going. I told them I did not know. In the morning I asked the Lord what He wanted to do and where to go. He merely said, "Go to the south." I got into the stage and rode eighty miles. The first man's house I stopped at was John Benbow's in Hereforshire. In half an hour after I entered the house I knew exactly why the Lord had sent me. There was a people there who had been praying for the ancient order of things. They were waiting for the Gospel as it was taught by Christ and His apostles. The consequences were, the first thirty days after I got there I baptized six hundred of those people. In eight months' labor in that country I brought eighteen hundred into the Church. Why? Because there was a people prepared for the Gospel, and the Lord sent me there to do that work. I have always had to give God the glory for everything good that has happened to me; for I have realized by what power it came.

When I got back to Winter Quarters from the pioneer journey, President Young said to me, "Brother Woodruff, I want you to take your wife and children and go to Boston, and stay there until you can gather every Saint of God in New England and Canada and send them up to Zion." I did as he told me. It took me two years to gather everybody, and I brought up the rear with a company. When I got into Pittsburgh with this company it was dusk, and I saw a steamer just preparing to go out. I asked the captain, "How many passengers have you?" "Two hundred fifty." "Can you take another hundred?" "I can." Then, said I, "I would like to go aboard with you." The words were hardly out of my mouth when the Holy Ghost said to me, "Don't you or your company go aboard that steamer." That was enough; I had learned the voice of the Spirit. I turned and told the captain that I had made up my mind not to go at present. The steamer started out. It was a dark night, and before the steamer had gone far she took fire, and all on board were lost. We should probably have shared the same fate had it not been for the monitor within me.

I refer to these things because I want to get the same Spirit. All of the Elders of Israel, whether abroad or at home, need that Spirit. When I was on my way east at one time, I drove into a man's yard in Indiana. Brother Orson Hyde had driven in and set his wagon in the door yard, and I set him by the side of it, I turned my mules and tied them up to an oak tree. I had my wife and two children with me in my carriage. We went to lie down, and the Holy Spirit told me to get up and move my carriage. I got right up. My wife asked me what I was going to do. I said I was going to move the carriage. She wanted to know what for. I told her I did not know. I moved the carriage about fifteen rods, looked around, and then went to bed again. The Spirit told me to get up again and move my mules. I did so. In twenty minutes there came up a whirlwind that blew the oak tree down and laid it right across where my carriage had been. By listening to that Spirit our lives were saved.

Now, it was not an angel that pointed those things to me; it was the Holy Ghost. This is the Spirit that we must have to carry out the purposes of God on the earth. We need that more than any other gift. I felt impressed yesterday to teach this principle to the Latter-day Saints. We are in the midst of enemies, in the midst of darkness and temptation, and we need to be guided by the Spirit of God. We should pray to the Lord until we get the Comforter. That is what is promised to us when we are baptized. It is the spirit of light, of truth and of revelation, and can be with all of us at the same time.

Brethren and sisters, God bless you. I am glad to meet with you. There are very few of you as old as I am. How long I shall tarry in this country I do not know; but while I do stand I want to do what good I can. These are principles that have rested a great deal upon my mind. If we labor for this spirit, we will have no quarrelling and no difficulty, so long as that is dwelling within us. God bless you. Amen.

--President Wilford Woodruff
given at Weber Stake Conference,
Ogden, Monday, Oct. 19, 1896

* * * * *

EXAMPLE

A child went forth and became what he saw.

--Walt Whitman

* * * * *

If you would lift me you must be on higher ground.

--Ralph Waldo Emerson

* * * * *

Of all commentaries upon the Scriptures, good examples are the best and the livliest.

--John Donne

* * * * *

We have committed the Golden Rule to memory. Let us now commit it to life.

--Edwin Markham

* * * * *

Parent's Responsibility

A careful man I ought to be
A little boy follows me.
I dare not ever go astray
For fear he'll go the self same way.

I must remember as I go,
Through summer's heat and winter's snow
I'm building for the years to be
The little chap who follows me.

I cannot once escape his eyes,
What ere he sees me do he tries.
Like me he says he's going to be
This little chap who follows me.

* * * * *

A father and his tiny son
Crossed a rough street one stormy day,
"See, papa," cried the little one,
"I stepped in your steps all the way."

Oh, in such a few words a child can deal
A painful thrust no coat of steel could stay.
It can pierce a man as a touch of steel
"I stepped in your steps all the way."

But they who thrust off greed and fear
Who love and toil and pray,
In their hearts it's a carol to hear
"I stepped in your steps all the way."

* * * * *

You Never Know

You never know when someone
May catch a dream from you.
You never know when a little word
Or something you may do
May open up the windows
Of a mind that seeks the light --
The way you live may not matter at all,
But you never know it might.

And just in case it could be
That another's life, through you,
Might possibly change for the better
With a broader and brighter view,
It seems it might be worth a try
At pointing the way to the right --
Of course, it may not matter at all,
But then again -- it might.

--Author Unknown

* * * * *

Growing Older

A little more tired at the close of day,
A little more anxious to have our way,
A little less ready to scold and blame,

A little more care for a brother's name;
And so we are nearing the journey's end,
Where time and eternity meet and blend.

A little less care for bonds or gold,
A little more zeal for the days of old;
A broader view and a saner mind,
And a little more love for all mankind;
And so we are faring down the way
That leads to the gates of a better day.

A little more love for the friends of youth,
A little more zeal for established truth,
A little more charity in our views,
A little less thirst for the daily news;
And so we are folding our tents away
And passing in silence at close of day.

A little more leisure to sit and dream,
A little more real the things unseen,
A little nearer to those ahead,
With visions of those long loved and dead;
And so we are going where all must go --
To the place the living may never know.

A little more laughter, a few more tears,
And we shall have told our increasing years.
The book is closed and the prayers are said,
And we are part of the countless dead;
Thrice happy, then, if some soul can say,
"I live because of their help on the way."

--R. G. Wells

* * * * *

FAITH

Faith without works is like a bird without wings; though she may hop with her companions here on earth, she will never fly with them in the Heavens.

* * * * *

Faith is a lamp in the hands of men. If it is never lighted, the world is seldom aware that they have passed.

--Douglas Meador

* * * * *

Faith is not a sense, nor sight, nor reason, but taking God at his work.

--A. B. Evans

* * * * *

Positive Attitude

If you think you are beaten, you are.
If you think you dare not, you don't.
If you'd like to win but think you can't,
It's almost a cinch you won't.
Life's battles don't always go
To the stronger or faster man.
But soon or late the man who wins
Is the one who thinks he can.

* * * * *

Patience

Just why I suffer loss I cannot know,
I only know my Father wills it so.
He leads in paths I cannot understand
But all the way I know is wisely planned.
My life is only mine that I may use
The gifts He lendeth me as He may choose
And if in love some boon He does recall
I know that unto Him belongeth all.
I am His child and I can safely trust
He loves and I know that He is just.

Within His love I can securely rest
Assured that what he does for me is best.

* * * * *

Faith

There comes a time for all of us
When we must say good-bye,
But faith and hope and love and trust
Can never, never die,
Although the curtain falls at last
Is that a cause to grieve?
The future's fairer than the past
If only we believe
And trust in God's eternal care --
So when the Master calls
Let's say that life is still more fair
Although the curtain falls.

* * * * *

Samuel Smiles suggests that the best kind of self-help in the area of building hope in the soul is to consider "hope is like the sun, which, as we journey towards it, casts the shadow of our burden behind us." This, too, will pass, the scriptures say, and that goes for the delightful moments as well as the trying ones. Hope sweetens the memory of experiences well loved. It tempers our troubles to our growth and our strength. It befriends us in dark hours, excites us in bright ones. It lends promise to the future and purpose to the past. It turns discouragement to determination.

* * * * *

Faith and Works

A man hired a boy to row him across a lake. About half way across he noticed a 'W' painted on one oar and an 'F' on the other oar. Upon inquiring as to the significance of these letters, he was told, 'F' stands for FAITH and 'W' stands for WORK. If I just row with faith I go in circles to my left. If I row with works I go in circles to my right. In order to go straight ahead I have to use both of them. In our lives the same principles apply...if we just use faith, or only works, we will go in circles. But we must use both faith and works in order to make a straight course through life.

* * * * *

Belief

Sir Isaac Newton, the British scientist, once had a skillful mechanic make him a miniature replica of our solar system, with balls representing the planets geared together by cogs and belts so as to move in harmony when cranked. Later, Newton was visited by a scientist friend who did not believe in God.

As Newton sat reading in his study with his mechanism on a large table near him, his friend stepped in. Scientist that he was he recognized at a glance what was before him. Stepping up to it he slowly turned the crank, and with undisguised admiration watched the heavenly bodies all move in their relative speed in their orbits. Standing off a few feet he exclaimed, "My! What an exquisite thing this is! Who made it?" Without looking up from his book, Newton answered, "Nobody."

Quickly turning to Newton, the infidel said, "Evidently you did not understand the question. I asked who made this?" Looking up now Newton solemnly assured him that nobody made it, but that the aggregation of matter so much admired had just happened to assume the form it was in. But the astonished infidel replied with some heat, "You must think I am a fool! Of course somebody made it, and he is a genius, and I'd like to know who he is."

Laying aside his book, Newton arose and laid a hand on his friend's shoulder. "This thing is but a puny imitation of a much grander system whose laws you know, and I am not able to convince you that this mere toy is without a designer and maker; yet you profess to believe that the great original from which the design is taken has come into being without either designer or maker! Now tell me by what sort of reasoning do you reach such an incongruous conclusion?"

* * * * *

The Story of Faith

A rustle of robes as the anthem soared gently away on the air;
The Sabbath morn's service was over, and briskly I stepped down the stair;
When, close in a half-illumined corner, where the tall pulpit's stairway
came down,
Asleep, crouched a tender wee maiden with hair like a shadowy crown.

Quite puzzled was I by the vision, but gently to wake her I spoke,
When, at the first word, the sweet damsel with one little gasp straight awoke.
"What brought you here, fair little angel?" She answered, with a voice like
a bell.
"I tum tus I've dot a sick mamma, and I want oo to please pray her well."

"Who told you?" began I, she stopped me, "Don't nobody told me at all.
And papa can't see, tos he's crying, and sides, sir, I isn't so small.
I's been here before with mamma, we've tummed when you ringed the big bell.
And every time I'se heard oo prayin' for lots o' sick folks to dit well."

Together we knelt on the stairway as humbly I asked the Great Power
To give back her health to the mother, and banish bereavement's dark hour;
I finished the simple petition and paused for a moment -- and then --
A sweet little voice at my elbow, lisped softly a gentle "Amen!"

Hand in hand we turned our steps homeward; the little maid's tongue knew no rest.
She prattled and mimicked, and cajoled -- the shadow was done from her breast.
We found that the dearly loved mother was past the dread crisis -- was safe.

They listened, amazed at my story, and wept o'er their darling's strange quest,
While the arms of the pale, loving mother drew the brave little head to her breast.
With eyes that were brimming and grateful they thanked me again and again,
Yet, I knew in my heart that the blessing was won by that gentle "Amen."

* * * * *

A Boy's Faith

My parents were living in Nauvoo, State of Illinois, when the incident I will relate occurred. There were ten children in the family, only one being a girl. I was at the time ten years old. We were very poor, owning only one cow, the milk from which we depended largely on for good. In the spring of 1842 the cow strayed off. My father and three older brothers spent weeks during the summer in vain looking for her, and about concluded that she must be dead, and almost gave up in despair. I had repeatedly asked father to let me go and hunt for her but he would reply, "What can you do when I and the older boys have traveled the country over for miles around in a vain search?" But young as I was, my faith was that I could find the lost cow.

One evening in August father came home very weary and discouraged after traveling all day for her. I said, "Father, if you will let me take Charley (an old horse) I will go and find the cow." He said somewhat angrily, "Well, go my boy and learn that you are not so smart as you think yourself to be."

Early next morning I started off, taking the "Big Mound," three or four miles east of the city, and in a prairie country. Here I had often herded cows with other boys from Nauvoo. Riding direct to the base of the big mound, I dismounted, and holding the horse by the bridle, knelt down and fervently prayed the Lord to direct me which way to go to find the cow. Then climbing up on the horse, I started due south; and notwithstanding there were numerous bunches of cattle in every direction, as far as the eye could reach, I did not turn to the right or left to examine any of them, although some were within a short distance to the direct course I seemed impelled to take. After traveling a number of miles in the open prairie, and passing hundreds of cattle, I came to a fence, the end of which I could not see either to the east or west, and how far it might be across the field, or what was on the other side, I did not know; but the Spirit which had thus far impelled me I could not resist, so I dismounted and let down the stake and rider of the fence, led my horse in, put up the fence, mounted and rode three miles due south across the field. When I came to the fence on the south side I again dismounted and let the fence down as before. Leading the horse through then putting the fence up, I found myself again in the open prairie, with numerous bunches of stock in every direction. Mounting the horse, I continued on my due south course, paying no attention to the stock on either side of me. When I had gone about a quarter of a mile from where I passed out of the field, I rode right on to the cow, feeding alone some distance from any other animals.

It was now late in the afternoon, and I was in a strange part of the country; but feeling elated and full of joy and thankful to my Father in Heaven, that he had heard and answered my prayers, I started to drive the cow in the direction of the city. In about two or three miles travel I came to the farm of old man Lot, on the Carthage Road just east of Nauvoo, where I had once been to a general master of the Nauvoo Legion, and then knew I was on the right way home, where I arrived late in the evening. My parents had been worried very much about me, but seeing the long-lost cow and my safe return, all anxiety and fear turned into thanksgiving, and we were a happy family.

--W. W. Cluff

* * * * *

FAMILY

A happier family is but an earlier heaven.

--Bowring

* * * * *

Pure hearts in a pure home are always within whispering distance of heaven.

* * * * *

The only time we fail in the home is when we give up on each other.

--Marvin J. Ashton

* * * * *

Zion is built of perfected family circles.

--John A. Widtsoe

* * * * *

Grime Time

Of mud you've got a faceful,
Your clothing is disgraceful,
And from your shoes and socks and sleeves
Sand spills out by the caseful.

You're home from playground's slaughter
In need of soap and water.
"Boys will be boys," the saying goes.
And boys, I guess, had "oughter."

But honey, you're my daughter!

--Nancy W. Olson

* * * * *

Home

Home...home...you've heard all the old quips about it...a place where you hang your hat...sign up for the family car...wait for the allowance dole... grab a snack.

You get so you sort of take the old abode for granted sometimes. It's there, it's familiar...it's just home, that's all.

But is that all? Have you ever been away somewhere and been stricken with a hungry longing for that place you call "home?" It's then you know that home is more than a roof over your head...and that it truly takes a heap of living to make a house a home for you or anybody else.

Home is where you loll on the floor and read Sunday's funnies...where a fragrance of fresh bread baking or pot roast cooking is tantalizing but promising...where your fifth grade masterpiece STILL hangs in the breakfast room...and the scratches of your pup's claws mark the back door.

Home is after-school-snacks of your own choosing...it's where your horde of books, snapshots, records, and things are stashed...it's birthday cakes and family reunions...it's everyone raking up the leaves in the fall and gardening in the spring...it's preparations for little brother's scout trips, and big brother's mission...it's praying together and singing together... sessions with Dad and church talks...sessions with Mom on clothes...it's tender, loving care when you're sick and a heap of understanding when you're blue...it's the place where you're loved the most by those who know you best.

Home is your own welcome mat to friends, where you can pay back their kindnesses to you...it's frantic preparations on Prom night...telephone calls for you...it's family squabbles, family fun.

It's not unlike other homes, yet it's special to you because your things, your loves, your happy growing up memories are there. It's a lot of things, home is, and all pretty special at that.

* * * * *

To All Parents

"I'll lend you for a little time a child of mine," he said,
"For you to love the while she lives and mourn
for when she's dead.
It may be six or seven years, or twenty-two
or three,
But will you, till I call her back, take care
of her for me?
She'll bring her charms to gladden you,
and should her stay be brief,
You'll have her lovely memories as solace
for your grief.

I cannot promise she will stay, since all from
earth return,
But there are lessons taught down there
I want this child to learn.
I've looked the wide world over in my
search for teachers true;
And from the throngs that crowd life's lanes,
I have selected you.
Now will you give her all your love, not
think the labor vain,
Nor hate me when I come to call to take
her back again?"

I fancied that I heard them say, "Dear Lord,
thy will be done!
For all the joy the child shall bring, the
risk of grief we'll run;
We'll shelter her with tenderness, we'll
love her while we may,
And for the happiness we've known
forever grateful stay;
But should the angels call for her much
sooner than we've planned.
We'll brave the bitter grief that comes
and try to understand."

* * * * *

Prayer For Parents

Dear Heavenly Father, make me a better parent. Teach me to understand my children, to listen patiently to what they have to say and to answer all their questions kindly. Keep me from interrupting them, talking back to them and contradicting them. Make me as courteous to them as I would have them be to me. Give me the courage to confess my sins against my children and to ask of them forgiveness when I know that I have done them wrong.

May not I vainly hurt the feelings of my children. Forbid that I should laugh at their mistakes or resort to shame and ridicule as punishment.

Let me not tempt my child to lie and steal. So guide me hour by hour that I may demonstrate by all I say and do that honesty produces happiness.

Reduce, I pray the meanness in me. May I cease to nag; and when I am out of sorts, help me, O Lord, to hold my tongue.

Blind me to the little errors of my children, and help me to see the good things that they do. Give me a ready word of honest praise.

Help me to grow up with my children, to treat them as those of their own age, but let me not expect of them the judgments and conventions of adults. Allow me not to rob them of the opportunity to wait upon themselves, to think, to choose and to make decisions.

Forbid that I should ever punish them for my selfish satisfaction. May I grant them all their wishes that are reasonable and have the courage always to withhold a privilege which I know will do them harm.

Make me so fair and just, so considerate and companionable to my children that they will have a genuine esteem for me. Fit me to be loved and imitated by children.

* * * * *

Description of a Grandmother, As Seen by a Grandchild

"A grandmother is a lady who has no children of her own, so she likes other people's little girls. A grandfather is a man grandmother. He goes for walks with the boys, and they talk about fishing and tractors and like that.

"Grandmas don't have to do anything except be here. They're old, so they shouldn't play hard or run. It is enough if they drive us to the market where the pretend-horse is and have plenty of dimes ready. Or if they take us for walks, they should slow down past things like pretty leaves or caterpillars. They should never, ever say 'Hurry up.'

"Usually, they are fat, but not too fat to tie kid's shoes. They wear glasses and funny underwear. They can take their teeth and gums off.

"It is better if they don't typewrite or play cards except with us. They don't have to be smart, only answer questions like why dogs hate cats and how come God isn't married. They don't talk baby talk like visitors do because it is so hard to understand. When they read to us, they don't skip or mind if it is the same story again.

"Everybody should try to have one grandmother, especially if you don't have television, because grandmas are the only grown-ups who have got time."

* * * * *

If For Girls

If you can hear the whispering about you
And never yield to deal in whispers, too;
If you can bravely smile when loved ones doubt you,
And never doubt, in turn, what loved ones do;
If you can keep a sweet and gentle spirit
In spite of fame or fortune, rank or place,
And though you win your goal or only near it.
Can win with poise or lose with equal grace;

If you can meet with unbelief, believing,
And hallow in your heart, a simple creed,
If you can meet deception, undeceiving,
And learn to look to God for all you need;
If you can be what girls should be to mothers
Chums in joy and comrades in distress;
And be unto others as you'd have the others
Be unto you -- no more and yet no less;

If you can keep with your heart the power
To say that firm, unconquerable "no;"
If you can brave a present shadowed hour
Rather than yield to build a future was;
If you can love, yet not let loving master,
But keep yourself within your own self's clasp,
And not let dreaming lead you to disaster
Nor pity's fascination loose your grasp;

If you can lock your heart on confidences
Nor ever needlessly in turn confide;
If you can put behind you all pretenses
Of mock humility or foolish pride;
If you can keep the simple homely virtue
Of walking right with God -- then have no fear
That anything in all the world can hurt you --
AND -- which is more --
YOU'LL BE A WOMAN, DEAR.

* * * * *

What Is A Girl?

Little girls are the nicest things that happen to people. They are born with a little bit of angel shine in them and though it wears thin sometimes, there is always enough left to lasso your heart -- even when they are sitting in the mud, or crying temperamental tears, or parading up the street in mother's best clothes.

A little girl can be sweeter (and badder) oftener than anyone else in the world. She can jitter around, and stomp, and make funny noises that frazzle your nerves, yet just when you open your mouth, she stands there demure with that special look in her eyes. A girl is Innocence playing in the mud, Beauty standing on its head, and Motherhood dragging a doll by the foot.

Girls are available in five colors -- black, white, red, yellow, or brown, yet Mother Nature always manages to select your favorite color when you place the order. They disprove the law of supply and demand -- there are millions of little girls, but each is as precious as rubies.

God borrows from many creatures to make a little girl. He uses the song of a bird, the squeal of a pig, the stubbornness of a mule, the antics of a monkey, the spryness of a grasshopper, the curiosity of a cat, the speed of a gazelle, the slyness of a fox, the softness of a kitten, and to top it all of, He adds the mysterious mind of a woman.

A little girl likes new shoes, party dresses, small animals, first grade, noise makers, the girl next door, dolls, make-believe, dancing lessons, ice cream, kitchens, coloring books, make-up, cans of water, going visiting, tea parties, and one boy. She doesn't care so much for visitors, boys in general, large dogs, hand me downs, straight chairs, vegetables, snow suits, or staying in the front yard. She is loudest when you are thinking, the prettiest when she has provoked you, the busiest at bedtime, the quietest when you want to show her off, and the most flirtatious when she absolutely must not get the best of you.

Who else can cause you more grief, joy, irritation, satisfaction, embarrassment, and genuine delight than this combination of Eve, Solome, and Florence Nightingale? She can muss up your home, your hair, and your dignity -- spend your money, your time, and your temper -- then just when your patience is ready to crack, her sunshine peeks through and you've lost again.

Yes, she is a nerve-racking nuisance, just a noisy bundle of mischief. But when your dreams tumble down and the world is a mess -- when it seems you are pretty much of a fool after all -- she can make you a king when she climbs on your knee and whispers, "I love you best of all!"

* * * * *

I Am A Teen-Ager

Never mind which one -- Just put me down as teen-ager:
I may be the one who lives next door -- or on the other side of town -- or across the tracks.
WHO KNOWS?

Maybe I'm the one who dumped garbage on your porch last Halloween --
or led yells at last night's exciting game.
I could be the news boy who throws your paper in the shrubbery with such amazing accuracy.
I'm the one who will date your daughter next Saturday night.
WHO AM I?

Why I'm the prom chairman --
I'm the guy who beat up some kid after the football rally.
I study while watching "Bandstand" on T.V. -- and baby-sit for you when you go out for an evening.
I beg for the car to go -- just messing around.
I'm a teen that's between childhood and adulthood -- and the pull of each of those phases of life gets me into trouble and makes me either happy -- or miserable -- a crazy mixed-up kid -- or the hope of the world.
WHO AM I?

I'm just a growing young person who lives near you, with you, or around you.
I'm a Protestant, Catholic, Jewish, White, Negro, or just miscellaneous -- a big thick slice of the jelly cake that twists all its young people up into one delicious roll.
But NO MATTER WHAT ELSE I AM,
I'm a Teen-Ager.

* * * * *

I Am A Parent

Not always the kind I'd like to be, call me just a mere parent.
I think I'm normal.
I find myself wondering if my son or daughter will ever grow up and display good manners and be reasonable and so, I nag, I nudge, I needle:
You see, I don't want to over step his rights, nor neglect mine.
Therefore, I worry, I stew, I fret.
I watch the clock's creeping hands.
I cringe at the sound of an ambulance.
I smile and drop off to sleep when I hear a car door slam.
I worry about grades, and companions, and the cost of giving to my community a good citizen.
Life has taught me a number of lessons, lessons hard to learn.
That being a parent is a full-time job,
That little, neglected daily problems can become time fuses that someday will go off,
That tensions within a home are normal and will continue to exist just as long as parents love children, and children love freedom.
Sometimes, I'm soft, and sometimes, I can be downright severe,
I'm often confused.

But let someone tell me how I must run my home, and I rise up in a
bristling independence,
No one has the right to hand me a list of inflexible do's and don'ts:
But, being a parent, I recognize, and respect the problems in thousands
of homes like mine.
Yes, I'm a parent, I like the job, for I believe in young people, all of them,
my son, your son,
My daughter, your daughter,
I covet for them a pleasurable time of growing up.
I want all of them to enter adulthood, clean, good, honest and right on schedule.

* * * * *

FATHER

A father is a guy who has snapshots in his wallet where his money used to be.

* * * * *

Those Boys Of Mine

Look at those boys just standing there
With straight-back, and curly and crew-cut hair;
So clean their faces with love do shine
Oh, God, how I wish those boys were mine.

Do you think I'd sit and silently wait
For some other man to come and take
Those boys of mine to mountain streams
To catch some fish, fulfill some dreams.

Their Dad's the man that a young lad needs
To nurture and feed those youthful seeds
That so strongly depend on a willing Dad
To bless the boy with the joy Dad's had.

So please don't wait for some other guy
To take your son while you wonder why
That boy of yours from the path did stray
When you were so busy at work today.

--Claudell Empey

* * * * *

Ten Commandments For Husbands

1. Remember that thy wife is thy partner, not thy property.

2. Do not expect thy wife to be wife and wage earner at the same time.

3. Think not that thy business is none of thy wife's business.

4. Thou shalt hold thy wife's love by the same means that thou won it.

5. Thou shalt make the building of thy home thy first business.

6. Thou shalt cooperate with thy wife in establishing family discipline.

7. Thou shalt enter into thy home with cheerfulness.

8. Thou shalt not let anyone criticize thy wife to thy face and get away with it, neither thy father nor thy mother nor thy brethren nor thy sisters nor any of thy relatives.

9. Thou shalt not take thy wife for granted.

10. Remember thy home and keep it holy.

--Roy L. Smith

* * * * *

The Hours I Spend With Dad

He doesn't stand out in a crowd, just an average, regular guy,
But to me he's a king and stands near ten feet high.
He loves and understands me, whether I am good or bad.
They'll make the man that I will be, the hours I spend with Dad.
As we don't have much money and can't afford long trips,
He taught me how to whittle; to make our own winged ships
That travel on the nearest creek. We sail to foreign lands;
He takes me all around the world, from snow to desert sands.
We carve men and airplanes loved by all small boys;
I receive more happiness from them than costly toys.
We go exploring in the woods; we tramp for miles around.
He never is too busy to explain the things we've found.
We watch a caterpillar; we see a red ant hill;
He says, "Don't move, you'll scare them. Watch...be very still!"
He huskers down beside me, begins, "Now listen, lad."
I absorb the wisdom which God has given Dad.
He seems to understand that I must make some noise,
And that I'm crammed with questions like all small growing boys --
Why rain and sun make colors, what makes them curve so high --
He explains the reason that the rainbow's in the sky.
We go to Church and Sunday School on every Sabbath day;
Sometimes I glance up at him when he bows his head to pray;
I've shed tears of happiness because I am so glad
That God has given me "Pa" and not some other dad.
After work, when he gets home, and if the wind is right,
We go hunt our fishing poles, perhaps the fish will bite.
We go digging angleworms beside the old cow-shed;
We walk together, just like men, with Duke, my pup, ahead.
The times when I am all mixed up, troubled, or feel bad,
I know that I can always talk it over with my dad.
And if I am in the wrong, he'll say, "Apologize!"

He lives the Word of Wisdom, the commandments, he's so wise.
"Love thy neighbour as thyself," that is my dad's code.
He's preparing me, while I'm still young, to travel life's long road.
The best that this world offers, I know that I have had;
I treasure every minute, the hours I spend with Dad!

--Louice Sexton Akin

* * * * *

FREE AGENCY

God gave us free agency, and then gave us the commandments to keep us free.

--Cecil B. DeMille

* * * * *

The Dead Duck

A wealthy plantation owner took Sam, his hired servant, hunting ducks with him. As they walked along, the Boss said, "Sam, you believe in God don't you?" And Sam replied, "Yes." The Boss said, "I don't." He then said, "Why is it, Sam, that I who don't believe in God have so much, and you who believes in God have so little? I have everything a man could want, but you have almost nothing."

Sam said, "Boss, give me a little while to think this matter over." So the boss agreed. Just then they came onto a lake and up flew a flock of ducks. The boss shot and dropped two ducks of which one was dead and the other wounded. Sam went out to get the ducks. The Boss told him to go and get the wounded one first...or he will get away: the dead duck will always be there. Upon returning, Sam said, "Boss, you have just answered your question. You are the dead duck. Satan knows I believe in God and he is doing all in his power to make me change my belief, and when he gets through with me, he knows that you will always be there."

* * * * *

The Things That Count

Not what we have, but what we use,
Not what we see, but what we choose --
These are the things that mar or bless
The sum of human happiness.

The things nearby, not things afar,
Not what we seem, but what we are --
These are the things that make or break
That give the heart its joy or ache.

Not what seems fair, but what is true,
Not what we dream, but what we do --
These are the things that shine like gems
Like stars in fortune's diadems.

* * * * *

An Arab Chief tells the story of a spy who had been captured and sentenced to death by a general of the Persian army. The general had fallen upon a strange and weird custom. He permitted the condemned person to make a choice. He could either face the firing squad or pass through the Big Black Door.

As the moment of execution drew near, the general ordered the spy to be brought before him for a short, final interview, the primary purpose of which was to receive the answer to the query: "Which shall it be -- the firing squad or the Big Black Door?"

This was not an easy question, and the prisoner hesitated, but made it known that he much preferred the firing squad. Not long thereafter a volley of shots in the courtyard announced that the grim sentence had been fulfilled.

The general, staring at his boots, turned to his aide and said, "You see how it is with men; they will always prefer the known way to the unknown. It is characteristic of people to be afraid of the undefined. And yet I gave him his choice."

"What lies beyond the Big Black Door?" asked the aide.

"Freedom," replied the general, "and I've known only a few men brave enough to take it."

* * * * *

FRIENDSHIP

Better are the blows of a friend than the false kisses of an enemy.

--Thomas A. Becket

* * * * *

Friendship improves happiness, and abates misery, by doubling our joy, and dividing our grief.

--Addison

* * * * *

To have a good friend is one of the highest delights of life; to be a good friend is one of the noblest and most difficult undertakings.

* * * * *

The only way to have a friend is to be a friend. The art of pleasing requires only the desire.

--Lord Chesterfield

* * * * *

A warm smile is an invitation to draw up a chair before the log fire of friendship.

* * * * *

As steadfast as the ages roll,
Binding closer soul to soul;
No matter how far, or heavy the load,
Sweet is the journey on Friendship's Road.

--J. B. Downie

* * * * *

Friendship is a chain of gold,
Shaped in God's all-perfect mold,
Each link a smile, a laugh, a tear,
A touch of the hand, a world of cheer.

--Helen Keller

* * * * *

"He who has a thousand friends
Has not a friend to spare.
But he who has one enemy
Shall meet him everywhere."

* * * * *

There are no strangers, just friends I have never met. I've never met a person I didn't like.

--Will Rogers

* * * * *

We might not all feel just like Will Rogers. Some of us might feel more like the little old black lady who said, "I loves everybody, is they black or is they white, I loves everybody." Then she shook her head and added, "But I don't like some of the things that some people does."

A person completely wrapped up in himself makes a small package.

--Harry E. Fosdick

* * * * *

Once in awhile a friend is found who's a
friend right from the start
Once in awhile a friendship's made that
really warms the heart
Once in awhile a friendship's found to
have a lifetime through
It really does happen, just once in awhile --
it happened to me and you.

* * * * *

I'd like to see the sort of friend that
you have been to me
I'd like to be the help that you are
always glad to be
I'd like to mean as much to you each
minute of the day
As you have meant, good friends of mine,
to me along the way.

* * * * *

When I have fears, as Keats had fears,
Of the moment I'll cease to be,
I console myself with vanished years,
Remembered laughter, remembered tears,
The peace of the changing sea,
And remembered friends who are dead and gone.
How happy they are I cannot know.
But happy am I who loved them so.

--Noel Coward

* * * * *

Little Town

I like to live in a little town,
Where the trees meet across the street:
Where you wave your hand and say "hello"
To everyone you meet.
I like to stand for a moment
Outside the grocery store
And listen to the friendly gossip
Of the folks that live next door.
For life is interwoven
With the friends we learn to know;
And we hear their joys and sorrows
As we daily come and go.
So I like to live in a little town,
I care no more to roam,
For every house in a little town
Is more than a house; it's home.

* * * * *

When trouble comes your soul to try,
You love the friend who just stands by.
Perhaps there's nothing he can do,
The thing is strictly up to you,
For these are troubles all your own,
The paths the soul must tread alone.
Times when love can't smooth the road,
Nor friendship lift the heavy load,
But just to feel you have a friend,
Who still stands by until the end.
Whose sympathy through all endures,
Whose warm hand clasp is always yours.

It helps someway to pull you through,
Although there is nothing he can do.
And so with fervant heart you cry,
"God Bless the friend who will stand by."

--Anonymous

* * * * *

A Friend

My soul cried.
The driving winds and rain lashed fiercely all about me.
As I stumbled, searching wildly in my mind,
Reaching out from the confusion in my heart.
    And she was there
    And understood
    And cried with me.
My soul gazed up.
The raging winds were stilled and the cool calm dark
Of night surrounded me. I looked up.
And spoke to God, and felt His peaceful presence there.
    And she was there
    And understood
    And prayed with me.
My soul soared.
The wind blew soft and cool against my face.
I stood barefoot on a grassy hill and watched the misty
    clouds drift over a silver moon, and thanked God
For the ecstasy of love.
    And she was there
    And understood
    And smiled with me.

--Jane Foote

* * * * *

If we knew each other better,
We would praise where now we blame.
We would know each bears his burden,
Wears some hidden cross of shame.

We would feel the heartaches better,
They have for so long born.
If we knew each other better,
We would praise instead of scorn.

If we knew each other better,
You and I and all the rest,
Seeing down beneath the surface
To the sorrow all unguessed,
We would quit our cold complaining
And a hand of trust extend,
If we knew each other better,
We would count each other one a friend.

We can know each other better
If we take time to try,
Little deeds of loving kindness
Make a better by and by.
Just a look of understanding
Brings a touch with all mankind;
We can know each other better,
Yes, seeking we shall find.

* * * * *

Around the corner I have a friend,
In this great city that has no end;
Yet days go by and weeks rush on,
And before I know it a year is gone;
And I never see my old friend's face,

For life is a swift and terrible race.
He knows I like him just as well
As in the days when I rang his bell
And he rang mine. We were younger then;
And now we are busy, tired men --
Tired with playing a foolish game,
Tired with trying to make a name.

"Tomorrow," I say, "I will call on Jim,
Just to show that I'm thinking of him."
But tomorrow comes, and tomorrow goes,
And the distance between us grows and grows.

Around the corner! -- yet miles away
"Here's a telegram, sir."
"Jim died today."
And that's what we get -- and deserve in this end --
Around the corner a vanishing friend!

--Anon

* * * * *

Leavin' The Old An' Greetin' The New

It's kinda tough t' hafta leave
So many folks you've learned t' know,
An' have 'em grip yer hand an' tell
How much they hate t' see you go!
It's kinda tough t' say goodbye
T' friends you've seen day after day --
It's hard t' break the happy bonds
O' comradship, an' move away.

It's hard t' pack up all yer things
An' leave a cozy home behind --
The place where joys have come t' you,
Where neighbors all have been so kind.
An' when, at last, yer dearest pal
Is tryin' hard t' make a bluff
At bein' brave, an' breaks right down,
It's kinda tough -- it's kinda tough!

But say! It's great t' find new friends
Just waitin' fer a chance t' show
How glad they are t' have you come
An' live with 'em! It's great t' know
That folks 're jus' about the same
No matter where you chance t' roam,
An' if you let 'em have their way
You'll soon be feelin' right at home.

So it's a long farewell, old friends;
May God be mighty good t' you!
Across the miles an' down the years
You'll find my friendship always true.
An' now I turn with eager heart
T' meet whatever life extends --
T' greet the folks that welcome me,
An' try t' make 'em all my friends!

--Lawrence Hawthorne

* * * * *

My Friend

Upon the waves of life's great seas
My Friend Ship smoothly glides
It's built to last eternally
Thru roughest waves and tides.

Friendship

It's foundation is strong, dependable;
It was built with love and care.
Its cabin is understanding
All troubles are housed there.

Good judgment and example
Are working at the helm
To keep the bow of loyalty
Pursuing its true realm.

With humility at the port
To balance starboard's worthiness,
No destructive overturn
Can spoil our happiness.

My ship is ever backed by trust
That watches at the stern
And in between both ends
Is the capacity to learn.

Good humor and fun adorn the deck
And though it receives hard wear
It still can boast of a glossy shine
That ever will be there.

And if perchance the boiler bursts,
As no doubt it might,
Forgiveness true is close at hand
To make all things aright.

There is no limit to my ship's space
Or to those it can afford.
Its friendly light encourages
New passengers aboard.

And if some flaw should enter in
My ship's strength to destroy,
There still is hope; we do not fear
But the oar of faith employ.

Then when at last we reach the shore
Of Eternal Destiny,
My Friend Ship will sail on and on
Throughout Eternity.

* * * * *

GOALS

The whole world steps aside for the man who knows where he is going.

* * * * *

It is more important to know where we are going than to get there quickly.

* * * * *

Nothing can stop the man with the right mental attitude from achieving his goal; nothing on earth can help the man with the wrong attitude.

--W. E. Ziege

* * * * *

As you ramble on through your life, brother,
Whatever be your goal --
Keep your eye upon the donut,
And not upon the hole.

* * * * *

There was a farmer who was a particularly successful farmer. He was proud of his work, and he always had straight, long rows with beautiful, golden corn, tall wheat and all manner of fine, healthy crops.

This farmer had a son who was of the age that he should learn to do the farm work. So his father took him out into the fields to teach him how to hoe, to plant seeds, how to irrigate, and how to do most of the other small chores around the farm. Then it came time that the farmer felt his son was old enough to learn how to plow the rows. He put him on the tractor and told him to plow straight, long furrows. The way to do this, he said, was to set your sight on something on the opposite side of the field, and with this goal constantly in mind, to steer straight toward it, not veering to one side or the other.

The farmer went into the house to enjoy an hour's rest, then came out later to check his son's work. To his dismay, the field was full of crooked rows. He was furious! He stormed over to the tractor to find out what was the reason for this foolishness.

The son's explanation: "Well, Dad, I did just what you said. I sighted in on something on the opposite side of the field, and I headed straight for it, and I never veered to one side or the other."

"Then why are the rows going every which way?"

"Well, the doggone cow kept moving!"

* * * * *

GOSSIP

I have never been hurt by anything I didn't say.

--Calvin Coolidge

* * * * *

Look out for the tongue; it is in a wet place and may slip.

* * * * *

Confucius say: "He who carries tail, makes monkey of self."

* * * * *

A rumor is one thing that gets thicker instead of thinner as it is spread.

--Richard Armour

* * * * *

Gossip -- Letting the chat out of the bag.

* * * * *

Even though the tongue weighs practically nothing -- it's surprising how few are able to hold it.

* * * * *

Some people are just like blotters -- they soak everything in, but they get it all backwards.

* * * * *

Quiet people aren't the only ones who don't say much.

* * * * *

A narrow mind and a wide mouth usually go together.

* * * * *

He who thinks by the inch and talks by the yard should be dealt with by the foot.

* * * * *

Gossip

A wise person doesn't blow his "knows" in public.

* * * * *

The second most deadly instrument of destruction is the H bomb. The bomb merely kills bodies and destroys cities; the human tongue kills reputations. Each bomb works alone; each tongue has a hundred accomplices. The havoc of the bomb is visible at once. The full evil of the tongue lives through all the years.

The crimes of the tongue are words of unkindness, of anger, of malice, of envy, of bitterness, of harsh criticism, gossip, lying, and scandal. Theft and murder are awful crimes, yet in any single year the aggregate sorrow, pain, and suffering they cause in a nation is microscopic when compared with the sorrows that come from the crimes of the tongue.

* * * * *

If all that we say
In a single day,
With never a word left out
Were printed each night
In clear black and white
'Twould prove queer reading, no doubt.

And then just suppose
Ere one's eyes he would close,
He must read the day's record through,
Then wouldn't he sigh
And wouldn't he try
A great deal less talking to do?

And I more than half think
That many a kink
Would be smoothed in life's tangled thread,
If one half that we say
In a single day,
Were left forever unsaid.

--Anon

* * * * *

If you see a tall fellow ahead of a crowd,
A leader of men, marching fearless and proud,
And you know of a tale whose mere telling aloud
Would cause his proud head to in anguish be bowed,
It's a pretty good plan to forget it.

If you know of a skeleton hidden away
In a chest, and guarded and kept from the day,
In the dark; and whose showing, whose sudden display
Would cause grief and sorrow and lifelong dismay,
It's a pretty good plan to forget it.

If you know of a thing that will darken the joy
Of a man or a woman, a girl or a boy,
That will wipe out a smile or the least way annoy
A fellow, or cause any sadness to cloy,
It's a pretty good plan to forget it.

--Anon

* * * * *

Thou Shalt Not Bear False Witness

Dr. Morley was a respected doctor in a small town of Ohio. He and his wife Nancy had enjoyed living in such a wonderful community with so many friends. How could one night make such a change in the lives of two people. Just the night before Dr. Morley had tried to help a friend who had had two too many drinks and in doing so had endangered his own reputation. Now Kathleen Little had spread malicious gossip that Dr. Morley was drunk too. Dr. Morley had never drank in his life nor even had liquor in his home, yet his career was at stake with such malicious gossip going around. The next day only one patient called at his office. He had scheduled surgery for a cancer patient and when no one arrived he called the father, Mr. Lopez, and told him how important it was that he got his son to the hospital for the operation as it could mean life or death for his boy, but Mr. Lopez wouldn't listen. Dr. Morley stressed how important it was that he take the boy to another doctor if he wasn't interested in his services, but to no avail. Tony Lopez died the next day from lack of medical attention.

Dr. Morley and his wife turned to their bishop for advice and help. Bishop Hansen was a kind, understanding man and had been a close friend of the Morleys for years. He, too, was upset with what had transpired. After visiting with the Morleys, he turned to them and said, "I have been asked to speak on television next Sunday. I haven't known what to talk about, but I do now." That Sunday after much fasting and praying, Bishop Hansen was ready. First he took a dish full of feathers and let a fan blow them over the room, then said, "Could anyone of you find every feather and bring it back after the wind has scattered them? It would be impossible. Malicious gossip is the same. There is no way of rectifying all the damage that can be done by gossip. I have a friend who is the very victim of such a thing. He was highly respected in our community, yet with idle gossip his reputation has been damaged. This has affected and will affect many. Already one life has been lost because of this. The medical center which was to benefit our community is at a standstill as this doctor's efforts were the very basis of our getting a medical center. One of the great commandments of our Lord is 'Thou shalt not bear false witness against thy neighbor.'" Kathleen Little sat listening, not moving. She knew that as a good Christian she had disobeyed one of God's great commandments. Bishop Hansen continued, "Gossip and Gospel are both found in the dictionary on the same page and the first three letters are the same, but how different their meanings -- Gossip is defined as idle talk; Gospel is defined as glad tidings. How wonderful it would be if everyone spread the Gospel instead of gossip."

* * * * *

GRATITUDE

Whatever your God has blessed you with, take it with grateful hand, nor postpone your joys from year to year, so that, in whatever place you have been, you may say that you have lived happily.

--Horace

* * * * *

The depth of our gratitude is the depth of our understanding.

* * * * *

The World Is Mine

Today upon a bus, I saw a lovely maid with
golden hair;
I envied her -- she seemed so gay -- and I
wished I were as fair.
When suddenly she rose to leave, I saw her
hobble down the aisle;
She had one foot and wore a crutch, but as
she passed, a smile.
Oh, God, forgive me when I whine;
I have two feet -- the world is mine!

And then I stopped to buy some sweets.
The lad who sold them had such charm.
I talked with him -- he said to me:
"It's nice to talk with folks like you.
You see," he said, "I'm blind."
Oh, God, forgive me when I whine.
I have two eyes -- the world is mine!

Then walking down the street,
I saw a child with eyes of blue.
He stood and watched the others play;
It seemed he knew not what to do.
I stopped for a moment, then I said;
"Why don't you join the others, dear?"
He looked ahead without a word,
And then I knew, he could not hear.
Oh, God, forgive me when I whine;
I have two ears -- the world is mine!

Gratitude

With feet to take me where I'd go,
With eyes to see the sunset's glow,
With ears to hear what I would know,
Oh, God, forgive me when I whine;
I'm blessed, indeed! The World Is Mine!

--Author Unknown

* * * * *

HABIT

The chains of habit are generally too small to be felt until they are too strong to be broken.

* * * * *

The best way to stop a bad habit is never to begin it.

--J. C. Penney

* * * * *

Habit is a cable, we weave a strand of it each day, until at last we cannot break it.

--Horace Mann

Bad habits are like a comfortable bed -- easy to get into, but hard to get out of.

* * * * *

There is an old saying that, "you can't kill a frog by dropping him into hot water." As you drop him into the hot water, he reacts so quickly that he immediately jumps out unharmed. But if you put him in cold water and gradually warm it up until it is scalding hot, you have him cooked before he knows it. The encroachment of bad habits in our lives is very much like this.

* * * * *

HAPPINESS

Happiness is that particular sensation you acquire when you are too busy to be miserable.

* * * * *

Happiness is neither having nor being, but becoming.

* * * * *

Happiness is habit -- cultivate it.

* * * * *

No one has ever injured his eyesight by looking on the bright side of things.

* * * * *

Unhappiness is not knowing what we want and killing ourselves to get it.

* * * * *

Happiness isn't always doing what you want to do; it's doing what you don't want to do, and being glad you did it.

--Jessie Evans Smith

* * * * *

The secret of happiness is not in doing what one likes, but in liking what one has to do.

--James M. Barrie

* * * * *

Happiness

You don't have to tell how you live each day
You don't have to say if you work or play
A tried, true barometer serves in this place
However you live, it will show in your face
The false, the deceit that you bear in your heart
Will not stay inside when it first gets a start
For sinew and blood are a thin veil of lace
What you wear in your heart you wear on your face

If your life is unselfish, if for others you live
For not what you get, but how much you give
If you live close to God in His infinite grace
You don't have to tell it, it shows in your face.

* * * * *

Happiness Is Everywhere

Where does happiness come from?
What makes happiness start?
How does it come out of nowhere
And into a person's heart?

Sometimes it's part of
A dream come true,
Or perhaps it's just doing
What we like to do.
Happiness comes from laughing...
Laughing together...
And from a bright change
In some unpleasant weather.
Happiness comes from a
Prayer we've said.
It's the feeling we get
When we're tucked into bed.
We're happy because of a
New friend we've met...
Or because of a gift
We had hoped we would get.
Sometimes happiness comes
Without any warning.
It may beam in our window
First thing in the morning.
Happiness comes from a
Secret we've shared.
Or from a special
Surprise we've prepared.
We often find happiness
In learning new things...
In a job we've done well
And the praise that it brings.
It's found in the wonder of
Blue sky above...
Or the magic of being with
Someone we love.

And when happiness seems to be
Nowhere around
Remember... it's waiting
Just to be found.

* * * * *

Cheerfulness

It costs nothing, but creates much. It enriches those who receive, without impoverishing those who give. It happens in a flash and the memory of it sometimes lasts forever. None are so rich they can get along without it, be it begged, borrowed, or stolen, for it benefits. Yet, it cannot be bought, begged, borrowed, nor stolen, for it is something that is of no earthly good to anyone until it is given away.

* * * * *

Our Best Analogies

The best law -- the golden rule.
The best education -- self-knowledge.
The best philosophy -- a contented mind.
The best war -- to war against one's weaknesses.
The best medicine -- cheerfulness and temperance.
The best music -- the laughter of an innocent child.
The best science -- extracting sunshine from a cloudy day.
The best art -- painting a smile upon the brow of childhood.
The best journalism -- printing the true and beautiful on memory's tablet.
The best telegraphing -- flashing a ray of sunshine into a gloomy heart.
The best biography -- a life that writes charity in the largest letters.
The best mathematics -- that which doubles the most joys and divides the most sorrows.
The best navigation -- steering clear of the lacerating rocks of personal contention.
The best diplomacy -- enacting a treaty of peace with one's own conscience.

* * * * *

Five Rules For A Happy Life

Many formulas have been given by many authors and psychologists for a happy life, but here are the five rules that most have agreed upon. To be truly happy an adult must be:

1. Capable of standing on his own feet, taking full responsibility for his own actions.

2. Careful to maintain a regard for other persons regardless of their race or religion.

3. Able to start work under his own power and not be driven to do a task.

4. Mindful of the fact that happiness comes only to those who have a purpose in life.

5. Able to take good fortune with a gracious smile and meet misfortune with faith in his ability to overcome it.

* * * * *

Homemaker's Creed

To live as humbly as I can.
To take what comes of good or evil and grow by my experiences into a better and a more understanding person.
To cling to the Faith which I possess and to live each day a little better than the day before.
To see others through their eyes and not through my own.
To be blind to the faults and see only the fine in every life.
To so live that I have no need of secret places to hide that which I would not have my friends know.
To live the same when I am alone as I do before the world.
To be exactly what my very best friend thinks I am.
To honor the teachings of my parents and when I am called to leave the sphere of action, to live in the memory of someone as a true friend.

--Mrs. Lila Newell

* * * * *

Thus I Think

It is a man's proper business to seek happiness and avoid misery.

Happiness consists in what delights and contents the mind; misery in what disturbs, discomposes, or torments it.

I will therefore make it my business to seek satisfaction and delight, and avoid uneasiness and disquiet; to have as much of the one, and as little of the other, as may be.

But here I must have a care I mistake not; for if I prefer a short pleasure to a lasting one, it is plain I cross my own happiness.

Happiness

Let me then see wherein consists the most lasting pleasures of this life; and that, as far as I can observe, is in these things:

First - Health, without which no sensual pleasure can have any relish.

Second - Reputation, for that I find every body is pleased with, and the want of it is a constant torment.

Third - Knowledge, for the little knowledge I have, I find I would not sell at any rate, nor part with for any other pleasure.

Fourth - Doing good, for I find the well-cooked meat I eat today does now no more delight me, nay, I am diseased after a full meal. The perfumes I smelt yesterday now no more affect me with any pleasure; but the good turn I did yesterday, a year, seven years since, continues still to please and delight me as often as I reflect on it.

Fifth - The expectation of eternal and incomprehensible happiness in another world is that also which carries a constant pleasure with it.

If, then, I will faithfully pursue that happiness I propose to myself, whatever pleasure offers itself to me, I must carefully look that it cross not any of those five great and constant pleasures above mentioned. For example, the fruit I see tempts me with the taste of it that I love, but if it endanger my health, I part with a constant and lasting for a very short and transient pleasure, and so foolishly make myself unhappy, and am not true to my own interest.

--John Locke

* * * * *

Desiderata

Go placidly amid the noise and haste and remember what peace there may be in silence. As far as possible without surrender be on good terms with all persons. Speak your truth quietly and clearly; and listen to others, even the dull and ignorant, they too have their story.

Avoid loud and aggressive persons, they are vexations to the spirit. If you compare yourself with others, you may become vain and bitter; for always there will be greater and lesser persons than yourself. Enjoy your achievements as well as your plans.

Keep interested in your own career, however humble; it is a real possession in the changing fortunes of time. Exercise caution in your business affairs; for the world is full of trickery. But let this not blind you to what virtue there is; many persons strive for high ideals; and everywhere life is full of heroism.

Be yourself. Especially, do not feign affection. Neither be cynical about love; for in the face of all aridity and disenchantment it is perennial as the grass.

Take kindly the counsel of the years, gracefully surrendering the things of youth. Nurture strength of spirit to shield you in sudden misfortune. But do not distress yourself with imaginings. Many fears are born of fatigue and loneliness. Beyond a wholesome discipline, be gentle with yourself.

You are a child of the universe, no less than the trees and the stars; and have a right to be here. And whether or not it is clear to you, no doubt the universe is unfolding as it should.

Therefore, be a peace with God, whatever you conceive Him to be, and whatever your labors and aspirations, in the noisy confusion of life keep peace with your soul.

With all its shame, drudgery and broken dreams, it is still a beautiful world. Be careful. Strive to be happy.

* * * * *

HONESTY

The trouble with some folks who say that there is no harm in the telling of 'little white lies' is that the tellers usually become progressively color blind.

* * * * *

Accuracy is the twin brother of honesty: inaccuracy is a near kin to falsehood.

--Tryon Edwards

* * * * *

This above all; to thine ownself be true and it must follow, as night the day, Thou canst not then be false to any man.

--Shakespeare

* * * * *

What a tangled web we weave when first we practice to deceive.

* * * * *

Honor

"My friends, I have been asked what I mean by 'word of honor.' I will tell you. Place me behind prison walls -- walls of stone ever so high, ever so thick, reaching ever so far into the ground -- there is a possibility that in some way or another I may be able to escape, but stand me on the floor and draw a chalk line around me and have me give my word of honor never to cross it. Can I get out of that circle? No, never! I'd die first!"

--Karl G. Maeser

* * * * *

On the points of good fellowship, the baker and the farmer agreed to exchange goods. The baker would receive from the farmer some butter, in exchange for some bread. Some time passed by and the baker began weighing his pounds of butter and each one weighed just a little less each time. The baker let it go on in this manner for a while. Then he thought it would be an advantage to the farmer to bring him to task by requesting him to meet before a jury.

The defendent came to court without any hesitency. He was asked by the jury to give his reason for disregarding the standards of honesty. But the farmer bashfully smiled and said, "Well, when I weighed my butter, I balanced it by the loaf of bread I received from the baker."

* * * * *

A fellow who pretends to be
A lot of things he's not
Overlooks the possibility
Of later being caught.

He follows a lot of people,
Some fall for such, it's true
But, as time wears at his pretense
Their opinion changes, too.

A priceless gift, it seems to me
That all would like to find
Is that supreme state of blessedness
That we call "Peace of Mind."

So -- why pretend a lot of things
Your "peace of mind" to mar
For deep down in your heart, you know
You are just what you are.

* * * * *

HUMAN RELATIONS

Tact is the ability to close your mouth before someone else wants to.

* * * * *

Cooperation is doing with a smile what you have to do anyway.

* * * * *

Social tact is making your guests feel at home, even though you wish they were.

* * * * *

Popularity comes from pleasing people, but greatness comes from pleasing God.

* * * * *

Conversation is the art of telling people a little less than they want to know.

* * * * *

The Ten Commandments of Human Relations

1. Speak to people -- there is nothing as nice as a cheerful greeting.

2. Call people by name -- the sweetest music to anyone's ears is the sound of his own name.

3. Have humility -- there is something to be learned from every living thing.

4. Be friendly -- if you would have a friend, be one.

5. Be cordial -- speak and act as if everything you do is a pleasure.

6. Be sincerely interested in others -- you can like almost everybody if you try.

7. Be generous with praise, cautious with criticism.

8. Give your word -- then keep it.

9. Be considerate of the feelings of others.

10. Be alert to give service -- what counts most in life is what we do for others.

* * * * *

I walked with my friend, a Quaker, to the newsstand the other night, and he bought a paper, thanking the newsie politely. The newsie didn't even acknowledge it.

"A sullen fellow, isn't he?" I commented.

"Oh, he's that way every night," shrugged my friend.

"Then why do you continue to be so polite to him?" I asked.

"Why not?" inquired my friend. "Why should I let <u>him</u> decide how I'm going to act?"

As I thought about this incident later, it occurred to me that the important word was "act." My friend <u>acts</u> toward people; most of us <u>react</u> toward them. His was a sense of inner balance which is lacking in most of us; he knows who he is, what he stands for, how he should behave. He refuses to return incivility for incivility, because then he would not be in command of his own conduct.

Nobody is unhappier than the perpetual reactor. His center of emotional gravity is not rooted within himself, where it belongs, but in the world outside him. His temperature is always being raised or lowered by the social climate around him, and he is a mere creature at the mercy of these elements.

Serenity cannot be achieved until we become the masters of our own actions and attitudes. To let another determine whether we shall be rude or gracious, elated or depressed, is to relinquish control over our own personalities, which is ultimately all we possess. The only true possession is self-possession.

--Sydney J. Harris

* * * * *

<u>Trust Thyself</u>

Emerson wrote: "There is a time in every man's education when he arrives at the conviction that envy is ignorance, that imitation is suicide, that he must take himself for better or worse as his portion; that though the wide universe is full of good, no kernel of nourishing corn can come to him but through the toil bestowed on that plot of ground which is given to him to till.

The power which resides in him is new in nature, and none but he knows what that is which he can do, nor does he know until he has tried...Trust thyself: every heart vibrates to that iron string."

There is a bit of advice that a person would do well to reflect upon every morning of his life. No one can even estimate the number of people who live nervous, anxious, unhappy lives because they daily attempt the impossible, which is to be like someone else. They are people who don't realize the truth of Emerson's words that envy is ignorance, that imitation is suicide. He must have used the word suicide because we have to kill that which is natural in ourselves when we attempt to be like someone else.

They need to recognize the truth, also, that the power which resides in them is new in nature, that it has never appeared before, in just that way, on earth. That if they'll learn about and develop their own powers, they'll have no need of envy or imitation.

Envy is ignorance because it means a person is ignorant of his own powers and abilities, his one-of-a-kind natural talent. He has never looked within himself for his own road to greatness, but, instead, seeks it in the lives of others. And when he fails to succeed as do those he envies -- as fail he must since he cannot possibly be exactly like them -- his image of himself shrinks. No understanding that he is unlike those he envies he does not realize that this simple fact lies at the bottom of his failure. Nor does he understand that he can be as successful as anyone on earth if he will build upon that power which resides in him.

As Emerson put it...the power which resides in him is new in nature, and none but he knows what that is which he can do, nor does he know...until he has tried.

This is why a parent or a wife is off base when they say to a child or husband, "Why aren't you like so-and-so? Look what he's doing." They don't understand that it's a human impossibility for him to be like so-and-so, and to do what he does in the same way.

Instead, they should say, "Don't worry about so-and-so. He's found his strength and he's building upon it. You have a strength of your own, and when you find it, you can build as high."

And when those great words: "Trust thyself: every heart vibrates to that iron string." When a person finds himself, when he stops imitating and envying others, there is something in his nature that says to him, "This is it. You've found your road at last."

It isn't luck, or the breaks, or anything else in circumstances or environment. It's finding yourself and building upon what you find just as have those whom so many envy.

Every person is born to be a star at something. The purpose of his life is to discover it, and then spend his years building upon that plot of ground it was given to him to till.

* * * * *

Jake

Bill Andrews was a big, awkward, homely guy. He dressed oddly with ill-fitting clothes. There were several fellows who thought it smart to make fun of him. One day one fellow noticed a small tear in his shirt and gave it a small rip. Another worker in the factory added his bit, and before long there was quite a ribbon dangling. Bill went on about his work and as he passed too near a moving belt the shirt strip was sucked into the machinery. In a split second the sleeve and Bill were in trouble. Alarms were sounded, switches pulled, and trouble was avoided. The foreman, however, aware of what had happened, summoned the men and related this story:

"In my younger days I worked in a small factory. That's where I first met Mike Havoc. He was big and witty, was always making jokes, playing little pranks. Mike was a leader. Then there was Pete Lumas. He always went along with Mike. He was a follower. And then I remember Jake. He was a little older than the rest of us -- quiet, harmless, apart. He ate his lunch by himself. He wore the same patched trousers for three years straight. He never entered into the games we played at noon, wrestling, horse shoe and such. He was indifferent.

"Jake was a natural target for practical jokes. He might find a live frog in his dinner pail, or a dead rodent in his hat. But he always took it in good humor.

"Then one fall when things were slack, Mike took off a few days to go hunting. Pete went along, of course. And they promised all of us that if they got anything they'd bring us each a piece. So we were all quite excited when we heard that they'd returned and that Mike had got a really nice big buck. We heard more than that. Pete could never keep anything to himself, and it leaked out that they had a real whopper to play on Jake. Mike had cut up the critter and had made a nice package for each of us. And, for the laugh, for the joke of it, he had saved the ears, the tail, the hoofs -- it would be so funny when Jake unwrapped them.

"Mike distributed his packages during the noon hour. We each got a nice piece, opened it, and thanked him. The biggest package of all he saved until last. It was for Jake. Pete was all but bursting; and Mike looked very smug. Like always, Jake sat by himself; he was on the far side of the big table. Mike pushed the package over to where he could reach it; and we all sat and waited. Jake was never one to say much. You might never know that he was around for all the talking he did. In three years he'd never said a hundred words. So we were all quite hypnotized with what happened next.

"He took the package firmly in his grip and rose slowly to his feet. He smiled broadly at Mike -- and it was then we noticed that his eyes were glistening. His adam's apple bobbed up and down for a moment and then he got control of himself.

"I knew you wouldn't forget me," he said gratefully; "I knew you'd come through! You're big and you're playful, but I knew all along that you had a good heart." He swallowed again, and then took in the rest of us.

"I know I haven't seemed too chummy with you men; but I never meant to be rude. You see, I've got nine kids at home -- and a wife that's been an invalid -- bedfast now for four years. She ain't ever going to get any better. And sometimes when she's real bad off, I have to sit up all night to take care of her. And most of my wages have had to go for doctors and medicine. The kids do all they can to help out, but at times it's been hard to keep food in their mouths. Maybe you think it's funny that I go off by myself to eat my dinner. Well, I guess I've been a little ashamed, because I don't always have anything between my sandwich. Or like today -- maybe there's only a raw turnip in my pail. But I want you to know that this meat really means a lot to me. Maybe more than to anybody here because tonight my kids," he wiped the moisture from his eyes with the back of his hand, "...tonight my kids will have a really..." He tugged at the string.

"We'd been watching Jake so intently we hadn't paid much notice to Mike and Pete. But we all noticed them now, because they both dove at once to try to grab the package. But they were too late. Jake had broken the wrapper and was already surveying his present. He examined each hoof, each ear, and then he held up the tail. It wiggled limply. It should have been so funny, but nobody laughed -- nobody at all. But the hardest part was when Jake looked up and tried to smile."

This was where the foreman left the story and the men. He didn't need to say anymore; but it was gratifying to notice that as each man ate his lunch that day, he shared part with Bill Andrews and one fellow even offered him his shirt.

* * * * *

Someone tells a story of the principal of a school in which boys were prepared for college who one day received a message from a lawyer living in a small town, requesting him to call.

When the teacher arrived at the office, the lawyer stated that he had in his gift a scholarship entitling a boy to a four-years' course in a certain college, and that he wished to bestow it where it would be best used.

"Therefore," he continued, "I have concluded to let you decide which boy of your school most deserves it."

"That is a hard question to decide," replied the teacher, thoughtfully. "Two of my pupils will complete the course this year. Both desire a college education, and neither is able to obtain it without assistance. They are so nearly equal that I cannot tell which is the better scholar."

"How is it as to department?" asked the lawyer.

"One boy does not more scrupulously observe all the rules of the school than the other." was the answer.

"Well," said the lawyer, "if at the end of the year one boy has not gone ahead of the other, send them to me and I will decide between them."

As before, at the closing examinations the boys stood equal in attainments. They were directed to call at the lawyer's office, no information being given as to the object of the visit.

Two intelligent, well-bred boys they seemed, and the lawyer was beginning to wonder greatly how he should make a decision between them. Just then the door opened and an elderly woman of peculiar appearance entered. She was well known as being of unsettled mind, and possessed of the idea that she had been deprived of a large fortune justly hers. As a consequence, she was in the habit of visiting the lawyers' offices, carrying in her hands a package of papers which she wished examined. She was a familiar visitor to the office, where she was always received with respect and dismissed with kindly words.

This morning, seeing that the lawyer was already occupied with others, she seated herself to wait his leisure. Unfortunately, the chair she selected was broken and had been set aside as useless. The result was that she fell in a rather awkward manner, scattering her papers about the floor. The lawyer looked with a quick eye at the boys, before moving himself, to see what they would do.

Charles, after an amused survey of the fall, turned aside to hide a laugh he could not control. Henry sprang to the woman's side and lifted her to her feet. Then carefully gathering up her papers, he politely handed them to her. Her profuse and rambling thanks served only to increase Charle's amusement.

After the lady told her customary story, to which the lawyer listened with every appearance of attention, he escorted her to the door, and she departed.

Then he turned to the boys, and after expressing pleasure at having found their acquaintance, he dismissed them. The next day the teacher was informed of the occurrence and told that the scholarship would be given to Henry, remarking:

"No one so well deserves to be fitted for a position of honor and influence as he who feels it his duty to help the humblest and lowliest."

* * * * *

The Art Of Getting Along

Sooner or later, a man, if he is wise, discovers that life is a mixture of good days and bad, victory and defeat, give and take. He learns that it doesn't pay to be a too sensitive soul; that he should let some things go over his head like water off a duck's back. He learns that he who loses his temper usually loses out. He learns that all men have burnt toast for breakfast now and then, and that he shouldn't take the other fellow's grouch too seriously. He learns that carrying a chip on his shoulder is the easiest way to get into a fight. He learns that the quickest way to become unpopular is to carry tales and gossip about others.

He learns that buck-passing always turns out to be a boomerang, and that it never pays. He comes to realize that the business could run along perfectly well without him. He learns that it doesn't matter so much who gets the credit so long as the business benefits. He learns that even the janitor is human and that it does no harm to smile and say "Good Morning," even if it's raining. He learns that most of the other fellows are as ambitious as he is, that they have brains as good or better, and that hard work, not cleverness is the secret of success. He learns to sympathize with the youngster coming into the business, because he remembers how bewildered he was when he first started out. He learns not to worry when he loses an order, because experience has shown that if he always gives his best, his average will break pretty well. He learns that no man ever got to first base alone, and that it is only through cooperative effort that we move on to better things.

He learns that bosses are no monsters, trying to get the last ounce of work out of him for the least amount of pay, but that they are usually pretty good fellows who have succeeded through hard work and who want to do the right thing. He learns that folks are not any harder to get along with in one place than another, and that the "getting along" depends about ninety-eight per cent on his own behavior.

--Wilferd Peterson

* * * * *

HUMOR

A sincere and devout man had the unfortunate habit of shouting whenever he offered a prayer in church. Once, after such a prayer, a small child remarked: "You'd think anyone who lived a good life like he does, wouldn't have to talk so loud to be heard in heaven."

* * * * *

One time a man who hadn't been to church for a long time was asked to give the closing prayer and he prayed for a long time and finally one brave deacon spoke up and said, "Amen." "Thank you." the man said. "I have been trying to think of that word for twenty minutes." and sat down.

* * * * *

Intelligence Personified

In the back woods of Tennessee two Mormon Elders called at a house. A lady came to the door and the Elders said, "Lady we have some literature on the death and crucifixion of Christ." "Oh, is he dead? I didn't even know he was sick or I would have gone over and sat up with him."

* * * * *

Where's My Man

At sweet sixteen, I first began
To ask the good Lord for a man.
At seventeen, I recall
I wanted someone strong and tall.
The Christmas I reached eighteen
I fancied someone blonde and lean.
And then at nineteen, I was sure
I'd fall for someone more mature.
At twenty, I thought I'd find
Romance with someone with a mind.
I retrogressed at twenty-one
And found college boys most fun.
My viewpoint changed at twenty-two
When "one man only" was my cue.
I broke my heart at twenty-three
And begged for someone kind to me.

Then begged at blase twenty-four
For anyone who wouldn't bore.
Now Lord, that I am twenty-five
Just send me someone who's alive.

* * * * *

There was a man who just loved to play golf and the biggest satisfaction he got out of it was bragging. He could talk a game of golf as well as he could play it. All at once he was called to be the bishop of his ward. As a result, he never had any time to play golf. If he had any time at all, it was on Sunday. He wanted to play golf so badly that it just kept working on his mind. It bothered him so much that he decided to play a game no matter what.

One Sunday, just as the sun came up, the bishop was out on the golf course. The arc angel who was assigned to watch over the bishop was very surprised to see him out on the golf course on Sunday and he ran to tell St. Peter.

St. Peter couldn't believe him and had to see it for himself. Sure enough, there was the bishop playing golf on Sunday. Then St. Peter told the arc angel that he would fix him. Just at that time, the bishop was coming to the hardest hole of the golf course which was a little hole on a back bend. He hit the ball and it bounced about three times and went right in -- the bishop got a hole in one!

The arc angel was surprised and said to St. Peter, "I thought you were going to fix him." St. Peter then said, "I did. Now who is he going to tell that one to?!"

* * * * *

One time there was a Sunday School music director who was named Hope. She was always very cheerful and smiled at her audience as she led the Sunday morning hymn services.

Now, Hope was expecting a baby. In fact, she was about two weeks overdue. But nevertheless, Hope still was found on Sunday morning in front of the chapel, leading the singing.

On this Sunday, the congregation was joyfully singing one of their favorites, "We Thank Thee, O God, For a Prophet," when they suddenly all burst into laughter. Hope couldn't understand what was so funny. Had she made a mistake? Was her slip showing? Was someone behind her making faces at the audience?

The audience finally settled down, finished the song, and Hope seated herself beside the organist, who pointed out to her these lines which the congregation had found particularly hilarious on that day -- "There is Hope smiling brightly before us, and we know that deliverance is nigh!"

* * * * *

Murphy's Laws

1. If anything can go wrong, it will.

2. Nothing is as simple as it seems.

3. Everything always costs more money than you have.

4. Everything takes longer than you expect.

5. If you fool around with something long enough, it will eventually break.

6. If you try to please everybody, somebody is not going to like it.

7. It is a fundamental law of nature that nothing ever quite works out.

8. Whatever you want to do, you have to do something else first.

9. It is easier to get into a thing than to get out of it.

10. If you explain something so clearly that no one can misunderstand, someone will.

* * * * *

The Puzzled Dutchman

A gentleman that did not believe in baptism by immersion was holding a meeting on the subject and tried to prove from the scriptures that 'into' did not mean into all the time but unto. "We read in the Bible," said he, "that Moses went up into the mountain, and that the Savior went up into the mountain. Now we do not suppose that either went into the mountain but went unto the mountain." He continued, "Just so with the Savior going into the water, he never went into but went unto or by the Jordan and then was baptized by sprinkling in the ordinary way." He carried the idea out in full and in due time closed his sermon. Then invitations were for anyone present to arise and express their thoughts. Many of the members arose and said they were well pleased with the sermon, and felt their souls had been magnified greatly by coming to the meeting. Then a friendly old gent of dutch decent broke the silence.

"Mr. Preacher, I vas glad I vas here tonight, for now I can believe things dat I could before. Oh! I vas so glad down into does not mean into at all, but just near unto. We read, Mr. Preacher, that Daniel went into the lion's den and came out alive. Dat never vas clear to my mind. Now it is all plain. Daniel did not go into the den of lions at all. He shust vent down near de den outside. And again ve read dat de tree Hebrew chillin vas cast into de firish furnace and came out alive. Now dat never vas, or dey would have burnt right away up. But now dat is all so plain. Dey vas near by de furnace, a good way off and not in de fire at all. And, Mr. Preacher, ve read dat Shonah vas taken into de whale's belly. Now dat was always a big fish story to me, but now it is all so plain to me. It meant he didn't get into the whale's belly at all; he just jumped on the whale's back and rode ashore. Oh! I vas so glad I was here tonight and now, Mr. Preacher, if you would explain to me shust one or two more passages of scripture I vill be glad I vas here tonight. It says de wicked shall be cast into de lake dat burns vit fire and brimstone, always. Oh! Mr. Preacher, if I vas a wicked man would I be cast into the lake or just down by a good ways off or just close enough to be comfortable? De udder passage says dat dey dat do all the commandments shall enter into the gates of the holy city. Oh! Mr. Preacher, I hope you tells dat into here hiss into and not shust close by, or near unto. You explain them to me and Oh I will be glad I vas here tonight.

* * * * *

Is There A Need For Good English?

The following excerpts are from letters actually received at the Salt Lake County Welfare:

1. I cannot get sick pay. I have six children. Can you tell me why?

2. This is my eighth child. What are you going to do about it?

3. Mrs. Brown had no clothing for a year and has been visited by the Clergy.

4. I am forwarding my marriage certificate and three children, one of which is a mistake, as you can see.

5. I am happy to say that my husband, who was reported missing, now is dead.

6. I am forwarding my marriage certificate and six children. I have seven, but one died, which has been baptized on half a piece of paper.

7. I am writing to say that my baby was born two years old. When do I get my money?

8. Please find for certain if my husband is dead. The man I am living with can't eat or anything until he knows.

9. I am very much annoyed to find you have branded my boy as illiterate. This is a dirty lie, as I was married a week before he was born.

10. In answer to your letter, I have given birth to a boy weighing ten pounds. I hope this is satisfactory.

11. Unless I get my husband very soon, I will be forced to lead an immortal life.

12. You have changed my boy to a girl. Will this make a difference?

13. Please send my money at once, as I have fallen into error with my landlord.

14. I have no children yet. My husband is a bus driver and works day and night.

15. In accordance with your instructions, I have given birth to twins in the enclosed envelope.

16. I want my money as quick as I can get it. I have been in bed with my doctor for two weeks and he doesn't seem to be doing much good. If things do not improve, I will have to get another doctor.

17. Please send my wife's form to fill out.

18. I have already wrote to the President and I don't hear from you. I will write to Uncle Sam and tell him about you both.

* * * * *

So Polly Goes

About the house our Polly goes
Tilted forward from her toes,
Doing, noting, singing, seeing,
Newly baked and fresh to being.

"I making fun.
There's just one sun?
I <u>soft</u> the kitty.
Daddy's <u>pretty</u>."

A certain modesty of soul
Makes her approach discreet.
"May touch?" "May bong?" "May peek?"
She asks. And once, "Okay to shriek?"

Balloons go <u>breezing.</u>
Gloves, not hands, are <u>very freezing.</u>
Water in the bath is <u>deeping.</u>
Sun in cloud is <u>fast asleeping.</u>

Now sure, now not, that all is right
So clear a candor yet knows night.
A kiss, to give or take, makes bright
Her never distant swift delight.

"I crying now.
I singing sweet.
Come here, Moon!
May eat my feet?"

"You sewed on me my big blue eyes?"
She asked without the least surprise.
And since her father's gone all day
"Remember Dad?" she'll often say.

On top of eyes there lives eyebrowses
Just like people live in houses.
Birds up there -- oh look -- they're flying!
Polly, too, can fly by trying.

About the house our Polly goes
Unerring, like a bud, she grows,
True to inner form and need,
Fed by easy love -- a seed
With genes of joy. Refract joy's light
Our Polly does,
And makes us gift of her delight.

--Helen Puner

* * * * *

<u>Children Should Be Seen Not Slurred</u>

Children have had a lot of bad publicity lately, outright slander, really. Between Jean Kerr's daisy-eaters and Elinor Goulding Smith's housemates, somebody who doesn't know children personally might think they were monsters. I, for one, like children better than people. I really do, and I can give you a hundred good reasons why.

For one thing, People are wet blankets. If somebody says, "Let's do this" or "Let's do that," People first think of all the reasons why they can't. They're too tired, or it's too close to dinnertime, or they have to put the screens up, or take the screens down. If they finally do it, after all that, they keep thinking about all those things and they don't have any fun.

Children, on the other hand, are enthusiastic. They're always ready to do practically anything, whether it's going to look at new puppies or swing in the back yard or shoot fireworks or make popcorn. They're never too tired. Children first think of all the reasons why they should do things. They like to play marbles, fly model airplanes, kick tin cans, dig for fishing worms, play cowboys, and turn somersaults.

Another thing. People are phony. You can't believe a word they say. They pretend to like other people while they are with them, and right after, they'll say they don't like them at all. If they get mad, they can't come right out and say no; instead they get ulcers or drive too fast or make sarcastic remarks or hold a grudge forever and ever. They even hide it when they feel happy.

Children, however, are candid. They don't pretend about what they like and don't like. If you say, "Would you like to have a peanut-butter sandwich?" or "Would you like to stay here with me?" or "Would you like to play outdoors?" they'll tell you. Children don't pretend to like you if they really don't; they act the way they feel. If they get mad, they simply throw a tantrum which blows over fast and then it's all finished and done with. They forgive and forget in just about two minutes flat. If they're happy, they really show it; they dance and skip and laugh, and everybody around feels happy, too.

People sleep too much. They take naps, even when nobody makes them. But children hate sleep. They love being awake because they love life so much. That's why they put up such a fight about going to bed. And they have no trouble bouncing out in the morning. Children are glad when morning comes -- like birds, they're gay as soon as they wake up. They never need coffee first.

People aren't very friendly, either. You don't see them going around making friends in the supermarket or on the bus or while they're in a park. Even if they're introduced they're afraid to ask about things they want to know. You don't hear People ask, "How old are you?" or "Do you want to be my friend?" or things like that. But Children are very Friendly. They don't care about anybody's race, creed or color. They like the TV repairman and the nurse in the doctor's office and the old man who feeds pigeons and the baby next door and the cleaning woman and practically everybody.

People don't really appreciate nature. All they know how to do is look at nature and take pictures of it and then look at them. They say, "Isn't this a lovely hill?" or "What a nice tree!" or "My, the lilacs are beautiful."

Children really appreciate nature. They roll like logs down the grassy slope, bumping along and giggling at the way the weeds tickle. Then they run down it with their arms spread out and they're airplanes or birds, and they feel the wind. They don't just look at the lilacs. They smell them, and then taste the leaves and take a flower apart to see how it's made and crawl through the bushes to find out what they're like underneath. They climb up a tree to sway on the branches and find out how rough the bark is and if there are bird's nests. Children don't just stand there looking at nature. They smell it and feel it and taste it and see how it looks from underneath and all around.

People are pretty dull. They aren't really interested in much. Children are interested in everything -- in telephones and God and bugs and stars and baseball and steam shovels and anything you can think of. They are bursting with curiosity and bubbling with questions.

People are always stewing about what other people will think. They do not do much of what they want to do. They get all dressed up when they go out so other people won't think they're sloppy and don't know any better, even if they're more comfortable in their shorts and old tennis shoes. They even go into debt so other people won't find out that they don't have as much money as they want to make them think they have!

Children don't give a hoot about what others think. When people say, "What will Mr. Brown think of a big boy like you acting this way?" or "What will the neighbors think of a big girl like you getting so muddy?" Children tell them, "I don't care." They never dress up unless they're made to. Children will even tell you how much money they have. They don't care if you know, even if they don't have a single cent.

People are always waiting until things are over. That way they spend a lot of time being bored, which shows up in their dispositions. Say they're riding along on a bus; they're just waiting until they get somewhere. If they're at the garage while the car is being fixed, they're just waiting until they can be on their way again. The minute they catch up to what they're waiting for, they start waiting for the next thing.

Children, on the other hand, enjoy things while they're going on. They have a good time counting telephone poles along the highway, watching the mechanic work on the motor, or skipping cracks in the sidewalk. That way they're happy as they go along and not all the time waiting to be happy.

Besides, people think for a thing to be good it has to cost money. Children know you can get lots of things for nothing. They can take vases and old inner tubes and bottles and a broken phonograph and an empty candy bowl out of the trash cans in the alley. They can pick up rocks with sparkles like diamonds in them and feathers and a big packing box for a fort without spending one single cent.

I could go on with all the reasons why I like children better than people, but it would take about a million years. What I'd rather do is have somebody explain this to me; when people say to other people, "You're so childish!" why do they say it in a derogatory tone? I think it's just about the nicest compliment there is.

* * * * *

Housekeeping Is A Man's Job

Every few seconds on the North American continent, a husband leans back in his chair, waggles a fork at an exhausted wife, and says: "Trouble with you is, you're not organized."

I went further. I said: "I have a theory that if men were to make a time-and-motion study of housework, the way they do in industry, they could cut down a lot of wasted time and effort."

My wife is not a girl to leave an untried theory lying around. Before I knew where I was at, she was visiting an old school friend out of town and I was stuck for a week with my two little girls, a refrigerator, a stove, a vacuum cleaner, a washing machine, an ironing board and four walls.

The week is over now. I haven't much to report about time and motion, except that in housework there is not enough of one and too much of the other. What I did find out was that a man can't keep house. No man. Your husband can't keep house. You can tell him for me, and if he doesn't believe me or you, he can come over and look at my fingernails, which are peeling like crisp celery.

A woman has an instinct for housekeeping that was already operating when she was a little girl dressing her doll, playing house and watching Mother cook. It continued through the hopeful teens by reading women's magazines, talking with other women and generally preparing to be a wife. A man spent all of his formative years asking his father how the clutch worked on the car, where he put the hammer, and scaring little girls with toads. I'm not discussing which is the most useful course. I'm merely pointing out that they lead to different types of human beings. A man keeping house is like a woman deciding to referee a prize fight or overhaul an internal combustion engine.

Let's take one simple example. How long do you cook spinach? Go ahead -- ask your husband how long you cook spinach. Are there books on it, like "Spinach, Its Preparation and Cooking Time?" The first batch I made I boiled for an hour and a half. It came out like heavy green out-door paint. Yet I'm sure that women have always had a rough idea when to take it out. Women take all these things for granted. For instance, my wife told me when she got home, "You stick a fork in it." This is typical feminine advice. Okay. I stick a fork in it. What's it suppose to do -- holler?

Another thing, all women know how to bring a meal out even. I always found myself opening a can of corn just as the meat was ready to take out of the oven. Twice my daughters and I sat down to one boiled potato apiece, with a full course meal on the stove not cooked yet. Another time I had a boat full of gravy a half hour before the roast was done. That was one trick that gave me a sort of perverted pride. My wife is still trying to find out how I did it.

In spite of all this, I seemed to be keeping up with things for the first couple of days. I suppose if you were to put a Congo witch doctor in a jet plane and start it off, he'd look as if he would be flying it for a couple of minutes.

My wife had said with a final leer, "As long as you're going to have time to burn, there's no point in my washing everything up before I go. With your system, it will be easier for you than for me to do anyway."

The washing itself wasn't so bad. I added a new tone to a few things by not washing a pair of purple overalls separately, but I did get all the clothes into the washing machine and pull the switch without any difficulty before I had to answer the door, get a piece of toast out of the toaster, answer the phone, and stop Mary screaming, "Jesus wants Me For A Sunbeam" at the top of her lungs. But, by the time I got the last piece hung out on the line at nine-thirty that night, I was losing ground fast. I hadn't been able to wash a dish since morning, and I was running out of fancy plates, and good silverware and had to serve the children their milk in paper cups.

Another thing, a woman has a flair for handling hair. She's always working at her own, and curls, braids, and pompadours come as easily to her as shaving does to man. I'd often watched my wife braid the kid's hair. It looked fairly straight forward. But the difference between knowing how to braid a little girl's hair, is the difference between knowing how to knit and knitting with four needles on horseback. I'd get the child I was working on to lie down flat on her face, then straddle her. I think this is probably the reason why I so often forgot to check on how the front was turning out. Normally, though, the finished product didn't look too bad for a few minutes. Then it would start coming apart. One day Mary came home from school with a note pinned to her that said: "Dear Mr. Allen. Mary is a bright little girl, but no child should be expected to do her work when he has to look at the black board through all that hair."

Another thing that escapes most men when they look around the average well-run home is the executive side of housekeeping. It all looks very simple when a woman is looking after it, but most men don't ever really absorb it. Little things, that in a semi-conscious way, I had watched my wife look after for years, became a baffling problem.

Anyway, it's more complicating than it looks. Even a thing like ordering the right amount of bread requires a special sense developed over a long period. I'd stand there imagining myself eating bread. Then I'd imagine Mary and Jane eating bread. I would feel each of us eating, say, about five slices. Then I'd have to estimate how many times five slices would go into a loaf.

In the meantime, the baker would be looking at me as if he were thinking, "this guy doesn't even make a good housewife," and inside the house other things would be burning, boiling over, getting dirtier and crying, -- I'd panic and order three loaves. I threw out so much bread in a week that every time I opened the side door so many sparrows would take off that it sounded like a four-motor job warming up for a flight to New York.

A woman, after a year or two of marriage, knows how to handle the traffic at the side door like a head purchasing agent of a supermarket. It's a talent that comes only with time. It also requires a woman's instinct to say, "No."

Every peddler realized he had a sucker the minute he saw my apron. I bought six scented pot holders, a tinted enlargement of my grandfather's last photo, a bouquet of paper roses, and two dozen wire things that looked like oversized safety pins. The man who made them said they were to pick up cups with.

A woman has to go to the side door every fifteen minutes not only to make fast decisions about merchandise, but to take care of more feuds, fights, and flights of temperament than the manager of an opera house. I didn't realize before that children spend the entire day biting, kicking, and hitting one another over the head with little yellow steam shovels. When they're winning, they stay outside. When they're losing, they come to the side door covered with mud and crying. Sometimes their mothers all start going to one another's side doors with pinched lips and flashing eyes. How a half dozen mothers on a street end up each year still speaking to one another and exchanging Christmas cards is another of those tricks of being a housewife that man couldn't pick up in less than five generations.

I made one determined try at putting an ingenious system of mine to work. I decided that instead of taking a half day to do the ironing, I'd do it bit by bit whenever I had a free moment. This was before I realized that housewives never have free moments. I started as a system, but ended as a grim running fight against increasing odds, ironing things, not a free moment, but as they were needed.

Yesterday the final breakdown came. I started off the day before trying out the last theory I will ever have about housework. I'd decided, way back when I was just a husband, that one mistake a woman made was devoting all her time until a quarter to nine to getting the children off to school. Children could be taught to get themselves off to school, I'd always say. Yesterday I decided to let them, while I did the dusting.

I'd never heard of a woman dusting before breakfast. I know now that the reasons no woman dusts before breakfast is that it can't be done. But I didn't know that yesterday. I sent the children into their room, put some prunes to soak for supper, sewed a button on a jumper and got started dusting the living room. I went into the children's room about twenty to nine, just to give them a final once-over before they left for school. I found Mary sitting without anything on doing water colors, and Jane, who was dressed in one of her mother's old dresses, a bed sheet, and a pair of my rubber boots, just starting to examine some old toys she had fished out of the closet.

I began to realize why wives occasionally sit down and cry. For a minute I considered doing it myself. But I was afraid the bread man would catch me. So I just sat down. I told myself to keep cool and calmly take stock of what had to be done. I'd have to tidy things up just to be able to walk around. Most of the ironing was still to be done. The stuff I'd managed to get through was stacked on top of the refrigerator. I had to put it there because I'd started putting the dirty dishes that I hadn't been able to get around to in the linen closet.

I decided that there was only one thing to do. I had to get the children off to school, late or not, forget about such details as sewing on buttons, abandon all my theories and work my fingers to the bone until I could see daylight. (I didn't realize how accurate that phrase was.)

I began moving like a faro dealer caught in a raid. I got the kids dressed, pinned notes to them saying they were late because I had thought they were showing spots, but I'd made a mistake and please let them in. I phoned the local lunch counter and told them to send six hamburgers at noon and six more at six o'clock; plugged the phone, put a note on the door telling everyone to come back tomorrow, and started to work.

I have just finished ironing and am waiting for the sun to come up. I worked all day and all night. My wife will arrive at 10:00 a.m. I am going to meet her, drive her home, then go downtown to a restaurant I know that caters to people off freight trains, order a cup of coffee and just sit there, noting that there are no little girls in the restaurant, no pigtails, no ironing boards, and that someone is going to do the dishes for me. Then I am going to start work on my time-and-motion study. I should have time, now that my wife will be home. But it's going to be a time-and-motion study for Wives. All the time I want is enough to go through the motions of shaving and getting out of the house in the morning before things start to happen.

--Robert Lewis Allen

* * * * *

St. Peter and Satan were having an argument one day about baseball. With a beguiling leer, Satan proposed a game (to be played on neutral ground) between a select team from the heavenly host and his own hand-picked Plutonian boys.

"Very well," the gate-keeper of the Celestial City agreed. "But, you realize, I hope, that we have all the good players and the best coaches, too."

"I know," said Satan calmly, "but we have all the umpires."

* * * * *

JUDGING

We always think every other man's job is easier than our own. And the better he does it, the easier it looks.

--Eden Phillpots

* * * * *

The unforgiving man assumes a judgment that not even the theologians have given to God.

--Sydney J. Harris

* * * * *

He who cannot forgive others breaks the bridge over which he must pass himself.

--George Herbert

* * * * *

To govern yourself, use your head; to govern others, use your heart.

* * * * *

Judge Not

Pray do not find fault with the man
Who limps, or stumbles along the road
Unless you've worn the shoes he wears
Or struggled beneath his load.
There may be tacks in him that hurt
Though hidden away from view
Or the burden placed on your back
Might cause you to stumble too.
Don't sneer at him who's down today
Unless you've felt the blow
That caused his fall, or felt the shame
That only he can know.
You may be strong, but still the blows
That were his, if dealt to you
In self-same way and self-same time
Might cause you to stagger too.

Don't be too harsh with him who sins
Or pelt him with word or stone
Unless you're sure, yea, doubly sure
That you've no sins of your own.
For you know, perhaps if tempter's voice
Should whisper soft to you
As it did to him that went astray
'Twould cause you to falter too.

* * * * *

The Blind Men And The Elephant

It was six men of Indostan,
To learning much inclined,
Who went to see the elephant,
(Though all of them were blind,)
That each by observation
Might satisfy his mind.

The first approached the elephant,
And, happening to fall
Against his broad and sturdy side,
At once began to bawl:
"God bless me! But the elephant
is very like a wall!"

The second, feeling of the tusk,
Cried: "Ho! What have we here,
So very round, and smooth, and sharp?
To me 'tis very clear,
This wonder of an elephant
Is very like a spear!"

The third approached the animal,
And, happening to take
The squirming trunk within his hands,
Thus boldly up to spake:
"I see," quoth he, "the elephant
Is very like a snake!"

The fourth reached out his eager hand,
And felt about the knee;
What most this wondrous beast is like.
"'Tis clear enough the elephant
Is very like a tree!"

The fifth, who chanced to touch the ear,
Said: "E'en the blindest man
Can tell what this resembles most:
Deny the fact who can,
This marvel of an elephant
Is very like a fan!"

The sixth no sooner had begun
About the beast to grope,
Than seizing on the swinging tail
That fell within his scope,
"I see," quoth he, "the elephant
Is very like a rope!"

And so these men of Indostan
Disputed loud and long,
Each in his own opinion
Exceeding stiff and strong
Though each was partly in the right,
All were in the wrong!

--John Godfrey Saxe

* * * * *

Guilty Or Not Guilty

She stood at the bar of justice,
A creature wan and wild,
In form too small for a woman,
In feature too old for a child.
For a look so worn and pathetic
Was stamped on her pale young face,
It seemed long years of suffering
Must have left that silent trace.

"Your name," said the judge, as he eyed her,
With kindly look, yet keen,
"Is____" "Mary Maguire, if you please, sir."
"And your age?" "I am turned fifteen."
"Well, Mary," and then from a paper
He slowly and gravely read
"You are charged here -- I am sorry to say it
With stealing three loaves of bread.

"You look not like an old offender,
And I hope that you can show
The charge to be false. Now, tell me,
Are you guilty of this, or no?"
A passionate burst of weeping
Was at first her sole reply;
But she dried her tears in a moment,
And looked in the judge's eye.

"I will tell you just how it was, sir:
My father and mother are dead,
And my little brothers and sisters
Were hungry, and asked me for bread.
At first I earned it for them,
By working hard all day,
But somehow the times were hard, sir,
And the work all fell away.

I could get no more employment;
The weather was bitter cold;
The young ones cried and shivered
(Little Johnnie's but four years old);
So what was I to do, sir?
I am guilty, but do not condemn;
I took -- Oh was it stealing?
The bread to give to them."

Every man in the courtroom --
Graybread and thoughtless youth --
Knew, as he looked upon her,
That the prisoner spoke the truth.
Out from their pockets came kerchiefs,
Out from their eyes sprung tears,
And out from old, faded wallets
Treasures hoarded for years.

The judge's face was a study,
The strangest you ever saw,
As he cleared his throat and murmured
Something about the law.
For one so learned in such matters,
So wise in dealing with men,
He seemed, on a simple question,
Sorely puzzled just then.

But no one blamed him, or wondered
When at last these words they heard.
"The sentence of this young prisoner
Is for the present deferred."
And no one blamed him or wondered
When he went to her and smiled,
And tenderly led from the courtroom,
Himself, the "guilty" child!

--Unknown

* * * * *

The Preacher Who Wouldn't Be

A church was in need of a pastor. One of the elders was interested in knowing just what kind of a minister they desired. He, therefore, wrote a letter, as if he had received it from an applicant. He read this letter before the pulpit committee:

Gentlemen:

Understanding that your pulpit is vacant, I should like to apply for the position. I have many qualifications that I think you would appreciate. I have been blessed to preach with power and have had some success as a writer. Some say that I am a good organizer. I have been a leader in most places I have gone.

Some folks, however, have some things against me. I am over fifty years of age, I have never preached in one place for more than three years at a time. In some places I have left town, after my work caused riots and disturbances. I have to admit that I have been in jail three or four times but not because of any real wrong doing. My health is not too good, though I still get a good deal done. I have had to work at my trade to help pay my way. The churches I have preached in have been small, though located in several large cities.

I have not gotten along too well with the religious leaders in different towns where I have preached. In fact, some of them have threatened me, taken me to court and even attacked me physically.

I am not too good at keeping records. I have even been known to forget them I have baptized. However, if you can use me, I shall do my best for you, even if I have to work to help with my support.

The elder read this letter to the committee and asked them if they were interested in the applicant. They replied that he would never do for their church. They were not interested in any unhealthy, contentious, troublemaker, absent-minded, ex-jailbird; in fact, they felt insulted that his application had been presented.

The committee asked the name of the applicant, whereupon the elder answered, "THE APOSTLE PAUL."

* * * * *

The Army Son

The Creightons were very proud of their son Frank. When he went to college, naturally they missed him; but he wrote and they looked forward to his letters and saw him on weekends. Then Frank was drafted into the army.

After he had been in the army about five months, he received his call to go to Vietnam. Of course, the parents' anxiety for his first letter was greater than ever before. And every week they heard from him and were thankful for his well-being. Then one week went by without a letter -- two weeks -- and finally three. At the end of the third week a telegram came, saying, "We regret to inform you that your son has been missing for three weeks and is presumed to have been killed in action while fighting for his country."

The parents were shocked and grieved. They tried to accept the situation and go on living, but it was tragically lonesome without Frank.

About three weeks later, however, the phone rang. When Mrs. Creighton answered it, a voice on the other end said, "Mother, it's Frank. They found me, and I'm going to be all right. I'm in the United States and I'm coming home soon."

Mrs. Creighton was overjoyed, with tears running down her cheeks she sobbed, "Oh, that's wonderful! That's just wonderful, Frank."

There was silence for a moment, and then Frank said, "Mother I want to ask you something that is important to me. While I've been here, I've met a lot of wonderful people and I've really become close friends with some. There is one fellow I would like to bring home with me to meet you and Dad. And I would like to know if it would be all right if he could stay and live with us, because he has no place to go."

His mother assured him it would be all right.

Then Frank said, "You see, he wasn't as lucky as some; he was injured in battle. He was hit by a blast and his face is all disfigured. He lost his leg, and his right hand is missing. So you see, he feels uneasy about how others will accept him."

Frank's mother stopped to think a minute. She began to wonder how things would work out, and what people in town would think of someone like that. She said, "Sure Frank, you bring him home -- for a visit, that is. We would love to meet him and have him stay for a while; but about his staying with us permanently, well, we'll have to think about that." There was silence for a minute, and then Frank said, "Okay, Mother," and hung up.

A week went by without any word from Frank, and then a telegram arrived -- "We regret to inform you that your son has taken his life. We would like you to come and identify the body."

Their wonderful son was gone. The horrow stricken parents could only ask themselves, "Why had he done this?" When they walked into the room to identify the body of their son, they found a young man with a disfigured face, one leg missing, and his right hand gone.

* * * * *

KINDNESS

A small child was asked to describe loving kindness. He said, "If I'm hungry and my mother gives me some bread and butter -- that's kindness. But if she puts lots of jam on it, that's loving kindness!"

* * * * *

There are two kinds of people in the world; those you love and those you don't know.

* * * * *

A good word is an easy obligation, but not to speak ill requires only our silence, which costs us nothing.

--Tillotson

* * * * *

There is no beautifier of complexion or form or behavior like the wish to scatter joy and not pain around us.

--Emerson

* * * * *

If you want your neighbor to see what the Christ spirit will do for him, let him see what it has done for you.

--Henry Ward Beecher

* * * * *

Courtesy

Courtesy is a science of the highest importance -- It is like grace and beauty in the body, which charm at first sight, and lead on to further intimacy and friendship.

--Montaigne

* * * * *

The whole of heraldry and chivalry is in courtesy -- A man of fine manners shall pronounce your name with all the ornament that titles of nobility could add.

--Emerson

* * * * *

Life is not so short but that there is always time for courtesy.

--Emerson

* * * * *

The small courtesies sweeten life; the greater, ennoble it.

--Bovee

* * * * *

We should be as courteous to a man as we are to a picture, which we are willing to give the advantage of the best light.

--Emerson

* * * * *

There is no outward sign of true courtesy that does not rest on a deep moral foundation.

--Goethe

* * * * *

Kindness

I shall pass through this world but once. If, therefore, there be any kindness I can show, or any good thing I can say it would be it now; let me not defer it or neglect it, for I shall not pass this way again.

--Etienne de Grellet

* * * * *

You can't get more than you give, anymore than you can take a pint container to a well and bring back a gallon of water. You can't give frowns and get back smiles; you can't give a loud angry voice and get gentleness from others in return. By the same token, you can't plant a kind word, a thoughtful deed, a generous gift, and not reap more of the same from someone, somewhere, sometime.

* * * * *

Kindness

Just a little act of kindness
Just a little word of cheer
Help to make our living pleasant
Minimize both doubt and fear.

Jesus said, "Be meek and lowly"
And He governs men with love
Just as God our Heavenly Father
Governs in the court above.

Jesus never hurt the feelings
Of a person great or small
Always he was kind and friendly
We're assured he loves us all.

All the world is now in turmoil
Caused by the gross unfriendliness
Peace will follow Christian living
Be the watchword Kindliness.

* * * * *

LIFE

Life is a grindstone; whether it grinds you down or polishes you up, depends on what you are made of.

* * * * *

To be what we are, and to become what we are capable of becoming, is the only end of life.

* * * * *

Isn't life beautiful?
Isn't life gay?
Isn't life a perfect way
To pass the time away.

* * * * *

Life is not a goblet to be drained; it is a measure to be filled. The foot-rule of life is philosophy which measures what we think about God. But religion is the square that measures what we feel and know about Him. So to quarrel with our lot in life is to detract from development.

* * * * *

All of us are expected to function successfully in some particular field -- some in more than one, but all in one.

* * * * *

Life alone can't give you joy,
Unless you really will it,
Life only gives you time and space,
It's up to you to fill it.

--Anonymous

* * * * *

The world is like a mirror
Reflecting what you do,
And if your face is smiling
Then it smiles right back at you.

* * * * *

What do we live for if not to make the world less difficult for each other.

--George Eliot

* * * * *

Making a living is a necessity, but making a life is a duty.

* * * * *

Fear not that your life shall come to an end, but rather fear it shall never have a beginning.

--Newman

* * * * *

If you would live your life with ease, do what you ought, not what you please.

* * * * *

There are three kinds of people: those who make things happen; those who watch things happen; and those who have no idea what has happened.

--Anonymous

* * * * *

When life falls into a rut, decay begins.

--Arthur Stilwell

* * * * *

The tragedy of life is what dies inside a man while he still lives.

* * * * *

<u>Life's Rewards</u>

The doctor knows what his trained eyes see
And he says it's the last of the ninth for me
So once more swinging while the clouds loom dark
And then I must leave this noisy park.

T'was a glorious game from the opening bell
Good plays, bad plays, thrills pell mell
The speed of it burned my tears away
But I thank God that He let me play.

* * * * *

For Sale:

One new and dew pearled day,
Dressed in a sunrise negligee,
Untarnished, washed by early rain,
A bargain you'll not get again.
A bargain going for a song,
A day but brief with memory long,
So treat with honor and with care,
Waste not with judgment false, unfair.
For Sale: a day as fresh as dawn.
What offer? Going, going, gone!

--Thelma Ireland

* * * * *

YESTERDAY is but a memory --
Tomorrow is only a vision --
Today, today Dear God
Bless my TODAY.

* * * * *

You can carry a pack
If it's strapped to your back;
You can carry a weight in your hands.
You can carry a bundle
On top of your head,
As they do in other lands.
A load is light
If you carry it right,
'Though it weighs as much as a boulder;
But a tiny chip
Is too heavy to bear
If you carry it on your shoulder.

--Anonymous

* * * * *

It is something to be able to paint a particular picture, or to carve a statue and so to make a few objects beautiful; but it is far more glorious to carve and paint the very atmosphere through which we look -- to affect the quality of the day -- that is the highest of arts.

--Henry David Thoreau

* * * * *

O! Give me patience when little hands,
Tug at me with ceaseless small demands.
O! Give me gentle words and smiling eyes,
And keep my lips from hasty sharp replies.
Let me not in weariness, confusion or noise,
Obscure my vision from life's few fleeting joys.
Then when in years to come, my home is still,
No bitter memories, its rooms may fill.

* * * * *

Life Insurance Policy

Could I interest you in a policy?
What kind is it you say?
Well, it's life insurance, friend
But in a different sort of way.

It's the very same insurance
That Christ brought to the Earth
And whatever you put into it, friend
You'll get your money's worth.

No, you don't pay so much in money
As you pay by living right
Just obey the gospel teachings
And put your sins to flight

Yes, it pays big dividends
But perhaps not right away
It insures your life eternal, friend
And you collect on Judgment Day

And contrary to worldly ways of man
You the reward will receive
Invest a lot in this policy, friend
And I promise you shall not grieve.

The Lord will do the collecting, friend
He comes around each day
And although you cannot see Him
He knows what you do and say.

It's the greatest policy that can be had
For it insures the souls of men
The Gospel of Jesus Christ, my friend
Really pays back in the end.

* * * * *

Life's Mirror

There are Loyal Hearts, there are spirits brave,
There are souls that are pure and true;
Then give to the world the best you have,
And the best will come back to you.

Give love, and love to your life will flow,
A strength in your utmost need;
Have faith, and a score of hearts will show
Their faith in your word and deed.

Give truth, and your gift will be paid in kind,
And honor will honor meet;
And a smile that is sweet will surely find
A smile that is just as sweet.

Give sorrow and pity to those who mourn;
You will gather in flowers again
The scattered seeds of your thought outborne,
Though the sowing seemed but vain.

For life is the mirror of king and slave --
'Tis just what we are and do;
Then give to the world the best you have,
And the best will come back to you.

--Madeline Bridges

* * * * *

The Loom Of Time

Man's life is laid in the loom of time
To a pattern he does not see,

While the weaver's work and the shuttles fly
Till the dawn of eternity.

Some shuttles are filled with silver threads
And some with threads of gold.
While often but the darker hues
Are all that they may hold.

But the weaver watches with skillful eye,
Each shuttle fly to and fro,
And sees the pattern so deftly wrought
As the loom moves sure and slow.

God surely planned the pattern:
Each thread, the dark and fair,
Is chosen by his master skill
And placed in the web with care.

He only knows its beauty,
And guides the shuttles which hold
The threads so unattractive
As well as the threads of gold.

Not till each loom is silent,
And the shuttles cease to fly,
Shall God reveal the pattern
And explain the reason why.

The dark threads were as needful
In the weaver's skillful hand
As the threads of gold and silver
For the pattern which He planned.

--Unknown

* * * * *

No Matter What Else

No matter what else you're doing,
From cradle days through to the end,
You're writing your life's secret story,
Each night sees another page penned.

Each month ends a thirty day chapter,
Each year the end of a part,
And never an act is mis-stated,
Nor even a wish of the heart.

Each morn when you wake the book opens,
Revealing a page clean and white,
What words and what thoughts and what doings,
Will cover it's surface by night.

God leaves that to you: you're the writer,
And never one word will grow dim,
Until one day you'll write the word 'finished,'
And give your life's book back to him.

--Jessie Evans Smith

* * * * *

There were two buckets sitting on the edge of a well. One turned to the other with mouth drooping down and said, "All I do is go down and come up and go down and come up all day long. No matter how many times I go down and come up, I always go down empty." The other little bucket smiled brightly, "That's funny. I have the same task. All I do is go down and come up and go down and come up all day long. But no matter how many times I go down and come up, I always come up full."

That's positive thinking. Hope is positive thinking. Hopeful people are happy people who take the changes and chances of life in their stride, worrying not so much about what happens to them as what they do about it. They look for the best in people and make haste to be kind, to help, to appreciate.

* * * * *

Several years ago a man was being interviewed on radio. He had started to walk across the United States on foot, from California to New York. He had reached a point halfway across. Reporters asked him about his experience. Finally, the question came, "Sir, what would you say has been your most difficult experience so far?"

The traveler thought long. Through his mind went the toilsome climb over mountain passes; hot dry stretches of desert. Sun. Wind. Then he said quietly, "I guess my greatest problem was that the sand kept getting into my shoes."

So that was it. The sand in his shoes. Not some great crisis that he had faced. Not some danger that had almost taken his life. But sand; sand that wore blisters on the soles of his feet. Sand that ground its way between the pores of his skin and irritated constantly, that made every step an agony. Sand in his shoes.

Life is like that. It is not always the great crisis in life that crushes. Not always the deepest sorrows or the great disappointments. Most often, it is the constant irritation of small things -- things insignificant in themselves. We can stand up to the big things of life. But the petty things can often cause our downfall. Until we say ofttimes it is just one thing after another. For the little things have a way of wearing down our inner reserves of strength.

It is that way in our personal lives too. It isn't the single drip of water that causes nerves to become taut. It is the continual dripping that makes folks mad.

--Harleigh M. Rosenberger

* * * * *

The only responsibility that a man cannot evade in this life is the one he thinks of least, his personal influence. Man's conscious influence, when he is on dress parade, when he is posing to impress those around him is woefully small. But his unconscious influence, the silent, subtle radiation of his personality, the effect of his words and acts, the trifles he never considers, is tremendous. Every moment of life he is changing, to a degree, the life of the whole world. Every man has an atmosphere which is affecting every other. So silent and unconsciously is the influence working, that man may forget that it exists.

Into the hands of every individual is given a marvelous power for good or for evil, the silent, unconscious, unseen influence of his life. This is simply the constant radiation of what a man really is, not what he pretends to be. Every man, by his mere living, is radiating sympathy, or sorrow, or morbidness, or cynicism, or happiness, or hope, or any of a hundred other qualities. Life is a state of constant radiation and absorption; to exist is to radiate; to exist is to be the recipient of radiations.

--William George Jordan

* * * * *

Twenty-Four Golden Hours

Charlotte had come to a hard time in her life. She was filled with discontent. Everything seemed wrong. Her ambitions were thwarted; her friends were commonplace; her home unattractive, her own personality unlovely, as she was well aware. The problems were too many for Charlotte. She seemed caught in a current of circumstances that was carrying her into an ugly and unsatisfying life, and she could not escape.

She went to the one person who seemed to be leading the kind of life that she very much desired. Margaret Ames, lovely, popular, gifted and successful, lived in a cottage studio set in a flower garden. There she painted those charming little water colors that were in such demand that they were always sold in advance. Margaret was so kind, so willing to help, that you dared go to her with your problems. In the charming studio Charlotte poured out the story of her heartache over her frustrated, unhappy life. She told all the details, the poverty, the ugliness, the disappointment about school, the unsympathetic family, the careless friends, her own lack of charm and beauty. Margaret after a gentle word of sympathy said, "You can change all that if you really have the will to do it."

"How? How?" cried Charlotte. "I'll do anything, no matter how hard."

"Will you indeed? It is not hard at all, it only takes time. You see, you must sow the seed for another kind of life, and wait with patience for it to grow. Here is a test to see whether you truly have the will: Live for twenty-four hours as if Christ were right beside you, seeing everything that you do. Then come to me again, and we'll talk it over. Will you do that?"

Charlotte was a Church member, but she never spoke of Christ like that -- almost as if he were a neighbor that one might speak to. Somewhat constrained and doubtful, she answered, "Yes, Mrs. Ames."

"Then come again tomorrow, sometime in the evening, and we'll talk about the change."

It was late afternoon when Charlotte went home. She knew that she was expected to help get the supper onto the table. She went to the drawer and took out a wrinkled tablecloth. When she spread it on the table she noticed several spoiled spots. And here she had her first thought of change.

"If Christ were going to eat with us, I wouldn't put on a soiled cloth," she said to herself.

She got a fresh cloth. And with the same thought she brought in a small bowl of flowers from the yard. She put the butter on a fresh plate instead of on the soiled one. She cut the bread with care. She mashed the potatoes, and beat them lightly, instead of putting them on plain boiled. She made her gravy smooth and rich. "If I'd known Christ would be here, I'd have managed something nice for dessert," she thought. She hoped that it was not sacrilegious to think of Christ in connection with desserts.

"Company tonight?" asked father, peering through his glasses as he came to the table.

"Just you, Daddy," smiled Charlotte. If Christ were present, of course you'd smile at your family and show them your very best manner.

Her mother, worn out and hot, and still dressed in her kitchen clothes, sat down saying, "I don't know what's got into her to fix up so for just us. I suppose she's expecting someone to drop in before we're done."

Charlotte bit back a hasty retort. She and Mother hadn't been getting along well lately. It seemed that mother wouldn't try to keep up-to-date, and that she never understood how a girl felt about things. Charlotte kept still until she thought of the proper thing to say in the presence of the unseen Guest. "I don't know of anyone I'd rather fix things up for than our own folks," she said.

The family simply stared for a minute. That wasn't like Charlotte. Then father said, "That's right, daughter. It's too bad we all don't think of that oftner." But Dick snickered. Charlotte's anger flared. There is nothing more maddening than to be laughed at when one is doing one's best. In another moment a sharp retort would have started a quarrel. But just in time Charlotte said to herself, "Christ is here," and said nothing aloud.

There was a short, uncomfortable silence. Dick was ashamed but wouldn't say so. But soon they were all talking quietly again.

"It is better," thought Charlotte, "to keep still when anyone else is exasperating. A quarrel makes mother really ill, and it gives me a headache, besides making me look like a beast. Besides, I think Dick's ashamed. I can tell, because he's so gruff."

"It's your turn to wash the dishes," said Agnes, when the two girls began to do up the work.

"All right," said Charlotte. Usually there was a sharp argument over whose turn it was. Charlotte got the water ready and began. Agnes continued to carry dishes out in silence. After a while she burst out: "It really was my turn, Charlotte. I was very selfish to let you begin. I'll take my turn tomorrow night, and the next."

"It's all right, Agnes. I really don't mind washing at all."

To her astonishment Charlotte knew that this was true. When you didn't mind washing it ceased to be the hard job that it had formerly been.

In the living room Charlotte slipped a magazine out from the bottom of the pile and began to read. She had brought the magazine home herself, and she kept it under cover. After a few minutes she put it down. It was not an immoral sheet; indeed, it was considered entirely respectable, but it was trashy, lurid, sentimental, a world removed from the wholesome type of love story. "I wouldn't be reading this if Christ were standing where he could read with me," she thought. And she carried it out, and put it in the wastepaper bag.

A party was in the making at Lucy's and she was invited to go. Should she go? Oh, yes! Christ went to parties. He seemed to like going, and he helped other people to have a good time. All through the gay evening Charlotte kept her thought, "Christ is beside me." She didn't think of herself very much. She helped the girls get the hasty snack prepared. She talked to a quiet, shy young man and drew him into the games. She took her turn at stunts and stories without self-consciousness, and she felt a genuine thrill when someone said in the dark ahead of her on the way home, "That Charlotte is a lot of fun, isn't she." She knew that the crowd hadn't been thinking her much fun lately until she tried this experiment tonight.

The next morning Charlotte went to work and applied this same experiment at work. Instead of hating her job like she had before, she tried being cheerful, helpful, and smiling through it all. Before long she was actually enjoying the job that she was tolerating long enough to earn the amount of money she needed to go to college and take a decorating course so that some day she could design beautiful clothes. No matter how rude some of the customers were, Charlotte found that a smile will melt even the rudest and unhappiest customers. The whole day Charlotte met every customer with an eager interest to serve acceptable. Closing time came before she knew it.

At eight o'clock she sat in Margaret Ames' studio again.

"I tried it, Mrs. Ames, just as well as I could, and, well, it made everything so different. I think I can see what you mean. Of course, it didn't change the things that are bothering me. I'm still poor, and can't go to school, and I live in an ugly house, and I don't know the sort of people I'd like to..."

"Ah, my dear! But you only started the seed-sowing twenty-four hours ago. When you first put the seed in, the garden doesn't look different does it? But it's on the way to becoming different. In three months it will be bright with bloom, not drab with dull, brown earth. That will be the way with you. You say these handicaps in your life haven't changed. But you've started to change them. Can you keep on as you've begun, and wait patiently for the Lord, as the Psalmist tells us? You will cease to be poor, and without opportunity. Friends will be drawn to you. Doors will open before you.

Your surroundings will blossom into beauty. You have the magic word. It is Christ. Fretting or even effort doesn't change things very much; but Christ does. Just remember to keep your daily walk very close to him."

"I'm going to do it," said Charlotte.

* * * * *

LOVE

Love, which is only an episode in the life of man, is the entire history of woman's life.

--Mad. de Stael

* * * * *

God has placed the genius of women in their hearts; because the works of this genius are always works of love.

--Lamartine

* * * * *

My bounty is as boundless as the sea,
My love as deep; the more I give to thee,
The more I have, for both are infinite.

* * * * *

Dear Lord, bless me that I may make this portion of eternity beautiful and happy to those I love and for those whose lives touch mine.

--Patricia Sykes

* * * * *

When love and skill work together, expect a masterpiece.

* * * * *

Love makes one richer than a mountain of gold.

* * * * *

The soul would have no rainbows if the eyes had no tears.

* * * * *

When I see you my stomach gets all over and over excited. Nothing much happens in my head, or that I can feel in my heart -- maybe, my stomach is in love with you.

* * * * *

Love is the feeling you feel when you feel you are feeling a feeling you feel you have never felt before.

* * * * *

Sacrifice brings forth the blessings of heaven. But giving brings forth the fruits of the spirit. The fruits of the spirit are love.

--Tay

* * * * *

Not knowing how to love means the loss of the meaning of life and its fulfillment.

--Pearl Buck

* * * * *

Love is a special way of feeling, rather it is a special way of being, of which feelings are a rich and intense part.

--Truman Madsen

* * * * *

Those who love not their fellow beings, live unfruitful lives.

--Shelley

* * * * *

Love is the master key that opens the gates of happiness.

--Oliver Wendell Holmes

* * * * *

The supreme happiness of life is the conviction of being loved for yourself, or more correctly, being loved in spite of yourself.

--Victor Hugo

* * * * *

They do not love that do not show their love.

--William Shakespeare

* * * * *

Riches take wings, comforts vanish, hope withers away, but love stays with us. Love is God.

--Lew Wallace

* * * * *

Trust

Trust is a fragile word for mortals
And passion a brilliant stone to crack it on.
But love, true love, is the velvet glove
That catches fragile trust before it's gone.

--Gay N. Blanchard

* * * * *

What Can I Give You

What can I give you, child, against the intruding years? What will keep each moment bright to withstand all the tears?

I can give you laughter...It will not be enough. I can give you courage for when the road is rough.

I can give you words of faith for when the night is long. And for the songless moment, I can give you a song.

I can give you promise of guidance from above: And always, always, always, I can give you love.

* * * * *

'Tis the human touch in the world that counts,
The touch of your hand to mine,
Which means far more to the fainting heart
Than shelter and bread and wine;

For shelter is gone when the night is o'er
And bread lasts only a day,
But the touch of the hand and the sound of the voice
Sing on in the soul always.

--Spencer Free

* * * * *

I Love You

I love you,
Not only for what you are,
But for what I am
When I am with you.

I love you.
Not only for what
You have made of yourself,
But for what you are making of me.

I love you
For the part of me
That you bring out.
I love you
For looking into my heaped up heart
And passing over all my weaknesses
That you can't help dimly seeing there;
And for drawing out into the light
All the beautiful belongings
Others may not have looked
Quite far enough to find.

I love you because you
Are helping me to make of my life,
A picture of endless beauty,
A song of rapture, dreams fulfilled,
A spiritual togetherness
With our Father in Heaven.
Yes, a creation together of
Eternal Joy and Love.

* * * * *

Love is found in unexpected places
It is there in the quiet moment
When we first discover a beautiful thing,
When we watch a bird soar high against a pale blue sky,
When we find a place that shelters us and is our very own.

Love starts in little ways
It may begin the day we first share our thoughts
with someone else...
Or help someone who needs us...
Or sometimes it begins because,
Even without words, we understand how someone feels.

Love comes quietly...but you know when it is there,
Because suddenly...you are not alone anymore...
And there is no sadness inside you.

* * * * *

One cold Christmas Eve day, a little boy about six or seven was standing out in front of a store window. The little child had no shoes and his clothes were mere rags. A young woman passing by saw the little boy and could read the longing in his pale blue eyes. She took the child by the hand and led him into the store. There she bought him some new shoes and a complete suit of warm clothing. They came back out into the street and the woman said to the child, "Now you go home and have a very Merry Christmas." The boy looked up at her and asked, "Are you Jesus' Momma?" She smiled down at him and replied, "No, son, I'm just one of his children." The little boy then said, "I knew you had to be some relation."

Love is a miracle! It can come to any of us at any age, at any time, and in any place. All we have to do is reach out and live, reach out and receive.

* * * * *

...When I first went to work as a nurse in the old folks' home, they gave me the most difficult cases, and one was an old woman who used to sit in a rocking chair all day long. Nobody liked her. The other nurses avoided her, and that's why I was given the assignment. I thought to myself, "If the Christian message of love means anything, it means something now with this woman." So I pulled up a rocking chair and just rocked along side this woman and loved her and loved her. The third day she opened her eyes and said, "You're so kind." Those were the first words she had spoken in three years. In two weeks she was out of the home.

"Now I never saw the patient whose life was transformed by love," said Mr. Jones; "But I did see the nurse who did the loving and here is another of the unarguable truths about love -- it makes the lover beautiful."

--<u>Guideposts</u>

* * * * *

Abou Ben Adhem

Abou Ben Adhem (may his tribe increase!)
Awoke one night from a deep dream of peace,
And saw within the moon light in his room,
Making it rich, and like a lily in bloom,
An angel writing in a book of gold:
Exceeding peace had made Ben Adhem bold,
And to the presence in the room he said,
"What writest thou?" The vision raised its head,
And with a look made of all sweet accord
Answered, "The names of those who love the Lord."
"And is mine one?" asked Abou, "Nay, not so,"
Replied the angel, Abou spoke more low,
But cheerfully still: and said, "I pray thee, then,
Write me as one that loves his fellowmen."

The angel wrote, and vanished, the next night
It came again with a great wakening light,
And showed the names who love of God had blessed,
And, lo, Ben Adhem's name led all the rest!

--James Henry Leigh Hunt

* * * * *

She asks only in return that when you look upon her your eyes shall speak devotion; that when you address her your voice shall be gentle, loving, and kind; that you shall not despise her because she cannot understand all at once your vigorous thoughts and ambitious designs; for, when misfortune and evil have defeated your greatest purposes, her love remains to console you. You look to the tress for strength and grandeur; do not despise the flowers because their fragrance is all they have to give. Remember, love is all a woman has to give, but it is the only thing which God permits us to carry beyond the grave.

--Drieser

* * * * *

Love Lightens Labor

A good wife rose from her bed one morn,
And thought, with a nervous dread,
Of the pile of clothes to be washed, and more
Than a dozen mouths to be fed.

"There's the meals to get for the men in the field,
And the children to fix away
To School, and the milk to be skimmed and churned,
All to be done this day."

It had rained in the night and all the wood
Was wet as it could be;
There were puddings and pies to bake, besides
A loaf of cake for tea.
And the day was hot, and her aching head
Throbbed as she wearily said,
"If maidens but knew what good wives know,
They would not be in such hurry to wed!"

"Jennie, what do you think I told Ben Brown?"
Called the farmer from the well;
And a flush crept up in his bronzed brow,
And his eyes half-bashfully fell.
"It was this," he said, and coming near
He smiled, and stooping down,
Kissed her cheek. "Twas this, that you were the
Best and dearest wife in town!"

The farmer went back to the field,
And the wife, in a smiling absent way,
Sang snatches of tender little songs
She'd not sung for many a day.
And the pain in her head was gone, and the clothes
Were white as the foam of the sea;
Her bread was light, and the butter was sweet
And as golden as it could be.

"Just think," the children called in a breath,
"Tom Wood has run off to sea!
He wouldn't, I know, if he'd only had
As happy a home as we."

The night came down, and the good wife smiled
To herself, as she softly said:
"'Tis so sweet to labor for those we love,
It's not so strange that young girls want to wed!"

--Anonymous

* * * * *

For You With Love

Love is the whisper of earth
When the stars pale
And the dawn-winds hail
A new day's birth...

The laughing abandon,
The shining glee
Of the fountains leap
And the headlong sweep
Of the sea...

Love is the memory
Time cannot kill,
The cherished tune,
Gay and absurd...

And the music unheard.

The silence that trembles
And seems to fill
The heart when the song
Of a bird
Is still...

Love is God's plenty...
An endless measure
Of gifts that descend
In sun and in shower
On mountain and plain...
The quickening rain,
And the storied treasure
At the rainbow's end...

Love is the coming alive
Of a golden bush
That cannot wait for spring...

Blossoms that bring
Joy to the day
And honey to the hive...

The call of the hills
And the answering ocean
When everything's a maze
And a blaze of color and motion...
Torrents of wonder, of waves,
And wings...
And the whole sky sings...

But first and last...
Time present, time future,
And time past...
Past all belief and thinking of...
Earth beneath and heaven above

Beginning and ending...

Forever new...

Love is You.

* * * * *

Eternal Love

In the broad expanse of space eternities ago,
We were created and assigned to go below;
It finally came my turn to bid my sad adieu,
To step upon the stage of life and make my great debut.

With a tear filled eye you said, "Goodbye,"
With a saddened heart, "Farewell," said I;
I turned to leave, but paused and then,
With a sudden jerk I turned again.

I know that God with His plan so deep,
Will cause my mind to fall asleep;
And forget the things that I know now,
Before I go to the earth below;
But one thing I'll remember and cherish evermore,
Is the beauty of your inner soul, so radiant and pure.

If it be His will, hope and pray,
We may meet and love again someday;
Oh, God I wish that I could stay,
But as I listened I heard Him say,
"Go now my child, make no delay."

And with your image burned into my soul,
I started off for my earthly goal;
But I'd vowed in my heart so full of pain,
That I'd recognize you if we met again;
Then the curtain was drawn and a veil was cast,
Across the happenings of the past.

All was forgotten except for the part,
Of your beautiful image I kept in my heart;
And God in His wisdom guided our feet,
So that down on earth once again we could meet.

Remember I said, "Have we not met before,
Perhaps on some Celestial shore,"
"Yes, I know you there, the one I sought,
So you see my love, I haven't forgot."

* * * * *

Dear Mary Marker:

It is not possible for me to enter my daddy in the "My Pop's Tops" contest, but I want to pay tribute to my daddy anyway, and to tell all other daddies like him, because they are very special fathers. So my mommie is writing this letter for me.

I love daddy first of all for accepting me just as I am without any questions, and for the happy home he has helped to create.

He loves me enough not to spoil me, and he cooperates with mommie to teach me to mind, so everyone will love me and I will not be unwelcome wherever I go.

Sometimes people refer to me as a "problem," but daddy is quick to explain that I am only a challenge.

He has so very much patience with me; he takes time to wait for me while I get things done in my own slow way. He encourages me and gives me confidence in myself.

He never gets angry when I break the record player, and I break it very often. He just hurries to get it fixed and comes home with more records because he knows how much I miss it.

Daddy and I are real pals. We spend hours playing together and watching the television he bought for me.

Sunday we go to church and Daddy is proud of me from the top of my curly head to the tip of my toes. He beams with pride when folks notice me, and he is never ashamed of me.

Daddy says I am an angel -- sometimes a good angel and sometimes a bad angel, but always an angel. He thinks Heavenly Father specially picked him out and mommie also to entrust a precious spirit to, that can do nothing very wrong and, therefore, will have nothing to answer for in the eternal world.

Until that day, the wonderful day when the three of us can stand together before our Maker and I can thank Daddy for seeing me so kindly through life, will you please tell him all this through your column, Miss Marker?

You see, I can only say a few words. I couldn't exist a single day without loving supervision and care, for I am mentally retarded. The world calls me a Mongoloid, but my daddy calls me SWEETIE PIE.

* * * * *

Our Brother's Keeper

A couple whom we shall call John and Mary had a nice home and two lovely children, a boy and a girl. John had a good job and had just been asked to go on business to another city and be gone several days. It was decided that Mary needed an outing and would go along too. They hired a reliable woman to care for the children and made the trip, returning a little earlier than they had planned.

As they drove into their home town feeling glad to be back, they noticed smoke, and went off their usual route to see what it was. They found a home in flames. Mary said, "Oh well, it isn't our fire. Let's go home." But John drove closer and exclaimed, "That home belongs to Fred Jones who works at the plant. He wouldn't be off work yet. Maybe there is something we could do."

"It's nothing to do with us," protested Mary. "You have your good clothes on. Let's not go any closer."

But John drove up and stopped and both were horrow stricken to see the whole house in flames. A woman on the lawn was in hysterics screaming, "The children! Get the children!"

John grabbed her by the shoulders saying, "Get hold of yourself and tell us where the children are!"

"In the basement," sobbed the woman, "down the hall and to the left."

In spite of Mary's protests John grabbed the water hose and soaked his clothes, put his wet handkerchief on his head and bolted for the basement which was filled with smoke and was scorching hot. He found the door and grabbed two children, carrying one under each arm like the football player he was. As he left he could hear some more whimpering. He delivered the two badly frightened and nearly suffocated youngsters into waiting arms and filled his lungs with fresh air and started back asking how many more were down there. They told him two more and Mary grabbed his arm and screamed, "John! Don't go back! It's suicide! That house will cave in any second!"

But he shook her off and went back feeling his way down the smoke-filled hallway and into the room. It seemed an eternity before he found both children and started back. They were all three coughing and he stooped low to get the available air he could. As he stumbled up the endless steps the thought went through his mind that there was something vaguely familiar about the little bodies clinging to him, and when at last they came out into the sunlight and air, he found that he had rescued his own children. The baby-sitter had left them at this home while she did some shopping.

* * * * *

The Miracle

The violent grinding of brakes suddenly applied, and the harsh creaking of skidding wheels gradually died away as the big car came to a stop. Eddie quickly picked himself up from the dusty pavement where he had been thrown, and looked around wildly.

Agnes! Where was the little sister he had been holding by the hand when they started to cross the street? The next moment he saw her under the big car that had run them down, her eyes closed, a dark stain slowly spreading on her little white face.

With one bound the boy was under the car, trying to lift the child.

"You'd better not try, son," said a man gently. "Someone has gone to telephone for an ambulance."

"She's not...dead, boss?" Eddie begged in a husky voice.

The man stooped and felt the limp little pulse. "No, my boy," he said slowly.

A policeman came up, dispersed the collecting crowd, and carried the unconscious girl into a nearby drug store. Eddie's folded coat made a pillow for her head until the ambulance arrived. He was permitted to ride in the conveyance with her to the hospital. Something about the sturdy, shabbily dressed boy, who could not be more than ten years old, and his devotion to his little sister, strangely touched the hearts of the hard-boiled hospital apprentices.

"We must operate at once," said the surgeon after a brief preliminary examination. "She has been injured internally, and has lost a great deal of blood." He turned to Eddie who, inarticulate with grief, stood dumbly by. "Where do you live?"

Eddie told him that their father was dead, and that their mother did day work -- he did not know where.

"We can't wait to find her," said the surgeon, "because by that time it might be too late."

Eddie waited in the sitting room while the surgeons worked over Agnes. After that seemed an eternity a nurse sought him out.

"Eddie," she said kindly, "your sister is very bad, and the doctor wants to make a transfusion. Do you know what that is?" Eddie shook his head. "She has lost so much blood she cannot live unless someone gives her his. Will you do it for her?"

Eddie's wan face grew paler, and he gripped the knobs of the chair so hard that his knuckles became white. For a moment he hesitated; then gulping back his tears, he nodded his head and stood up.

"That's a good lad," said the nurse.

She patted his head, and led the way to the elevator which whisked them to the operating room -- a very clean but evil-smelling room, with pale green walls and innumerable shiny instruments in glass cases. No one spoke to Eddie except the nurse who directed him in a low voice how to prepare for the ordeal. The boy bit his quivering lip and silently obeyed.

"Are you ready?" asked a man swathed in white from head to foot, turning from the table over which he had been bending. For the first time Eddie noticed who it was lying there so still. Little Agnes! And he was going to make her well.

He stepped forward quickly.

Two hours later the surgeon looked up with a smile into the faces of the young interns and nurses who were engrossed in watching the great man work.

"Fine," he said. "I think she'll pull through."

After the transfusion Eddie had been told to lie quietly on a cot in the corner of the room. In the excitement of the delicate operation he had been entirely forgotten.

"It was wonderful, Doctor!" exclaimed one of the young interns. "A miracle!" Nothing, he felt in his enthusiastic recognition of the marvels of surgery, could be greater than the miracles of science.

"I am well satisfied," said the surgeon with conscious pride.

There was a tug at his sleeve, but he did not notice. In a little while there was another tug -- this time more peremptory -- and the great surgeon glanced down to see a ragged, pale-faced boy looking steadily up into his face.

"Say, Doc," said a husky voice, "When do I croak?"

The interns laughed and the great surgeon smiled. "Why, what do you mean, my boy?" he asked kindly.

"I thought...when they took a guy's blood...he croaked," muttered Eddie.

The smiles faded from the lips of the doctors and nurses, and the young intern who had thought there was nothing greater than the miracles of science, caught his breath suddenly. This ragged lad had climbed to the very height of nobility and sacrifice, and showed them a glimpse of the greatest miracle of all -- a selfless love!

But Eddie must never know this. The lesson was too poignantly beautiful to be wasted. The great surgeon motioned the others for silence.

"I think after all you will get well, Eddie," he said gruffly. "You and little Agnes."

--Arthur Styron

* * * * *

MAN'S WORTH

I cannot conceive of a greater loss than the loss of one's self-respect.

--Mahatma Ghandi

* * * * *

The life of every man is a diary in which he means to write one story, and writes another, and his humblest hour is when he compares the volume as it is with what he vowed to make it.

--J. M. Barrie

* * * * *

If you want to leave your footprints in the sands of time, wear your work shoes.

* * * * *

The Lord is not going to fill an empty well, but if you fill it with good things, He may help you draw out the things you need.

* * * * *

No one can make you feel inferior without your consent.

--Eleanor Roosevelt

* * * * *

If you treat a man as he is, he will remain as he is, but if you treat him as if he were what he ought to be, and could be, he will become what he ought to be, and should be.

--Goethe

* * * * *

The soul is dyed the color of one's leisure hours.

* * * * *

Great minds have purposes -- others have wishes.

--Washington Irving

* * * * *

Man's Worth

When you meet a really great man, he seems so simple and modest that you almost have a new faith in your own possibilities.

* * * * *

I always like to hear someone talk about themselves because you never hear anything bad.

--Will Rogers

* * * * *

The Lord does not ask about our ability,
Nor our inability,
But only about our availability.
And if we prove our dependability,
The Lord will take care of our capabilities.

* * * * *

An Indispensible Man

Sometime when you're feeling important,
Sometime when your ego's in bloom,
Sometime when you take it for granted
You're the best qualified in the room;

Sometime when you feel that your going
Would leave an unfillable hole --
Just follow these simple instructions
And see how it humbles your soul.

Take a bucket and fill it with water --
Put your hand in it up to your wrist;
Pull it out and the hole that's remaining
Is a measure of how you'll be missed.

You may stir up the water galore
But stop -- and you'll find in a moment
It looks quite the same as before.

The moral in this quaint example
Is "Do just the best that you can."
Be proud of yourself, but remember
There is no indispensible man.

* * * * *

The Measure Of Man

Not -- "How did he die?"
But -- "How did he live?"
Not -- "What did he gain?"
But -- "What did he give?"

These are the units to measure the worth
Of a man, as a man, regardless of birth.

Not -- "What was his station?"
But -- "Had he a heart?"
And -- "How did he play his God-given part?"

Was he ever ready with a word of good cheer.
To bring back a smile, to banish a tear?

Not -- "What was his church?"
Nor -- "What was his creed?"
But -- "Had he befriended those really in need?"

Not -- "What did the sketch in the newspaper say?"
But -- "How many were sorry when he passed away?"

* * * * *

How To Measure A Man

A man's no bigger than the way
He treats his fellow man!
This standard has his measure been
Since time itself began!

He's measured not by tithes or creed.
High-sounding though they be,
Nor by the gold that's put aside.
Nor by his sanctity!

He's measured not by social rank,
When character's the test;.
Nor by his earthly pomp or show,
Displaying wealth possessed!

He's measured by his justice, right,
His fairness at his play,
His squareness in all dealings made,
His honest, upright way.

These are his measures, ever near
To serve him when they can;
For man's no bigger than the way
He treats his fellow man.

--Author Unknown

* * * * *

The Monkey's Disgrace

The monkeys sat in a coconut tree
Discussing things as they are said to be.
Said one to another, "Now listen you two:
There's a certain rumor that can't be true.
That man descended from this noble race
The very idea is a disgrace.

No monkey ever deserted his wife,
Starved her babies and ruined her life;
And you've never known of a mother monk
To leave her babies with others to bunk.
Or pass them on from one to another
Till they scarcely know who is their mother.

And another thing you'll never see;
A monkey build a fence 'round a coconut tree
And let the coconuts go to waste,
Forbidding all other monks to taste.
Why, if I put a fence around a tree,
Starvation would force you to steal from me.

Here's another thing a monk won't do:
Go out at night and get on a stew,
Or use a gun or a knife
To take some other monkey's life.
Yes, man descended, the ornery cuss;
But, brother he didn't descend from us."

* * * * *

Trees And Man

The tree that didn't have to fight
For sun and sky and air and light,
But lived out on the open plain
And always got its share of rain,

Never became a "Forest King,"
But lived and died a scrubby thing.

The man that never had to toil,
The man who never tasted spoil,
Who never had to win his share
Of sun and sky and light and air,
Never became a manly man.
But lived and died where he began.

Good timber does not grow with ease
The stronger the winds the tougher the trees,
The further the sky the greater the length
The more the storms the more the strength,
By sun and cold and rain and snow
In "trees or man" good timbers grow.

Where thickest stands the "Forest Growth,"
We find the "Patriarchs" of both,
Who hold a converse with the stars
Whose broken branches show many scars
Of many winds and much of strife,
This is the common law of life.

* * * * *

The Touch Of The Master's Hand

'Twas battered and scarred, and the auctioneer
Thought it scarcely worth his while
To waste his time on the old violin,
But he held it up with a smile.

"What am I bid, good friends?" he cried.
"Who'll start the bidding for me?
One dollar! Only one? And who'll make it two?
Two dollars, once. And three!

Three dollars, once. And three dollars, twice.
And going, and going," but no...
From the back of the room a grey-haired man
Came forward and picked up the bow.

And wiping the dust from the old violin,
And tightening the loose strings,
He played a melody pure and sweet
As caroling angels sing.

The music ceased, and the auctioneer
With a voice that was quiet and low,
Said, "What am I bid for the old violin?"
As he held it up with the bow.

"One thousand dollars, and who'll make it two?
Two thousand dollars, and three!
Three thousand, once. And three thousand, twice.
And going, and going, and gone!" said he.

The people cheered, but some of them cried,
"We don't quite understand
What changed its worth." Swift came the reply.
"'Twas the touch of the Master's hand."

And many a man with life out of tune
And battered and scarred with sin,
Is auctioned cheap to the thoughtless crowd
Much like this old violin.

A mess of pottage, a glass of wine.
A game, and he travels on.
He's going once, and going twice.
And going, and almost gone.

But the Master comes, and the thoughtless crowd
Never can quite understand
The worth of a soul, and the change that is wrought,
By the touch of the Master's hand.

--Myra Brooks Welch

* * * * *

A Mission Triumphant

At a council assembled in Heaven,
Where presided the great Magistrate,
Came the spirits in anticipation
To make plans for their second estate.
Each was given his own special mission,
And a talent to use and display;
And with joy each received his assignment
With instructions to keep faith and pray.

Now one spirit transcended the others,
So outstanding in talent and grace;

So majestic in stature and bearing,
With a light in his angelic face.
And the Magistrate turned to address him:
"Lo, your mission is unlike the rest;
They are going to earth to be tested,
But, my son, you are going to test."

"You will sift out the hearts of my people,
You will test them for true charity;
What is done to the least of my children,
That is the measure they mete out to me.
You will challenge the faith of your loved ones,
And the stranger you meet on life's way;
You will undergo great tribulation,
And your spirit will feel deep dismay."

"When your sojourn on earth is completed,
And your message imparted to me,
The, as humble and pure as you left Me,
You'll return to my presence again."
For a moment the spirit was troubled,
Ere the conflict within him had won,
Then he spoke, "I am willing, Dear Master
For Thy will and not mine shall be done."

Now the time had arrived for departure,
And the spirits were ready to go;
But one paused at the throne of the Father
And spoke in a voice sweet and low,
"Hold my hand so I won't be afraid, Lord,
I am eager to go down to earth."
So with God's hand in his, he departed,
And entered the channels of birth.

On a bright golden day in October,
All our family was radiant with joy,
For Heaven had sent a choice spirit
In the form of a dear baby boy.
How excited I was on that morning
As I ran to my schoolmates and cried,
"Oh, guess what, I've a new baby brother!"
And my small heart was bursting with pride.

How his hair was the color of Autumn,
He had brown eyes and rose-petal skin.
Through those eyes we were often permitted
A quick glimpse of the angel within.

Thus, joy lingered awhile in our cottage,
And my father would whistle a tune.
My mother would scour and polish
And would smile at her baby and croon.

Happiness was short-lived in our household,
For grave sorrow stole in at the door.
My father's gay whistling faltered,
And my mother's sweet voice sang no more.
Our baby was entering boyhood.
And his strong body grew as it should,
But the mind did not function correctly
And we soon knew that it never would.

For the rest of his life he was destined
To remain a perpetual child;
He would laugh and then cry like a baby,
With emotions subdued, and then wild
My dear parents dreams were now shattered,
And their fond hopes reverted to grief;
They discarded the plans for his future,
And their heartache could find no relief.

But as time passed, we learned to accept it;
We would all laugh together and play;
And my brother was petted and pampered,
And usually given his way.
And his physical growth still continued
All according to natural plan
And his body received strength and passion
While developing into a man.

And society must have its way now,
So our darling was taken away.
He was placed in a state institution,
Where the rest of his life he must stay.
I prayed day and night for my brother,
And in mercy, God answered my prayer,
For one evening I knelt at my bedside
And received inspiration while there.

My dear brother and those who live with him
Are fulfilling a mission sublime,
And they will return to the Father
To receive crowns of glory, in time,

In the meantime, they're not being tested
It is we who are taking the test;
And in serving the least of God's children,
We truly are serving the best.

How dare we presume to neglect them,
And leave them alone to their fate.
Those children should dwell in a palace,
To be served by mankind while they wait.
We should deem it an honor to know them,
And to do everything that we can
To comfort, to live, and protect them,
They should not be forgotten by man.

Even though there are those who will shun them,
There are those who will bless them with love;
And I, somehow, am sure that our actions
Are now being recorded above.
So I no longer fear for my brother,
For I know, though I don't understand,
That he'll travel life's highway in safety,
For his God is still holding his hand.

--Joan Bills

* * * * *

I never knew how old the old man was. It never occurred to me that he was any age at all. He had worn the same battered hat and the same shaggy moustache ever since I could remember. Even the yellow stains on the moustache hadn't changed since we started knocking around together like men since I was nearly six. He treated me like an equal. I remember the day I had a bit of trouble with the other members of the family and decided to run away. I was a red hot six-year-old and the Irish was showing.

"You sure you've got everything you'll need?" the old man asked solicitously. "Matches, hatchet, air rifle to shoot birds with?"

I picked up my grub sack. "I'm going now," I said, full of dignity and trepidation. "Goodbye."

"Would you mind shaking hands?" the old man said and shoved out his paw.

I shook his hand and went off to my tent. I planned to depart before dawn. "You know how lonely it can be in a tent even in the side yard when night falls." The house was maybe thirty yards away, but my pride had removed it a million miles. I couldn't make a fire because I had no firewood. Mosquitos were beginning a concerted dive on my carcass and I was hungry. Night marauders were coming on and I huddled disconcertedly while an owl hooted and the whippoorwills made a symphony of sadness. Suddenly, footsteps padded across the lawn.

"You all right in there?" the old man's voice was soft. "Anything I can do?"

"I'm fine," I said, choking back the sobs.

"Well," the old man said, "I'm kind of a committee speaking on behalf of your ma and pa and grandma. They reckon that maybe there was wrong on both sides. Mind you, we ain't asking you to give in or anything that would offend your sense of what is right and wrong. It's just that we are having deepdish apple pie for dinner and it seems a shame to waste the spare slice."

Even at six years old I knew a concession when I saw one. "I'm willing to talk business if you are," I said, keeping my voice cool and bored. What I wanted to do was jump up and wrap myself around his neck and weep out of sheer relief, not knowing then that the old gent had really pulled me off the hook and left my self-respect intact.

--Robert Ruark

* * * * *

The Littlest Screw

There was once upon a time a village that was beautiful and well kept. The people were very proud of their village and loyal citizens. They held a meeting one day to decide what type of monument could be erected on the town square -- a final touch -- something both useful and lovely. They thought for sometime and finally decided to erect a beautiful, impressive clock.

They sent for the best materials -- for they wanted the finest clock they could have. The materials needed should be able to stand all kinds of weather and not tarnish, rust, or warp -- the very finest of clockmakers was brought to the town to do the work.

Finally, it was finished and all the people came to see the clock and as each went around the clock looking at the exquisite workmanship, they each commented on the huge, impressiveness of the main spring that made the clock run. And each time something was said about the big spring a little screw located just above the spring wiggled and twisted and in envy said, "I'm not important, I'm not needed. No one notices me."

The day went on and more and more people came to see the clock and over and over again the little screw would comment and wiggle and twist and feel very much unnecessary and unhappy. Toward the end of the day just as the last few people were viewing the clock, someone made a remark about the main spring. And it was the last straw for the little screw -- it gave a twist and jerk and came right out of its place and as it fell to the base of the clock said, "No one notices me -- I'm not important." But when the screw came out, the big main spring also fell out of place. You see, the whole clockwork depended on the little screw!

* * * * *

The Revealing Angels

Suddenly, and without warning, they come. The Revealing Angels come. Suddenly and simultaneously, through the city streets, through the quiet lanes and country roads they walked. They walked crying, "God has sent us to find the vilest sinners of earth. We are to bring them before Him, before the Lord of Life!"

Their voices were like bugles, and then all war, all strife, all the voices of the world grew still. No one talked, no one retorted, but many strove to flee away. Robbers and thieves and those sunk in drunkenness and crime ran to hide.

But the Revealing Angels passed them by, saying, "Not you! Another day when we shall come again unto the haunts of men, then we will call your names. But God has asked us first to bring to Him, those guilty of greater shames than lust or theft or drunkenness or vice, yea, greater than murder done in passion, or self-destruction done in despair. Now, in His Holy Name, we call 'Come one and all, come forth, reveal your faces!'"

Then through the awful silence of the world, where noise had ceased, they come, the sinful hosts. They come from lowly places, and from lofty places, some poorly clad, but many clothed like queens. They come from scenes of revelry and from toil, and from places of sin, from palaces, from homes, from boudoirs and from churches. They come like ghosts. The vast brigades of women who had slain their helpless unborn children!

With them trailed lovers and husbands who had said, "Do this!" And those who had helped for hire (doctors). They stood before the Angels, before the Revealing Angels they stood, and they heard the Angels say:

"These are the vilest sinners of all, for the Lord of Life made sex that birth might come; made sex and it's keen, compelling desire, to fashion bodies wherein souls might go."

"From lower planes to higher, until the end is reached (which is beginning), they have stolen the costly pleasures of the senses. They refused to pay God's price. They have come together, these men and women, as male and female, they have come together in the great creative act.

"They have invited souls and then flung them into space; they have made a jest of God's design. All other sins look white beside this sinning. All other sins may be conditioned, forgiven, all other sinners may be cleansed and shriven. Not these, not these! Pass on and meet God's eyes!"

The vast brigade moved forward, and behind them walked the Angels, the sorrowful Revealing Angels.

--Ella Wheeler Wilcox

* * * * *

MARRIAGE

Buying a marriage license doesn't guarantee a happy marriage any more than buying a hunting license will guarantee a successful hunting or fishing trip.

* * * * *

Can You Afford Marriage?

The Bride, white of hair, stoops over her cane,
Her footsteps, uncertain, need guiding,
While down the church aisle, with a wan-toothless smile,
The groom in a wheel chair comes riding.

And who is this elderly couple thus wed?
You'll find when you closely explore it,
That here is the rare, most conservative pair,
Who waited till they could afford it!!!

* * * * *

The Seed

One day -- so long ago -- God gave me a seed...a seed of love to plant and nurture so it would grow.

Even as the rosebud slowly opens to the golden rays of light to become a rose -- full-blooming, with soft, velvety petals holding jewels of dew, my love for you unfolded petal by petal so that now I am to become your wife.

Soon we, together, will go the Temple of the Lord and there will seal our love with a bond, stronger than iron, to join us together for eternity.

Our love shall know no bounds -- time loses all value when I realize that forever you shall be mine, and I shall belong to you. No power exists which can separate us or destroy the love upon which we are building an everlasting home.

With a kiss across the altar in the Lord's own house I become your helpmeet and companion, not for only time but for all eternity.

I know that in the minutes, hours, days, and years to come my love for you shall continue to grow and that eternal happiness and joy shall be ours.

How great the wisdom and the love which gave to us this pearl of great price -- a never-ending love.

--Mary MacNeill

* * * * *

So Dear To My Heart

Today is my wedding day, I'm happy as I can be
For I have found my own true love, whom God has meant for me.
It's all so very wonderful that words just can't express
The joy of love so sweet and good, which makes my happiness.

As I look back on all the years of waiting for this time
When I can clasp my hand in his and know he will be mine.
To know that he is virtuous...he saved himself for me.
And he can look into my eyes and purity he sees.

Because I've been so careful when choosing friends along the way,
That their ideals were good and true, as I'd like mine to stay.
When temptation came and Satan was knocking at the door,
We'd turn our heads and walk away. Then he was easier to ignore.

At times like these my memories would take me back to Mother
Who taught me purity of heart. She gave me more than any other.
Her heart was ever full of fear for she knew that Satan was strong.
But her faith in me kept me clean and pure -- I never wanted to do wrong.

So I've prepared myself for today a very long time ago.
I've kept myself in very close check, so my virtue I'd always know.
Today when I go to the temple...When across the altar we kneel,
He'll know I've been true and faithful to the ideals and truths we feel.

In the temple I'll place my hand in his with the Lord standing very close by.
We'll be married forever and ever, be together even after we die.
I know the angels will sing in the heavens, it will be so dear to my heart
For today we'll be in the House of the Lord where our marriage vows will start.

Oh, I'll love and cherish my husband, God meant him just for me.
Our home will be filled with choice spirits, throughout all eternity.
Blessings and joy I've always dreamed have come to me this day.
Because I've stayed pure in heart -- There is no other way.

So girls and boys, we plead with you, to keep your bodies clean.
You too will find your precious love and these blessings you'll surely glean.

When temptation comes your way -- Don't let it bother you.
If you stay pure and virtuous...God will make your dreams come true.

--Carold Holland

* * * * *

A Bride's Prayer

Oh, Father, my heart is filled with happiness so wonderful that I am almost afraid. This is my wedding day and I pray thee that the beautiful joy of this day may never grow dim with the years of regret for the step I am about to take. Rather, may its memories become more sweet and tender with each passing anniversary.

Thou has sent to me one who seems all worthy of my deepest regard. Grant unto me the power to keep him ever true and loving as now. May I prove indeed a helpmate, a sweetheart, a friend, a steadfast guiding star along the temptations that beset the impulsive hearts of man.

Give me the skill to make home the best loved place of all. Help me to make its glow shine farther than any glare that would dim its radiance. Let me, I pray thee, meet the little misunderstandings and cares of my new life bravely. Be with me as I start on my mission of womanhood, and keep my path from failure. Walk with us, even to the end of our journey.

Father, bless my wedding day, hallow my marriage night, sanctify my motherhood -- if thou seest fit to grant me that privilege. And when all my youthful charms are faded, and physical fascination give way to the greater charm of blessed companionship, so may we walk hand in hand down the highway, lighted by the sunshine that comes from living righteously for time and all eternity.

Amen.

* * * * *

Temple Marriage

Now, springtime was here and two lovers stood
Side by side in the soft warm breeze
That carries the sweet perfume that comes
From the breath of the apple trees.

Oh, John, I'm so happy tonight," said she.
"Will happiness always stay?"
"Ah yes, my darling --" as he held her close,
"Tomorrow's our wedding day."

"But John," said Mary in an uncertain tone
"Are you sure that your views are right?
You know how Mother seemed sort of sad
When we spoke with her there tonight."

"Oh yes, I know, but Mary, my dear,
There's plenty of time for that.
You know, our mothers both
Are inclined to worry and chat.

"The temples restrict certain things, they say,
For instance my cigarette --
It's difficult breaking a habit like that,
And well, I couldn't -- not yet.

And then there's the tithing, a tenth to pay,
And we'll just be starting out.
It would be a struggle for us, you see,
And lots we'd have to do without."

"Oh yes, John dear, you're right I suppose --
Mother's just old-fashioned, I guess.
And there's something I've sort of considered, too,
For instance, that lovely dress --

The one I wore to the ball last week,
The neck's cut extremely low.
Why, I'd never be able to wear it again,
The garments I'm sure would show.

"And there's all my blouses, so dainty and sheer,
The things that I simply adore.
I just couldn't think of discarding all of them,
It wouldn't be worth it, I'm sure."

So they continued there under the stars
In the scent of the apple trees,
Discussing the bad points, while none of the good
Either lad or lassie could see.

Yes, they were still young, there was plenty of time --
The temple marriage could wait.
They'll enjoy their own way of life for a while.
And go at some later date.

Many months had passed since the night they stood
In the scent of the old apple tree.
Tonight John waited outside her door
To learn what the news would be.

As the hours flew by, his nerves grew tense
While anxiety filled his heart.
When the nurse appeared, her countenance grave,
He rose with a sudden start.

Ah yes, 'twas a boy -- he had hoped for that,
"But what of Mary?" gasped he,
"Come, don't keep me waiting, is Mary all right?
She's all that matters to me."

In silence she beckoned him through the door
Where Mary lay, still and white.
Beside the bed he fell to his knees --
Head bowed, and his hands clenched tight.

"Lord God, hear my pleading, don't take her away --
I need her, don't you see?
If thou wilt but grant me this one request,
I'll give my service to thee."

With trembling form John stooped and pressed
A kiss on the pale white brow.
A faint smile flickered across her lips --
Thank God, he could keep her now!

How merciful, God, in that hour of need,
While John in his anguish was blessed.
God heard of his pleading and hastened at once
To grant him his one request.

The months passed by, a year had lapsed,
John's part of the bargain forgot --
His promise to God on that fateful night
He scarcely had given a thought.

All seemed going well, the world was indeed
A heaven for Mary and him,
Their cottage complete, and life but a dream
For them and their Baby Tim.

Success was the word, John's fields were aglow
With crops that he planted last spring.
To Mary he promised the finest wear
With the money the harvest would bring.

The time arrived, the harvesters came
Their labor beginning next day,
But lo, through the night came hailstones --
The crops could scarcely be gathered for hay!

This wasn't enough, in their little farmhouse
A fire broke out next day.
Before help was brought, the ravishing flames
Swept all their belongings away.

It wasn't so bad, the neighbors were kind,
And hastened to help make amends,
For Mary and John were the likeable kind
And always had plenty of friends.

John didn't give up, though life became
A struggle for Mary and him.
With their perfect love they'd still make a go,
And they were thankful they had Baby Tim.

But winter came with sickness and colds
And baby was stricken one day.
With folks quarantined, there wasn't much help,
The doctor was some miles away.

Together they watched through the long dreary night,
Each moment their darling grew worse.
If only the dawn of the morning would break,
The blackness of night to disperse.

Through the small cottage window John peered, through the night,
Where darkness was growing more dense.
The wind in its fury was shaking without,
The snow was piling high on the fence.

Ah, gloom filled their cottage that fierce winter night,
And their hearts were burdened with fear
As they knelt by the crib and appealed to God
While the shadows of death crept near.

"Lord God, have mercy! Don't take him away --
We're needing him, don't you see?
If thou wilt but grant us this one request --"
A pause -- John ended his plea.

Ah yes, it was John who uttered that prayer
While Mary with anguish wept.
But God heeded not, John knew it wouldn't be so.
In silence their baby slept.

As months passed by with cold winter's snow
'Twas dreary for Mary and John.
In years they knew without Baby Tim
Forever, they couldn't go on.

And they longed for the spring with flowers to bloom,
The Robin to sing its first song.
It was then they planned a journey to take --
The one they had neglected so long.

Now springtime was here and the two lovers stood
Side by side in the soft warm breeze
That carried the sweet perfume that comes
From the scent of the apple trees.

"Oh, John, I'm so happy tonight," said she,
"Will happiness always stay?"
"Ah yes, my darling," he held her close,
"Tomorrow's our wedding day."

"And Mary, I know that our views are right --
God's promptings have told me so.
In no other way could we find the joy
That tomorrow we both shall know."

"Yes, John" said Mary, "I know that I was wrong,
Mother wasn't old-fashioned at all,
It was God who was pleading in her sad eyes,
And we failed to answer the call."

Thus they talked of their failings long into the night,
And of their love for their darling Tim,
How God might have spared their dear little child
If only they'd harkened to him.

As the sun sank low over the hills next day,
Its glorious rays to unfold,
The Temple spires that reached toward the heavens
Were lighted with shimmering gold.

A symbol of faith to shine all the way
As onward through life they trod,
Till they anchored the ship that would sail them beyond
To meet Baby Tim -- and God!

--Lydia Bennett Egbert

* * * * *

MISSIONARY WORK

The Lord so loved me that He chose me to serve Him.

* * * * *

You can count the seeds in a single apple, but you can't count the apples in a single seed.

* * * * *

"Let's work! I shall go to my grave saying that missionaries generally speaking never rise in their entire life above the stature they carve out for themselves in the mission field."

--Henry D. Moyle

* * * * *

To A Mormon Elder

You will never know of the gladness you brought
To a heart overburdened with care,
Of the beautiful wonderful changes you wrought
In a life once so pitifully bare.

You will ever know that you brought Christ so near
Who had once seemed so far, far away,
That you gave Him to me as a big brother so dear
Whom I understand now when I pray.

And I'll never know of others whose lives
You've brightened just as you have mine,
Of many a soul who now hopefully strives
With Jesus for a comrade divine.

But our Heavenly Father who watches will know
And will nurture each seed that you've sown,
That when harvest time comes in the fields here below
He may gather sheaves for His own.

And when He has called you, your record to share
On that glorious beautiful day,
You'll find souls that are faithful and hearts that are true
Because you have journeyed this way.

* * * * *

Missionaries' Girls

Somewhere between the whirl of teen-age dates and the responsibility of matrimony, we find a lone creature called the Missionary's Girl.

They come in two varieties...engaged and hopefuls. They come in assorted sizes, weights, and colors, blue being the most common.

Missionaries' girls are found at home, missing parties, staying away from dances, paying their own way to the show, buying stationery by the gross.

Missionaries love them, young girls look up to them, parents tolerate them, postmen hate them, and weekly letters support them.

A missionary's girl is a composite. She has the appetite of a mouse, the enthusiasm of a wet noodle, the patience of Job, the persistence of a stainless steel salesman and the imagination of Scherazade.

She likes letters from the mission field, invitations to his home, long distance telephone calls, items for his scrapbook, pictures of him, and other girls who are waiting. She isn't much for Saturday nights at home, people who say, "Two years is a long time." and new clothes with no one to wear them for, sad movies and music, movies with love scenes, knitting, wedding receptions, little sisters who date, calendars, and "Dear Janes."

A missionary's girl is an odd object: She can get lonesome, discouraged, and temporarily lose faith in the whole missionary system. No one else can write such cheerful letters in such a rotten mood. No one else can get such a thrill at the end of the day by the words, "Why yes, I believe there is a letter for you." Nobody else is so early to bed and so early to rise.

A missionary's girl is virtue with no chance to be otherwise. Faith with twenty-four months to wait, prudence with 69¢ in her savings account, and beauty with no one to give a darn.

Yes, she is all this, but it will all be forgotten the day he receives his letter of release and on his arrival home she will probably utter the speech she once considered trite, "It hasn't seemed like any time at all!"

* * * * *

Loving a missionary isn't all play,
The life it demands of you isn't so gay.
It's mostly the having, but not to hold;
It's being too young and feeling so old;
It's a life of skimmed milk -- without any cream,
And being in love with a wonderful dream.

Yes, loving your guy means "Goodbye" at the plane.
And two years must pass before you see him again.
You reluctantly, painfully let him go,
While you are aching inside for wanting him so.
Then you wait for his word that everything's well,
And bide through a miserable letterless spell.

Then comes the mail, you are giddy with joy.
And you pounce like a child with a shining new toy.
You realize that he is so far away,
And your love for him grows greater each day.
You are proud of the job he is helping to do,
And you know he is doing it, thinking of you.

Loving a missionary is undefined fears,
And crying at night till there aren't any tears.
Then seeking comfort, you kneel down to pray,
And put your whole heart in the words that you say.
And you find that your feet are on the sand and not sod.
And your source of strength comes only from God.

* * * * *

Prayer For A Missionary

Father in Heaven
Hear this my plea,
For I have a loved one
In service to Thee.

Give him the wisdom
To know what to do.
Give him the courage
To stand for what's true.

Develop his faith
So he'll always pray
To Thee for guidance
From day to day.

Keep him forever
Safe from all harm
That we at home
Will be free from alarm.

Give him the strength
To escape every snare.
Overcome all temptation
Be free from all care.

Give him patience
To understand
The customs and people
Of a strange land.

Let him radiate love
That he may be
Able to turn
Many hearts unto thee.

And let him know
That I wait cheerfully
For that glorious day
Thou return him to me.

--Janelle Smith

* * * * *

The Reason Why

When I tried and failed in every way
To find a soul to teach someday,
After a long week, I had toiled
To find my work had all been foiled,
At last I finally knelt in prayer
And said, "O, Lord it isn't fair
That I should work so hard for you
And yet my people all fall through.
I've come out here for two long years
And endured hardships and overcome fears.
I have preached the Gospel with all my might
From early morning till late at night
All of these rules I have applied
Yet everything has failed that I have tried.
O, Lord, you know I'm working hard;
Isn't it about time I got my reward?
Please tell me what I should do
That I might be able to satisfy you."

The answer came to me
And set my mind and conscience free
He said, "My son, it's the same old story;
Your eyes are not single to my glory.
The reason you have tried in vain
Is because you are trying to build your fame
The reason I have let you fail
Is because you let your pride prevail,
I've let you wander in the dark and fumble
Because I'm trying to make you humble
And the reason your people all fall through
Is because your work is not true.
My son, I'm afraid you're just a fake;
You're not baptizing for my sake.
You think of numbers ten by ten
To raise your stature in the eyes of men.
You're thinking only of your own success
And that type of person I will not bless.
Your actions and your thoughts are before my eyes.
I'll never give my blessings to you
Until your heart is pure and true."

I knelt in prayer and said to Him:
"O, Lord, forgive me for this sin,
What a fool I've been to surmise
That my thoughts were hidden from your eyes.

You won't let divine blessings impart
To satisfy the lusts of my evil heart.
I'm thankful you revealed this unto me
My eyes were blind, but now I see.
O, Lord, I'm really a foolish man,
Without your help I can't work your plan.
Remove from my heart that awful greed
And help me to plant that fertile seed.
From this time on, let it be
That my labors are directed only to thee."

* * * * *

MOTHER

To "His" Mother

"Mother-in-law" they say, and yet,
Somehow I simply can't forget
'Twas you who watched his baby ways,
Who taught him his first hymn of praise;
Who smiled on him with living pride
When he first toddled by your side;
And as I think of this today,
Methinks that I'd much rather say
Just "Mother."

"Mother-in-law" but oh, 'twas you
Who taught him to be kind and true;
When he was tired, almost asleep,
'Twas to your arms he used to creep;
And when he bruised his tiny knee,
'Twas you who kissed it tenderly;
When he was sad you cheered him too,
And so I'd rather speak of you
As "Mother."

"Mother-in-law" they say, and yet,
Somehow I never shall forget
How very much I owe
To you who taught him how to grow,
You trained your son to look above,
You made of him the man I love;
And so I think of that today,
Ah! Then with thankful heart I'll say
"Our Mother."

--Minnie Price

* * * * *

Ten Commandments For Wives

1. Honor thine own womanhood that thy days may be long and happy in the house which thy husband provideth for thee.

2. Expect not thy husband to give thee as many luxuries as thy father hath given thee, after many years of labor and economy.

3. Forget not the virtue of good humor, for verily, all that a man hath will he give for a woman's smile.

4. Thou shalt not nag.

5. Thou shalt coddle thy husband, for verily, every man loveth to be fussed over.

6. Remember that the frank approval of thy husband meaneth more to thy happiness than the side-long glances of many strangers.

7. Forget not the graces of cleanliness and good dressing.

8. Permit no one to assure thee that thou art having a hard time of it, neither thy mother nor thy sister nor thy maiden aunt nor any of thy kinfolk, for the judge will not hold thee guiltless for letting another disparage thy husband.

9. Keep thy home with all diligence, for out of it will come the joys of thine old age.

10. Commit thy ways unto the Lord thy God and thy children shall rise up and call thee blessed.

--Roy L. Smith

* * * * *

A Mother In Heaven

"This I beheld, or dreamed it in a dream --"

I was suddenly aware that I was being propelled through space. The weightlessness of my bodily parts and the frictionless speed that I somehow was aware of, contributed to the unreality. I remembered thinking that if I truly was in space breathing would be difficult or impossible. But I felt no discomfort as a vast panorama of heavenly bodies and universes flashed through my consciousness.

I was just beginning to relax and abandon myself to the caprice and fantasy of a strange dream, when I arrived. Don't ask me where I arrived to, for I could not tell you. I just knew that I had arrived. Somehow, I had been placed in a room, or at least an area of size and dimension. It was furnished with chairs, tables, and carpets, and I suddenly felt I had been there before. The distinct impression crossed my mind that this room resembled the celestial room of the Temple. Its simple beauty and purity of design caught my eyes and each object seemed to be transcendantly beautiful in itself. As I stood in quiet awe at my surroundings, I felt a presence. I knew someone was with me, and as I turned to look about, that presence appeared. It didn't seem to arrive, it was just there. I <u>should</u> say SHE was there.

I beheld a woman who appeared even more beautiful because of the love that seemed to flow between us. I remembered my own mother who was even more beautiful because of the tender love she gave me. This same feeling now invaded my inner being as I beheld this personnage.

Her smile, the movement of her hand, the tender eyes all gave me the feeling that I had known her. She was dressed in a white flowing robe-like gown that was trimmed with other white materials that differed in texture. It is difficult to describe her beauty, and I cannot express to you my feelings, except to say that I -- I loved her.

She moved to a chair and beckoned me to her. I sat at her feet and she took my hand in hers. I guess I sat in amazement admiring her soft countenance when she suddenly spoke. I hadn't really expected her to do so, and her words startled me.

"How have you been, my daughter?"

It wasn't only the words, but how she said them that caused feelings of recognition to well up within me. Her emphasis on "my daughter" was not just the usual impersonal reference so often used by an older person. I <u>felt</u> like her daughter and wanted to tell her so, but I'm sure that I mumbled badly the answer to her question.

Again, she asked, "Have you been happy?" I was a little more composed by this time and reasonably explained the love I had for my wonderful husband and children. I'm afraid I rambled a bit in explaining the good times that were mine in life. I seemed to forget the unhappiness and the disappointments, as the joys and satisfactions really did dominate my life.

She touched my cheek in a loving caress as she once more spoke.

"Have you walked uprightly before your Father and fulfilled the vows and covenants that you made with us before?"

She was so kindly and concerned in her question that I could see a negative answer would break her heart.

"Mother --" I started to answer, (why did I say Mother?). "Mother, I am sure that I have fallen short in many things, but I love you and the Father and have held true to the vows and covenants which were given me in a time past. I have tried to live my life so as to return to you and the presence of God the Father. Having tasted once again of your presence, I will double my efforts to merit this blessing."

My new confidence with words was tempered with the thought that She knew what I was going to say before I said it. I knew She saw within me and could read my feelings as plainly as She heard the spoken word. I could speak no guile in her presence and indeed had no intentions of doing so. The fact that She was there precluded any thoughts not of a celestial nature.

She rose from Her chair and placing Her hands on my shoulders as she looked deep into my eyes, perhaps even into my soul, and said,

"Your Father and I love you. You were Ours before being born in the flesh. I gave you up for a season so that you could grow and develop and achieve a fleshly body from your earthly Mother. She and I are equally concerned for your welfare. We are partners in your eternal progress and are both as close to you as your faith will allow." So <u>this</u> was who She was!

I choked back the tears when she folded me in Her arms. The words were simply drowned in my emotion. I wanted to tell her of my love and respect. I wanted to covenant with her to become more like Her. I wanted to declare my allegiance to the Father and pledge my charity to all men. I wanted to confess my sins and cast them from me. But I could not speak. I knew, however, that She knew my thoughts, and Her knowing smile made me but love her the more.

She left as she came -- Her presence was just no longer there, and I suddenly found myself back in the world of noise, bustling movement, and earthly relationships.

How could I tell anyone of my experience, for --

This I beheld, or dreamed it in a dream.

"But truth is reason, truth eternal tells me I've a Mother there."

--Earnest Widtsoe Shumway

* * * * *

Men Are What Their Mothers Make Them

It was Saturday morning. Mrs. Ormon sat on her porch in the warmth of the May sunshine watching her husband plant their vegetable garden. Suddenly a great longing to see the boy who had helped him the year before came over her. But she knew that could not be, for he was finishing his first year at a college some distance away and would not be home till the first week in June. Even Mother's Day could not stretch their budget for an extra trip home.

She was roused from her thoughts by the mailman whistling the strains of "Mother McCree."

"That is worth paying for, your whistling, I mean," she called to him as he was putting her mail in their box by the side of the road.

"For that compliment, I'll bring your letter and give it to you myself. Sure, and it's from that big handsome son of yours away at college. I'm mighty proud of him, you should be."

"Thank you, Mr. McDougal, I am proud, but a little lonely, too, this morning."

"The letter will cheer you up. I'll be going along so you can read it."

With a smile, Mrs. Ormon opened her letter and began reading:

Dear Mother:

Wish I could be talking to you instead of writing, but that cannot be, but someday, Mother, I'll be so successful, -- I hope -- that I can come home every Mother's Day. But this time, this letter and the small remembrance I am sending must suffice.

Now, Mother, don't say "you shouldn't have" about the gift. I couldn't think of getting a corsage for Barbara to wear last night and not remember my favorite girl on her special day.

"And who is Barbara?" I hear you ask. You would like her, Mother. She invited me to go with her to a party given by one of her sorority friends. She's beautiful, easy to talk with, and a good dancer...It was a formal affair, and Barbara looked like a million in her dress, but it was modest, Mother, which is more than I can say for some of the creations that the girls wore.

You should have seen me in a tuxedo, the first I've worn. No, dear little Mother, I didn't have to rent one so I'm not low on cash as a result. My roommate had one and he was generous enough to let me wear it...It fit perfectly..Strange how the wearing of a tuxedo made me feel important and dignified and sophisticated. If I do say so, Barbara and I made a handsome couple.

I enjoyed the dancing, every moment of it, but when we were seated for a midnight banquet and pretty little waitresses began filling the small crystal goblets with wine or champagne -- I'm not familiar with such drinks, as you know, so I can't say for sure -- I knew a few moments of panic. It was if hot fingers were clutching at my throat. I knew what I should do, Mother, for the Word of Wisdom has always been lived in our home. But could I be different and face the consequences...Would it really matter to do as the rest just this once and be recognized as one of the crowd and belonging. I looked at Barbara and read a challenge in her eyes. The smiling waitress was but a few plates away. Indecision seemed choking me.

Suddenly I was a boy again. It was the morning of my twelfth birthday, a bright, sunny morning, the day I arrived at the important age when I could be ordained a deacon and begin scouting. The scout oath passed through my mind and I remembered you had given me the scout handbook to study a few months before so I would be all ready to be a real scout when I was twelve. Again I saw my birthday cake with its roses and candles and "Happy Birthday, Richard!". Once more my eyes rested on your gift, a book, A YOUNG FOLKS HISTORY OF THE CHURCH, in which you had written, "You will receive the Priesthood today. Magnify it." Again, I was holding a sealed letter I found in the book. On the outside of the envelope you had written "To be opened on your twenty-first birthday, and telling the kind of man I think you will be then."

It was as though a clean canyon breeze blew across my soul. My mind cleared. I turned to the little waitress about to fill my glass, smiled, and said, "No, thank you." Then I turned to meet the scoffing rebuke I expected to see in Barbara's eyes. Instead, I saw them light with the gladness of relief, and smiling, she, too, said to the waitress, "No, thank you." To my astonishment, several others at the table refused, and some of the filled goblets were never raised to the lips of those who had lacked the courage to say no.

When I said good night to Barbara at her door, her eyes were shining, as she said, "Thanks, Richard. I'm so grateful to you and proud of you. I have never tasted liquor of any kind, and now I am sure I shall be able to keep my record clean. I had decided to do whatever you did."

Thanks, Mother, for all you have taught me, and thank dad for me. Had it not been for your teachings in many different ways, I would not have been able to say no. And, Mother, I still have two more years before I can open your letter. I shall try to live so I can read it unashamed and with no regrets.

Good night, Mother, and all my love.

Your son, Richard

Tears were running gently down Mrs. Ormon's face as she finished the letter. Thankfulness welled up in her heart. She knew the sweetness of humility as she breathed a prayer of gratitude.

"Why the tears, my dear?" It was her husband who spoke. "Not tears of sorrow, I am sure, for there's a radiance in your eyes. You are beautiful Mother, 'smiling through.' Here, let me dry your eyes." He did so, then kissed her tenderly. "Now tell me all about it."

For an answer she handed him her letter. When he finished reading he turned to her and there were tears in his eyes, also, and he said softly, "Emerson was right: 'Men are what their mother's make them.'"

She looked in her husband's eyes for a long moment. There was tenderness in her voice and love and gratitude as she answered gently, "I believe you are right, my dear." She paused briefly and then continued, "What a wonderful mother you must have had."

The sacred moment was broken by the click of the gate. The boy from the florists handed her a long slender box, received her "thank you" and went on his way.

With eager, trembling fingers she removed the wrapping, opened the box, and saw one long-stemmed perfect white rose. On the card was written:

"The white rose of purity. Love, Richard."

* * * * *

The Little Parable For Mothers

The young Mother set her foot on the path of life. "Is the way long?" she asked. And her guide said, "Yes. And the way is hard. And you will be old before you reach the end of it. But the end will be better than the beginning."

But the young Mother was happy, and would not believe that anything could be better than these years. So she played with her children, and gathered flowers for them along the way, and bathed them in clear streams, and the sun shone on them and life was good and the young Mother cried, "Nothing will ever be lovelier than this."

Then came night, and storm, and the path was dark, and the children shook with fear and cold, and the Mother drew them close and covered them with her mantle, and the children said, "Oh, Mother, we are not afraid for you are near and no harm can come." And the Mother said, "This is better than the brightness of day, for I have taught my children courage. Today, I have given them strength."

And the next day came strange clouds which darkened the earth -- clouds of war and hate and evil, and the children groped and stumbled, and the Mother said, "Look up. Life your eyes to the light." And the children looked and saw above the clouds an Everlasting Glory, and it guided them and brought them beyond the darkness. And that night, the Mother said, "This is the best day of all, for I have shown my children God."

And the days went on, and the weeks and the months and the years, and the Mother grew old, and she was little and bent. But her children were tall and strong and walked with courage. And when the way was hard, they helped their Mother, and when the way was rough, they lifted her, for she was as light as a feather, and at last they came to a hill, and beyond this hill they could see a shining road and golden gates flung wide.

And the Mother said, "I have reached the end of my journey. And now I know that the end is better than the beginning, for my children can walk alone, and their children after them."

And the children said, "You will always walk with us, Mother, even when you have gone through the gates."

And they stood and watched her as she went on alone, and the gates closed after her. And they said, "We cannot see her, but she is with us still. A Mother like ours is more than a memory. She is a Living Presence."

--Temple Bailey

* * * * *

OPPORTUNITY

Opportunity knocks. Temptation kicks the door down.

* * * * *

Opportunities are never "lost." Someone else will take the ones you miss.

* * * * *

A sign on the door of Opportunity reads "Push."

* * * * *

Opportunity always looks better going than coming.

* * * * *

Opportunities are the offers of God.

* * * * *

The wise man will make more opportunities than he finds.

* * * * *

The greatest opportunity of life is life itself.

* * * * *

The door of opportunity is wide open if you are prepared.

* * * * *

Success: Think big -- catch the whole vision -- opportunity does not knock, it is created.

--Paul Dunn

* * * * *

Education has opened many, many doors. However, there are still innumerable doors shut tight -- unopened yet. These are the doors of the future. Perhaps one of my children will open one of these doors -- I shall help give him the key.

* * * * *

Four things come not back,
The spoken word,
The sped arrow
The past life,
The neglected opportunity.

--Arabian Proverb

* * * * *

Yes, You Can Succeed

"Figure it out for yourself, my lad:
You've all that the greatest men have had;
Two arms, two hands, two legs, two eyes,
And a brain to use if you would be wise,
With this equipment they all began.
So start from the top and say, 'I can.'

"Look them over, the wise and great;
They take their food from a common plate,
And similar knives and forks they use,
With similar laces they tie their shoes.
The world considers them brave and smart,
But you've all they had when they made their start.

"You are the handicapped you must face;
You are the one who must choose your place.
You must say where you want to go,
How much you will study the truth to know;
God has equipped you for life, but He
Lets you decide what you want to be.

"Courage must come from the soul within,
The man must furnish the will to win.
So figure it out for yourself, my lad:
You were born with all that the great have had.
With your equipment they all began,
Get hold of yourself and say, 'I can.'"

--Anonymous

* * * * *

I Met A Man

I met a man once who said:

I missed out on my college days. You see, I didn't enter into it quite all the way. I was afraid, I guess. I wanted to try for a part in the school play once, but I didn't. I intended to. I went up to the room the night they were reading parts, but I didn't go in. There were so many there who could do it better than I, and I turned away and went down the hall. I wanted to try for the football team, too, but I told myself I was light and turned away from the practice field. And, it's funny, but do you know I can't go to see a football game now, or hear one on the radio, and I can't go to see a college play, because I see myself out on the field or on the stage as I might have been if I hadn't been afraid. And I find myself wishing I could go back to college to live those days over again.

I met a man once who said:

I missed out on my college days. You see, I didn't enter into it quite all the way. Working my way through school took all my time, or I told myself it did. The fellows used to go bumming around at night and sometimes they'd ask me along, but I never did. I always told them I had to study. It seemed to me a lot of foolishness, the way they used to hang around the college drug store, or loiter on the library steps, or go to the snake dances or rallies. I even missed the football games. Froth, I called it. Wasted time! I was in school to study. And it's funny, but do you know I turn away now every time I see a group of college men gathered in a drug store or on a corner of the campus. And every time I see two old college men slap each other on the back and say, "Remember the time we..." I gulp a little because I missed out on all that, and I find myself wishing I could go back to college to live those days over again.

I met a man once who said:

I missed out on my college days. You see, I didn't enter into it quite all the way. I never got acquainted with a professor. Or even a textbook. No, seriously, I never learned the thrill of digging fossils on the mountain side. Or working till dark over a test tube. Or getting on the trail of something in the library and searching it down feverishly for hours. I told myself that people who did that sort of thing were queer. And I said that professors were dull and I complained about the classes. I could learn more out of school, I said. I slid through someway without ever letting my mind grow curious. And it's funny, but do you know I feel kind of regretful now whenever I talk to a scholar. Or go in a library, or wander through a museum. I missed out on all that. And I find myself wishing I could go back to college to live those days over again.

I met a man once who said:

I missed out on my college days. You see I didn't enter into it quite all the way. When I went there I wanted to meet the one girl and I wanted to dream dreams with her and make eternal pledges. But I read a lot of things about the "romantic fallacy." And about the "facts" of love and marriage. And some of the other fellows said, "Love is only sex." They said, "You've got to be hard about these things." And they gritted their teeth on the word hard and went in for sex. I let myself believe them and believe hard. I threw away the dreams and pledges, and then one day I met a girl who could have been the dream girl, but I didn't believe in dream girls. "I'm hard," I said. And gritted my teeth. "Love is only sex," I said and went in for sex. I didn't enter into love all the way, and aim at perfection, I married another girl, and have a family now. But I missed out on all the dreams and pledges. And, it's funny, but do you know that every time the wind blows across a campus in the springtime I wince a little inside. I didn't let myself believe in perfection. I was satisfied with something less. And now, when I see a boy and girl look at each other a certain way, I find myself wishing I could go back to college...to live those days over again.

I met a man once who said:

I missed out on my college days. You see, I didn't enter into it quite all the way. When I went there as a freshman, they had us climb to the top of the "Y" on the mountain. I participated that night in lighting it, but, I considered the school to be a university just like any other university. I became somewhat irritated over having to take religion courses in order to graduate. I must be honest and say that I discovered that I never understood the meaning of the great principles that were being discussed. I never really internalized them. It was only after I was out of college that the scale fell from my eyes and I discovered that those principles, if understood, accepted, and lived, would bring me the greatest joy that I could ever know. It was only then when I was in the later years of my life, that I made the Personal Committment to try to live those principles and to represent Him in the devotional in which a great man talked about those principles and I found myself wishing that I could go back to college and live those days over again.

--Thomas Wheelwright

* * * * *

PRAYER

Life is fragile -- handle with prayer.

* * * * *

Prayer is the key that opens the day and the lock that guards the night.

* * * * *

He prays well who is so absorbed with God that he does not know he's praying.

* * * * *

When we pray unto the Father in the name of Jesus for specific personal things we should feel in the very depths of our souls that we are willing to subject our petitions to the will of our Father in Heaven.

--Marion G. Romney

* * * * *

Have you ever knelt down to pray and after addressing Diety, wondered if you had turned off the lights, wound up the clock, made a certain phone call? Get up, check your light, make your phone call, wind the clock, and then kneel again in humility, when ready, and have a heart-to-heart talk with your Father in Heaven.

* * * * *

Pray as though everything depended upon God, and work as though everything depended upon you.

* * * * *

A Prayer

Where there is hatred, let me sow love. Where there is injury, pardon. Where there is doubt, faith. Where there is despair, hope. Where there is darkness, light. Where there is sadness, joy. O Divine Master, grant that I may not so much seek to be consoled as to console; to be understood, as to understand; to be loved, as to love; for it is in giving that we receive; it is in pardoning that we are pardoned, and it is in dying that we are born to Eternal Life.

--Francis of Assisi

* * * * *

Renewal

To keep God at the center of one's life requires frequent renewal of power through prayer. But such renewal is not measured by the amount of time it takes, rather by the degree to which one is able even for a short time to have relaxed and unhurried communion with God. One can pray inwardly at any time and anywhere -- but one prays best either alone or with understanding friends. To avoid neglecting to pray, it is best to have a time-habit and a place-habit. This is so important that it is worth great effort, in spite of the hurry of life and our lack of privacy.

--Georgia Harkness

* * * * *

Answers

Answers to prayer often come in unexpected ways. We pray, for instance, for a certain virtue; but God seldom delivers Christian virtues all wrapped in a package and ready for use. Rather he puts us in situations whereby his help we can develop those virtues. Henry Ward Beecher told of a woman who prayed for patience, and God sent her a poor cook. The best answers to prayer may be the vision and strength to meet a circumstance or to assume responsibility.

* * * * *

Prayer

If radio's slim fingers can pluck a melody
From night, and toss it over a continent or sea;
If the petaled white notes of a violin
Are lifted across a mountain or a city's din;
If songs, like crimson roses, are called from thin blue air
Why should mortals wonder if God hears prayer?

I often say my prayers, but do I ever pray?
And do the wishes of my heart go with the words I say?
I may as well kneel down and worship gods of stone,
As offer to the Living God a prayer of words alone.
For words without the heart the Lord will never hear;
Nor will He to those lips attend whose prayers are not sincere.

* * * * *

Prayer

I know not by what methods rare
But this I know
God answers prayer
I know that He has given His word
Which tells me
Prayer is always heard.
And will be answered soon or late
And so I pray
And calmly wait.
I know not if the blessings sought
Will come just in
The way of thought
But leave my prayer with Him alone
Whose will is wiser
Than my own
Assured that He will grant my quest
And send some answer
Far more blessed.

--Eliza M. Hickok

* * * * *

Whenever I am troubled
And lost in deep despair
I bundle all my troubles up
And go to God in prayer.
I tell Him I am heartsick
And lost and lonely, too
That my mind is deeply burdened
And I don't know what to do.
For I know He stilled the tempest
And He calmed the angry sea
And I humbly ask if in His love
He'll do the same for me.
And then I just keep quiet
And think only thoughts of peace
And if I abide in stillness
My restless murmuring's cease.

* * * * *

Prayer

My soul usually weeps and my heart always cries
When I think of the sorrow and grief,

That can come to a man who won't even try
To kneel and ask God for relief.

We all have our pains and troubles to bear
Each minute of every day
And Satan's the kind who'll always be there
To tell us we needn't pray.

He wants us to quit, to give up the ghost
To darken God's shining ray
By making us think the battle is lost
And it's God who darkened our day.

But, this I can say with all the strength of my soul
The Lord's not the one who has moved
It's just part of the way to put our names on the roll
Of those whom our God has approved.

We all must be tested some time in our life
So He'll know if we really care
But He'll never give us the pain or the strife
We have not the strength to bear.

So when Satan does come to lead you astray
Look to your God through prayer
And when you've survived the trials of the day
You'll find He was always there.

--Rydman

* * * * *

Prayer

Here is the story of the roofer who was repairing the roof on a three-story house. He was in a heavy snow area and the "pitch" of the roof (the slant) was very steep. All of a sudden his feet lost their hold and the worker began to slide. As he picked up momentum, he thought of the certain death which awaited him if he slid off the edge onto the concrete below. His life flashed before his eyes as he recalled that he hand't always done what he ought to have done. He suddenly became very repentant and he began to pray in this manner: "O God, I know I have been a poor member of your Church, but I will do better, I promise! If you help me live, I will dedicate myself to your service. I will spend my whole life being good -- all my energy, talents, time, and money will be yours -- PLEASE, PLEASE, if you'll only stop me from sliding down this roof and falling off the edge."

Just as he was really warming up his promises to the Lord, a protruding nail caught his clothing and stopped his sliding. Relieved, he interrupted his fervent prayer: "Whew! Never mind, God, I took care of it myself."

* * * * *

These Things I Ask For

I care not whether worldly wealth is mine,
Nor if fame and fortune linger at my door,
Yearning for thrills is now all bur forgotten,
As childhood fades these things alone I ask for.

Laughter, for the world is bleak without it;
Music, for my heart is full of song;
Virtue, so I might walk with head erect;
Strength, to help some weary soul along;
Love, that my heart may e'er be tender;
Comfort, I, too, have known grief's stinging lash;
Honor, that my soul may not be tarnished;
Judgment, to separate the pure from trash;
Wisdom, better to cope with problems;
Loyalty, to give my country aid;
Endurance, for I know too well my weaknesses;
Courage, to speak for justice unafraid;
Observing eyes, to see the needs of others
And to lend a hand, as on life's course they plod;
And last, but to me the most important,
The Power of Prayer, for I would talk with God.

--Charlene Bailey Hardcastle

* * * * *

A Portrait Of Prayer

Prayer is a dialogue, not a monologue. It opens a spiritual channel between man and his Immortal Guide. President McKay said that prayer is "a message of the soul...The language is not mere words but spirit vibration."

Prayer can predict our progress. If it is a true blueprint of our intent, it will articulate the best of each of us.

Prayer constitutes deep thoughts and institutes deeper ones. It is part of the key to wisdom. The Prophet Joseph was instructed by Moroni: "Forget not to pray, that thy mind may become strong."

Prayer requires faith, and builds it, and permits each of us to experience the feelings of gratitude, humility, and hope.

Prayer provides relief from mundane burdens through sharing the responsibilities of life with another. It is an invigorating prescription, an antidote for unnecessary cares and qualms, a catalyst for further spiritual endeavors.

Prayer provides an individual with an honest analysis of himself. It teaches him the ability to appraise himself realistically and rightly -- not as compared to the neighbors next door, the group at the office, or his graduating class, but to himself and how well he is running the race of life as an individual, evaluated only according to his inherent "talents" and his use of them.

Prayer teaches, indeed admits, the reality of God. It is a testimony of faith, a daily autobiography, a person portrait.

Prayer can resolve any doubt, remove any fear, guide and inspire, and teach the eternal truths.

* * * * *

PREPARATION

All who have meditated upon the art of governing mankind have been convinced that the fate of empires depend upon the education of youth.

--Aristotle

* * * * *

If a man empties his purse into his head, no man can take it away from him. An investment in knowledge always pays the best interest.

--Benjamin Franklin

* * * * *

Too Late

We always find there is something
We wish we had done before
Someone we love sleeps softly
Onto the other shore
Some message of love unspoken
Some tiny word of praise
That might have helped to brighten
The passing of the days.

Why are we always so busy
So blind to our brother's need
We never know of his burdens
Or how much a kindly deed
Might give him the strength and courage
To meet the tests of late
It's often the same old sad story
Too little, and yes, too late.

* * * * *

When You Meet A Tiger

Dear Son:

Last night as we were watching T.V. you asked me a question I did not answer. Since my jet does not land for a couple of hours, I have decided to write an confidential reply.

You'll recall that it was hard to recognize the sly tiger in the jungle show and the great power he seemed to have. As he snarled with that angry, singsong whine and leaped, you turned to me and asked, "Dad, what do you do when you meet a tiger?"

Well, son, when a man meets a tiger he should be prepared, for if he is not, the tiger will destroy him. If we were living where tigers are feared by man and by all other animals because of their viciousness, cruelty, and treachery, I would suggest that you avoid meeting a tiger at night or where grass and undergrowth stand high. To meet a tiger you had best be in a cage, perched on an elephant's back, or with a powerful rifle across your lap. Even then, it is dangerous. A tiger's terrible claws can slash through even an elephant's thick skin. If a man meets a tiger, he must know what he is doing and have courage.

I doubt that either of us will ever meet an honest-to-goodness live tiger -- at least, I hope not.

But there are other kinds of tigers, just as sly and vicious, and as harmful and deadly as the tigers in India. I call them invisible tigers. Invisible tigers like real-life tigers, are treacherous, both night and day. They are hard to recognize, for they too blend into the tall grass and undergrowth of people and their conversations. They damage a man's soul. To fight them you have to recognize them, surround yourself with a protective shield and powerful weapons, including courage.

There are several rules it would be wise to follow when you meet a tiger:

Rule No. 1 -- Tag the Tiger

To tag tigers you really need to be sharp. Because you cannot see them, you must depend largely on what you hear. If someone dares you to do something you know is wrong, or calls you "chicken" when you refuse, or assures you "It really is O.K.," or "Everybody's doing it," you can bet your life you have met an "invisible tiger." This tiger is temptation. Of the many varieties of invisible tigers, teen-agers are most vulnerable to "show-off" tigers, "Follow-the-crowd" tigers, tigers of "rebellion," "break the Word of Wisdom" tigers, "break the law of chastity" tigers. You can be sure these tigers are lurking close by when you say to yourself such things as "No one will know," or "Just once won't hurt."

Rule No. 2 -- Turn Up the Volume

Inside you is a secret place for things you have been taught, and these things play back to you as you go about your day. Sometimes the play back is not very loud. So when you meet a tiger, turn up the volume.

Rule No. 3 -- Set Your Sights

Slaying your invisible tigers is something you have to do. Setting sights is deciding what to do. In these days, it becomes very difficult to set sights, because your friends have greater influence over you than when you were young. They will be unkind to you at times and will even persecute you by calling you names. It becomes a problem to make up your mind. Invisible tigers do not drop dead from old age or accident...so you need to decide how you are going to handle them. Keep asking questions that need mature answers; weigh one idea against another; listen to your inner promptings -- and then decide. As you test and compare and decide, your ability to eliminate invisible tigers will grow in leaps and bounds.

Rule No. 4 -- Use Your Shield

This shield is the protection afforded by your Heavenly Father through prayer. If you will pray to God and seek his guidance, he will guide you and surround you with protection more effective than a tiger cage. Your Father in Heaven loves you, and you need only to seek his help and try your best to do right.

Rule No. 5 -- Cap with Courage

After you have tagged the tiger, turned up the volume, set your sights, and used your shield, the final rule is to slay the tiger with the courage of your convictions. You are certain to have static from some of your friends, but you can claim no fame through inaction, or going with the crowd, or running away. Courage in doing right is its own reward.

You are very choice to your mother and me and we know that you will always have the courage to fight the tigers you meet.

Love,

DAD

* * * * *

PROPHETS

To Joseph

I came today where you once lived,
The fields, where as a boy, you roamed.
I toured the sites of Palmyra town
And loved the beauties of your home.

I saw the Peter Whitmer home and grounds
Where once the Church began,
The Martin Harris place, your home and farm
Where lived God's greatest man.

I climbed the hill that you once climbed
To meet an angel sent from God.
As I recalled his mission there,
So many truths I understood.

I knelt today where you once knelt,
On sacred, holy ground.
Among the quiet trees I felt
His spirit all around.

Unlike you, though, I needn't ask
Which Church is right on earth.
Instead, because you filled the task
I bore a witness of that truth.

The streets where you once walked, I walked,
Those straight, four-acre blocks.
Great homes, with proper space you planned
And with your people built.

I saw the temple site so long destroyed
Preserving holiness by our Father's hand.
In Brigham's home I felt His Spirit,
And knew that there He talked to man.

I stood today in Carthage Jail
And felt the sacredness of death.
I think I felt a little pain
As I recalled your dying breath.

The open window, the bullet holes,
And, oh, that stain of blood.
And then, I knew that truth you knew,
The truth for which you died.

--Sharon Miller

* * * * *

Joseph Smith -- The Man And The Prophet

A life that has become a candle of the Lord, is a life that all would wish to see more clearly. Such a life was Joseph Smith's, a life of monumental splendor. The second greatest man to ever walk the face of the earth was Joseph Smith. Those who knew the prophet, came from around the world and they say him in a variety of roles. Their description of the prophet reflects their own background. Let me give you the impressions of those who knew and admired the prophet:

A thirteen-year-old lad, small for his age, watched the prophet during Zions Camp March. He idealized his strength and says, "He was a tall, well-built man." A convert girl, age twenty, was most impressed by his "blue eyes, light hair, and very fine white skin." A convert from the Quaker Movement, observed that he was not as "sedate and serious" as his brother, Hyrum, and noted that he was "always so neat." A lad from England, impressed with British Royalty observed that "he wore no whiskers, and that altogether he presented a very formidable appearance being a man of gentlemanly bearing." The daughter of a wealthy southern family, an accomplished horsewoman, admired the prophet's mastery of his black horse, Old Charley. And a girl of literary talent who left her home at sixteen to come to Nauvoo, says, "His majesty of appearance was something wonderful. You would think he was much taller and much larger than even he was." And later she wrote, "There are no pictures of him in existence, that compare with the majesty of his presence."

Looking more deeply into his personality and character, they portray a remarkable blend of qualities. They speak of his solemnity in sacred circumstances, yet are pleased at his great wit, repartee, and hearty laughter.

They are inspired by his powers of spiritual concentration. They say he often bowed his head in deep reflection. "Why don't you hold up your head like a man?" asked one youth. The prophet simply pointed to some ripe grain, bent under a full head. But they are equally struck at his versatility in changing pace: He could move from studying Hebrew or Greek or counseling to playing ball, or wrestling, jumping at a mark, or pulling up stakes, and back again. At sixteen, Samuel Miles recognized his "easy, jovial appearance when engaged in sports, but also his firm dislike of that which was degrading."

They describe him as a rugged, outdoor man, often in rough clothes or in coats with thin elbows to be found haying or chopping or shooting. Young Joseph nobels learned of the restoration, while working at the prophet's side in the hay field. Yet Emmeline Wells recalls his great love of poetry, of the "grand in nature." Hiram Clawson tells of his delight in drama and Wandall Mace says his love for sacred music was unmatched. He wept when a small congregation sang, "Glorious Things Are Sung of Zion."

They bask in the power of his testimony which seemed, "to shake the earth" in meetings where even the children observed "the most profound silence." They say he "had the appearance of one that was heaven born while preaching." Yet they record his honest confessions of need.

They comment on his manly endurance and lamblike submission to divine impressions, even when it wrenched "his very heart strings." They also speak of his lionlike rebuke, followed by a reassurance of love. "I am determined," he said, "while I lead this Church, to lead it right." They speak of the dizzying depths of his teaching and, with Horace Cummings, say that the prophet always showed an unsatisfied anxiety to communicate his experience. And so the list continued. They found a man so tender that he never passed a child without speaking. A man of "indomitable perseverance" who was also "ceaselessly forgiving." A man inclined to silence with his own thoughts, but also inclined to such soulful brotherhood that his wife observed, "He can never eat without his friends." A man so eager and full of zest for life that his very presence, say the Pratt brothers, was "soothing, comforting, and nourishing." But a man who with his superlative blessings also endured unspeakable suffering.

A man who led like Moses, spoke like Peter and wrote like Paul. And as he grew older, what do we learn about his mind and spirit and heart. They say he was "as unassuming as a little child," whose kindness was as "though we had all been his own brothers and sisters." Yet they stood in increasing awe.

Of his mind: Emmeline Wells, a precocious girl who tried to listen to his every word, said, "He was beyond my comprehension." Jedediah Grant who delivered many missionary sermons before he was eighteen and who later became the father of Heber J. Grant, says, "He could take the wisest of elders and circumscribe their very thoughts." Edward Stevenson, who became an assistant Church Historian, says, "I began to believe that he possessed an infinity of knowledge." Mercy Thompson says, "To him all things seemed simple and easy to be understood, and thus he could make them plain to others as no other man could that I ever heard."

In the course of a brief few years, the Prophet Joseph was able to read Egyptian -- the ancient hieroglyphics -- German, Hebrew, and Greek. I suppose he would not have been proficient in speaking any of them, but he understood them and conversed on biblical writings in those various languages. On one occasion he mentioned a great number of languages and said, "If I live long enough I will master them all." It seemed as though the gates of heaven were opened, and a living stream flowed directly to him.

Of his warmth and love: Seventeen-year-old William Taylor spent two weeks with him while in hiding. "I have never felt the same joy and satisfaction in the companionship of any other person." John Smith was fifteen when he made a forced march with a segment of the Nauvoo Legion to protect the city. He looked up from a log where his feet left blood marks in the snow to see the prophet in tears. "God bless you my dear boy, God bless you." "The sensation and impression can never be forgotten," says he. Joseph once hugged his cousin George and said, "I love you as I do my own life." George was overwhelmed. "I hope," he said, "my whole life and actions will ever prove my feelings and the depth of my affection for you."

Imagine yourself age twenty-three, charged with perhaps the most crucial task of translation in history. Acting as your secretary is your new bride. At the moment you cannot afford food, nor even paper on which to record the translation. In these circumstances, you are inspired with a divine call and a promise to be published to all the world. "This generation shall have my word through you." And you say, "I am the chosen seer spoken of by Nephi. I am the son of ancient Joseph."

Joseph's brother, William, adds another page to the story. On his deathbed Joseph Smith Sr. gave blessings to all his sons and daughters. His fathers had promised Joseph before: "Your heart shall meditate great wisdom. Your intelligence shall circumscribe and comprehend the deep things of God. Your mouth shall utter the law of the just." And now he said, "Joseph, my son, you shall even live to finish your work." Joseph cried out weeping, "Oh, my father, shall I?" "Yes," said his father. "This is my dying blessing upon you, in the name of Jesus Christ."

In these and other ways the prophet knew two things: His promised destiny, and its price: willingness to sacrifice all unworthy things for the "excellence of the glory of Christ." Thus when Elizabeth Rollins asked him how he gained such peace and assurance, he replied, "I have the oath of God upon it." And David Osborne, a boyhood admirer, heard him say, "If I obtain the glory which I have in view, I expect to wade through much tribulation."

He seemed to see each person in terms of a like origin and a like destiny. He was a seer of both their past and future. As a missionary in his twenty's when he came back to Salem, Massachusetts, he was instrumental in the conversion of many people. The prophet said that the time he spent while on a mission was full of some of the most exciting and rewarding experiences of his life. One prophetic word often changed whole lives. Putting his hand on a lad he had never before seen, he said to the father, "Brother Lorenzo, this boy will live to aid in carrying the Gospel to the nations of the earth." "His words thrilled me like fire," the boy remembers, "and from that hour, I looked forward to that day."

Many who listened to his prayers -- intimate, expressive -- and imbued with the spirit -- were kindled to take pattern in their own homes and learned that the heavens could literally open. "Forget not to pray, that thy mind may become strong..." So Moroni enjoined the prophet at age seventeen. He did not forget. In the crests and crises of his life, his query was constant, "Oh, Lord, what shall I do?"

Daniel Tyler heard him pray before an assembly of the saints in Kirtland, kneeling before them: "He addressed his maker as though he was present listening as a kind father would listen to the sorrows of a dutiful child. There was no pretentiousness, no raising of voice, but a plain conversational tone, as a man would address a present friend. It appeared to me as though in case the veil were taken away, I could see the Lord standing facing his humblest of all servants I had ever seen." His experience of the sacred grove went with him wherever he ministered. No witness he ever bore carried more convincing power.

The prophet called young people to the same holiness and wholeness in Christ. It is significant that at the time, the prophet spoke publicly of the "perfect love" of Christ, without which, he said, we are liable to fail. The vision of the degrees of glory was given in the presence of several elders at Hiram, Ohio. Philo Dibble was present. He saw nothing, but was filled with the warmth and light of the spirit. He studied the faces of Joseph and Sydney and heard them say what they later wrote. "And now after the many testimonies which have been given of Him, that he lives. For we saw him, even on the right hand of the Father, and heard the voice bearing record that He is the only begotten of the Father."

Those who were blessed in having a living relationship with Christ, understood Joseph's final words as he went to his death as he spoke to Stephen Markham: "My conscience is void of offense." A model is always a better motivator than a medal. This is why the life, and not just the pronouncements of Jesus Christ, are so everlastingly crucial. And so is any life illuminated and empowered by Him. Such a life was Joseph Smith's.

--Sherman Kent Sowby

* * * * *

President Brigham Young
(Anecdotes of the Great Pioneer and Leader)

The true character of any man is revealed as quickly through an anecdote as through pages of description. If Boswell had not written the thousand-and-one incidents and repartee of the famous old, lumbering Dr. Johnson, we should still be measurably ignorant of that grand old, pock-marked, witty, stupendous genius.

Dr. Johnson called, (so Boswell tells us, in one of these delightful anecdotes) according to appointment, at the house ofa nobleman to dine with his lordship. The powdered and bewigged footman who answered the bell looked at the great, awkward figure before him, with its seedy coat, unclean linen, and the coarse, bloated face above it all, then said contemptuously.

"The place of admittance for your kind is at the back door."

"Ah, but," answered the visitor, "I came as the guest of his lordship."

Another scornful look, and the flunky replied,

"My master expects Dr. Johnson."

"Yes," answered the imperturbable old genius, "I'm Johnson."

"What!" cried the servant. "You? The famous Dr. Johnson? Why you don't look as if you could say Boo, to a goose."

"Boo!" sung out Johnson, in his deep, bass voice.

"Come right in, Doctor," answered the non-plussed servitor, "his lordship is in the drawing room."

While the deepest currents of human life may not thus be discovered, certainly these bubbles on the stream show with sufficient accuracy the sweep and swirl of the currents and whirlpools below.

Perhaps no trait of Brigham Young's character was more marked than his love and tender care for the helpless. Poverty -- and health -- did not appeal to him very much. But childhood, helpless old age, sickness or weakness, all these brought out the best that was in him.

"Provide work," was his cry. "The giving of alms raises a generation of paupers." This was his thought. "Let the aged, even, do something for what they receive, that they may not lose their independence."

On one cold, rainy day, a child came to his office with a message for the President's private secretary.

The child's feet were soaking wet. The President saw her, and noticed at once her condition.

With a gentle word, to reassure the little one, he set her on a chair, near the blazing grate, and drew off, with tender care, the wet shoes and stockings. The stockings were shaken and hung carefully to dry, and the shoes placed at the exact nearness to the fire to dry without burning or undue stiffening. Then the little feet were rubbed warm and dry with his own pocket-handkerchief, while he talked cheerfully and simply to the amazed child. After a while, he rubbed and softened the shoes, drew on both stockings and shoes, and sent the happy child home with a peppermint drop to add to her afternoon's enjoyment.

He had a most peculiar way of amusing babies; he would take them on one knee, and then commence a sort of "Too-roo-loo-rool-lool-or-loo," which was a sure antidote for weeping babies. The unusual noise, not loud, nor harsh, but withal musical, yet very peculiar, would dry up an incipient torrent on a baby's cheek, and leave the infant in a vague wonder as to where itself and the world "were at."

Only once did I see my father whip a child: and that was at prayer time.

A lovely, rosy, blue-eyed, romping baby of two years, father's youngest child born in the Lion House, was as full of frolic and noise, naturally, at prayer time as at any other time of the day. Father had requested the child's mother to keep the baby quiet during the prayer itself. This rule was fairly well observed. But the tiny tyrant knew her own power, and her mother's weakness. So, occasionally, she would wiggle out of the restraining arms, as the mother kneeled at her chair, and go laughing and dancing across the long prayer room.

One awful night, baby May again broke from her mother's care, in the midst of the solemn, heartfelt prayer, and ran mockingly straight for her father's bowed form.

Suddenly the prayer was stilled, no one moved, nor scarcely breathed; but those who were hardy enough to look around, saw father quietly arise, pick up the child, spank it heartily, place it quietly on the mother's chair, then, going back to his own place, he resumed his prayer, just where he had left off. That child never again disturbed a prayer.

Seeing one of his daughters trying to make an obstinate child mind, he said, "Never ask a child to do a thing you are sure it won't do."

At one time, a feast was provided for President Young and those with him who were attending a conference in a distant stake. The sharp eyes of the President noted the ones who were seated at his own table, and at the other tables, as well as those who had no place at all.

The conference and the feast were both held in an old-fashioned bowery.

At the close of the afternoon service, he asked the people if they would come to a meeting on the morrow, and if they would provide another feast, if he would stay over.

A glad consent was given.

The next day, at noon, the feast was again spread. After everything was ready, the president drew near his former table, to which he was led by the mistress of the feast.

"I wish you to entertain my friends today," he said.

So saying, he stepped away to the outer edges of the bowery, where were gathered the poor, the aged, the halt and blind. Inviting all of these, he led the way to his own table where he seated these astonished guests with gracious courtesy. No reference was made to what he had done, but he entertained them all with delightful grace, and left his lesson to sink deep into the hearts of those who had prepared the feast.

He knew everybody; it was a mystery to me for years how he could retain a mass of seemingly unrelated facts, as pertained to individuals everywhere. But his secret was simple; the moment he saw a new face, he either called the stranger to him or inquired about him. The name of the stranger was the least part of the desired information; where did he come from, where was he born, who were his parents and grandparents? Any relation in the valley? What was the stranger's occupation, habits and ambitions? All this formed many connecting links with which to fasten on memory's chain the individual and his history.

Surely everyone remembers his first encounter with that wittiest of Utah's sons, Scipio A. Kenner.

After the usual fire of questions, he put the last, a stumper, to the poor young fellow who remembered his early baptism, but subsequent wanderings from the church.

"Are you a 'Mormon?'" asked the President of the nervous, non-plussed youth before him, who had come a-courting one of the President's pretty daughters. "Are you a 'Mormon?'"

"Slightly," answered the curly-headed boy. And the big grain of truth in the small answer tickled the President mightily. It amused him for years. He always called the lad "Scipio Sinner" after that.

Brigham Young was a small eater, and would fain have lived much simpler than his loving family and friends would permit him to do.

He often said he was raised on johnny cake, baked potatoes, and buttermilk, and no feast could so please him as these three simple articles. But like many other Yankees, he had an appetite for cream.

"I am very fond of skimmed milk," he would say, "but please give me the skimmings." Often when an elaborate menu was spread for him, he would say quietly, "Sister, can you give me a bowl of bread and milk -- with a little skimmings?"

In 1868, he began his reform movement to induce the people to observe the Word of Wisdom more closely. At this time, too, he taught the people to cease eating pork. He announced this as a revelation, and he strictly lived up to it himself.

In traveling around, he would sometimes spy a plate of doughnuts on the table, a dainty of which he was very fond. Then would surely follow the question, "Sister, what were your doughnuts fried in?" If the answer was "lard," he said nothing more. But if the lady replied, "Well, sir, I fried them in suet or drippings," he would say jubilantly, "Pass the doughnuts."

I have yet to hear from man or woman who had the last or best word with Brigham Young. Some tried it, and even now recall, with more or less gusto, their own brightness or impertinence, as the case may be. But if such would tell the whole story, the truth of what has just been stated would be apparent.

A three days' conference was held, at one time, in a northern stake. A certain good brother, who formed one of the President's party from Salt Lake City, was a long-winded and very prosy speaker. But like some others, he was very fond of preaching. And during the long meetings he had not once been asked to speak.

The afternoon of the last session had arrived, and this brother was smarting with indignation at his supposed neglect. After the opening hymn, President Young turned to this brother, and said, "Brother So-and-so, will you open the meeting with prayer?" The President composed himself, and the brother began; but the brother did not stop. Quarter of an hour, half an hour, and still another quarter of an hour dragged along, and the brother was still praying. He was putting his long pent-up sermon into a series of thanks to the Lord. Finally he closed, and sat down. Gravely the President turned to the choir, behind him, and announced in his resounding voice, "Choir, please sing, and we'll dismiss."

--Sura Young Gates

* * * * *

REGRET

Melody in F

How frequently I wryly grin
And think about what might have been:
If I'd said "Yes" instead of "No" --
If I'd gone fast instead of slow --
If I'd looked far instead of near --

If I'd made each move in reverse --
If I'd be better off -- or worse??

I'd rather be a Could Be
If I could not be an Are;
For a Could Be is a May Be,
With a chance of touching par.
I'd rather be a Has Been
Than a Might Have Been by far;
For a Might Have Been has never been,
But a Has was once an Are!

* * * * *

Dear L.D.S. Girls:

Hello! Some of you know me, some of you don't; but I hope you will all listen very carefully to what I have to say!

I have been a member of the L.D.S. Church all of my life, living in an active, Church going family. I have a brother on a mission for the Church and another brother planning to go on one. I have earned individual awards for six years and have received superior ratings in speech and music festivals in Church and school. I graduated from high school last year, and until a month ago I had a good job.

Sounds pretty good, right? Please read on.

I am going to tell you where I am and let you wonder for a moment how I got there. I am presently sitting in a hospital bed. My mouth is wired closed for repairs to the bones in my face. My jaws hurt terribly, and have for a month. I am being fed through a tube in my stomach. With luck, I will be able to begin eating by mouth again in a month and a half.

My beautiful long hair was completely shaved off shortly after I entered the hospital and I am wearing a wig donated by a local wig store. Beneath the wig I wear a temporary protective plate on my forehead where some bone with dirt and hair was removed. Later, they will operate to insert a plate.

So far, I have had six operations, and can look forward to five or six more, plus the plastic surgery. Hopefully, I will eventually be fixed up to look like I used to look, thanks to a team of skilled doctors and the help of my Heavenly Father. The only walking I do now is from my room to the other end of the hospital for daily physical therapy hours. Some say I will be able to lead a normal life, marriage, children...with a normal looking body (minus one eye and a sense of smell.)

With the hundreds of people praying for me, I HAVE to get well! God answers prayers...I know this, because I am slowly getting better. I shall thank Him eternally for the second chance He gave me.

It will be about two more months before I can go back to my family, to Church, and to dates with my fiance. Our marriage plans had to be postponed, but then when we marry, it will be in the temple, so that we will be together for time and all eternity.

Thank goodness, my Mom, Dad, Fiance, and fifteen-year-old sister can come to see me every day at the hospital. I only see my little brother and two sisters on special occasions when I meet them in the hospital lobby.

By the time I return to work, I will have been gone three months or more. Hopefully, I will get my job back.

Sounds pretty good? No, not really! And I wouldn't want you to trade me places, any more than you would want to trade with me.

What got me in the hospital? I fell down on one thing which Church teaches us girls! Modesty in dress. And I know I am not alone. What bothers me is that many of you girls are doing the same thing I was doing when I received my injuries. I am madly in love with my L.D.S. fiance, but still I had to wear short skirts (three or four inches above the knee) to attract guys. Makes sense? Not hardly.

Well, I attracted a guy alright...a young negro who wanted sex and nearly killed me because I wouldn't give it to him. That is where my not heeding the counsel of the Church and my parents got me.

I had read in magazines and newspapers about other girls who got jumped while walking home from work. But things like that couldn't happen to me! They just happen to other girls, I told myself. Don't kid yourselves, girls! That can happen to any one of you.

Please don't invite it. I did, very unknowingly. My parents and teachers all told me, but I didn't pay enough attention.

When I get home, I will un-hem every one of my skirts to knee length. And I will help my three younger sisters to do the same. I would hate for anything like this to happen to them. That is one experience no one forgets, or wants to go through again. Please protect yourselves!

I hope that all L.D.S. girls can learn from my experience and not have to learn it the hard way, as I did.

From now on, there is only one guy I'll ever try to attract with my clothes.

Sincerely,

"One Who Has Learned"

Dear L.D.S. Girls:

The contents of this letter above are not the figment of the imagination. Everything contained therein is true.

It was written by someone I know very well and love very much. It could have been written by someone you know. Or, it could have been written by YOU, perhaps?

Just like so many of you, she knew what she was supposed to do, but she just didn't always do it. Now, she will never again be quite the same person she was before.

In the incident she describes, she was attacked and assaulted. She struggled to be free from his grasp, tried to plead with him, became infuriated when he tried to get what he shouldn't have, and hit him several times. With the last bit of strength and consciousness she had, she knocked the board from his hands.

The severe beating she received from him resulted in a fractured skull with open wound...brain exposed; both jaws and nose broken; nose membrane gone; sense of smell gone, one badly damaged eye and one eye gone... literally.

She was left for dead in the desert where she was found some fifteen hours later, wearing only her blouse covered with a coat. She certainly should have died, except for the power of the Priesthood, the faith and prayers of hundreds of good people, and her faith and fighting spirit. Also, for the fact that God must have had a special mission for her to perform.

She has stated many times that she would go through it all again, if it need be, before she would willingly submit to an immoral act. In this respect she can face God and her loving fiance with self-respect. Their love for each other has grown into something that can never be destroyed.

Now, my dear, beloved sisters, children of God, please stop and ask yourselves, "What do I really want?"

None of us want bad things to happen to us, but merely not wanting them will not prevent them from happening. I wouldn't want this to happen to any one of you, any more than I wanted it to happen to my sister.

If we desire a blessing from the Lord, we must keep the laws upon which that blessing is predicated. Please, just stop and think about what you may be doing, and thank your Father in Heaven for the commandments He has given to you. May God's choicest blessings be upon each and every one of you, is my sincere prayer.

Sincerely,

An L.D.S. Youth

* * * * *

Minnie The Cook

About fifteen years ago I was a student at the University of Michigan living in a sorority house with fifty other girls. Of course, we were all remarkably intelligent and sophisticated.

Many nights, after we had said our ritual farewells to the young lions we all thought we would marry one day, some of us would cluster around the big coffee urn in the kitchen at 1322 Hill Street.

Resplendent in our seventy-five pin-curls each and our chic red flannel nightshirts, we drank gallons of coffee and discussed how we were going to solve the Problems of Society -- in about a month and a half after we graduated.

Minnie, our cook, always left a little something on the back burner for these late-night planning sessions -- much to the consternation of the housemother, who thought the less we ate the sooner we'd be in bed, and the sooner she'd be able to balance her food budget.

One of my all-time favorites was Minnie's barbecued hamburger. None, before or since, has come close to hers for sheer good taste.

A couple of years after I graduated I had made very little progress with the Problems of Society, but there had been one significant distraction: A terribly intelligent and sophisticated young man had asked me to marry him, and I thought it sounded like a good idea.

The loyal "sisters" planned a bridal shower back at the old sorority house. Undergraduates, alumnae, and friends gathered, and I opened box after box of beautiful gifts. There were imported crystal goblets, place settings of silver and china, silver hollowware pieces, and delicate table linens.

About half way through the very proper party, someone took me aside and said Minnie wanted to see me in the kitchen.

I found her standing next to the big old stove, looking just as I had remembered her -- if I had remembered her at all, which I realized, painfully at that moment, I had not.

She was short and insignificant-looking, with her glasses slipping down toward the end of her nose (as they always did) and a few strands of graying hair creeping out from under the net she wore while she was "on duty."

She shoved a hand into the pocket of her great white apron and pulled out a piece of paper. As she handed it to me she said, "I want to give you something too. I had trouble cutting it down, but I think it's all right now."

On the paper in Minnie's almost unreadable scrawl was her recipe for barbecued hamburger -- adjusted from enough to serve fifty to enough to serve four.

In my intelligence and sophistication I couldn't think of a thing to say. I was embarrassed, and angry with her for embarrassing me. What could I say about this "nothing" gift when I had just been given a whole roomful of beautiful and valuable gifts?

There were tears in Minnie's eyes, but none in mine, as I stuffed the paper in a pocket and thanked her politely, but insincerely.

Something -- perhaps the one grain of sense I inherited from my French ancestors -- made me keep that scrap of paper.

A few years later, when the linens were long gone and the crystal was chipped and the silver had become a gigantic bore to polish, Minnie's barbecued hamburger was cheering a hungry family of five with solid regularity.

It is a special favorite of our three children, who Minnie in her wisdom knew would come to fill my days with real joy and sweep away that phony elegance.

Once, several years ago, when we were in Ann Arbor for a football game, I found Minnie still in the kitchen on Hill Street. I tried to thank her then properly for her loving and useful gift, but she was very old and growing deaf and I don't know if she understood.

Perhaps by sharing her recipe with you I can ease the ache I still feel whenever I remember that bridal shower and those terribly intelligent, sophisticated, and -- in their own way -- beautiful years.

Minnie's Barbecued Hamburger

1-1/2 lb. ground beef
1 small onion, finely chopped
1/2 cup celery, finely chopped
1/4 cup green pepper, finely chopped
Salt and pepper to taste
1 Tbsp. prepared mustard
1 Tbsp. vinegar
1 Tbsp. brown sugar
1 cup chili sauce
1 Tbsp. worcestershire sauce

Brown ground beef with onion, celery, and green pepper in large skillet or heavy pan. Add remaining ingredients and simmer for about 45 minutes. If ground beef is very fat, remove excess fat as it accumulates.

Spoon onto split hamburger rolls and serve immediately.

* * * * *

My Hot-Shot Driving Ruined A Girl's Life

I called for Cathy at quarter after eight that Saturday evening in June. Final exams were just over, and we were going to celebrate. Nothing large, just a movie and maybe a pizza later.

Cathy wasn't ready as usual. While waiting, I got to talking to her twin brother, Chuck, about scuba. We're both skin-diving nuts. Chuck and Cathy were in my junior class in high school.

Pretty soon Cathy ran down the stairs. She was wearing a white dress. She was tanned and all and looked terrific. We weren't going steady, but I was planning to ask her soon.

Cathy skipped down the porch steps after kissing her folks goodnight. They stood there, looking at her proudly, the way parents do when they think their kids aren't looking. Chuck hollered goodbye.

Cathy got into the car. I slipped behind the wheel and grinned at her. She grinned back and winked. I liked Cathy. I liked her a lot.

I drove out onto the main road, and traffic was pretty heavy because the big shopping center near town stayed open late at night. The movie was only three miles away.

Cathy and I talked about the exams, how we'd be seniors next year, and then, for no reason, I began clowning. I used to kid around a lot in the car, pulling all kinds of tricks. I had a whole bagful. I got a kick out of doing them.

This time I made like a jet pilot. I put my hand over my mouth to make my voice sound like it was coming from a two-way radio. "Flight 22, calling the tower. Ready for take-off. Over."

I pretended to listen for instructions, then barked screwball 'orders' to the co-pilot, the navigator, even the stewardesses. I was having myself a ball. Cathy was laughing, and that made me invent more wacky things. All the time I was doing about 40-45 in this traffic.

Finally I decided to 'take-off.' I leaned all the way back in my seat and pulled at the wheel, like I saw them do in the movies. I got sort of carried away. I was leaning as far back as I could, and even had lifted myself up from the seat a few inches to get "airborne."

A light just ahead was turning red. I needed only a split second to stop but I didn't have it because of my position at the wheel. I couldn't get my foot to the brake, so I ran through the light.

The truck whammed into me at the intersection. I felt a sharp pain when my head and left shoulder hit the door, then I blacked out.

I heard the siren before I opened my eyes. When I came to, I was lying on the road. I saw a police car race up. Everything was noisy and confused. People were calling and horns were blowing.

I looked at my car. The truck had backed off and the whole side was smashed in where Cathy had been sitting. I saw a bundle of white inside. I tried to lift myself up, saying something about getting to her, but a hand held me back.

For some freak reason all I got was a bump on the head, but for weeks we didn't know if Cathy would live.

I called the hospital almost every hour. I went down to see her but only the family was allowed. I also tried to see Chuck and Cathy's parents at their house -- but they were always out.

Finally I got the news. Cathy wasn't going to die. As soon as I heard I ran a mile and a half to Cathy's house, hoping to see Chuck and her folks.

I rang the bell and Chuck opened the door. He looked at me a second, then slammed the door in my face. His eyes were all red.

It shook me up. I went back home and an hour later I found out why from Anne, one of Cathy's girlfriends. Cathy would live all right, but she would have to spend the next twelve months in a special hospital, and then maybe another year at home. It might be a long time before she would walk again, if ever, or go to school. There was something else. She wouldn't look like Cathy any more.

When I had heard all this, everything I had been holding back all that month burst out in me. I took out my car keys and heaved them as far as I could. Then I locked myself in the basement and cried like a kid.

It didn't dawn on me until that minute that I was entirely to blame for what happened. I guess I had been too shook up to think clearly. But now it hit me like a pile driver. My stupid clowning had wrecked Cathy's life.

The thought was so terrible, I started to shake. I stuck my closed fists over my eyes, like I did when I was a kid and wanted to hide from something. But I couldn't hide. I only saw the accident more clearly than ever in my mind. I lived through it again and again. I dug my fists deeper into my eyes, but I still saw the car all smashed and the bundle of white on the front seat.

I sat there in the dark until long past midnight. I thought back on all the other kook things my friends and I had pulled in our cars, just for kicks, hot-shot drivers, we called ourselves.

There was one stunt where the driver would stick both hands out the window or on top of his head. Another fellow was crouched out of sight, doing the steering. The idea was to scare...people. They'd think nobody was steering. Here was one always good for a yak. When the car stopped for a light, one fellow would distract the attention of the driver, then another would call out, "go ahead," before the light changed. Automatically, the driver would step on the gas. The idea was to make him look foolish, but he'd also come near a crack-up.

We'd one-hand all over the place, take curves at high speed, weave like crazy and pull a hundred stunts. We never thought something might happen.

In a few days, a cop came to the house. A criminal charge had been filed against me for wreckless driving. Cathy had been questioned at the hospital and had told the story. A hearing was held, and my driving license was revoked.

Next day, I packed and hitch-hiked to a resort section where I got a job as a waiter. I worked harder than anybody there. After Labor Day, I came back home and started my senior year.

Everybody in town knew about the accident and why it happened. Things like that get around fast.

The first day in school, the principal made an announcement in assembly about driving habits. Heads turned toward me. I stared straight ahead.

I used to be pretty popular but I noticed that groups began breaking up when I was around. Guys I knew kept making excuses when I suggested we get together. Funny, because these were guys I used to horse around with in cars. Later, a doctor told me they shared my guilt for the accident. They saw themselves in me and hated it.

Once I called a girl for a date. She turned me down cold. "I fly only in jets with experienced pilots," she said as she hung up.

After the term began, I met Cathy's mother in a supermarket. I started to ask about Cathy and tell her how I felt. She looked at me a second, then slapped my face. She broke out crying, and a friend helped her out of the store. Later, I found out that Cathy's family had moved away and that she was in a hospital in a far off state. I never heard about her again.

Things got worse for me. During a scrimmage at football practice, I took a long pass and started running with the ball. Behind me, a voice yelled: "Look at that boy fly." That day I quit the team.

Little by little I became a real loner at school. I left the math club, the school paper. I couldn't study either. I found my mind fuzzing up when I tried to concentrate. I started losing weight. Finally I dropped out of school. My father tried to talk me out of it, but I had my mind made up. My mother was dead and my father worked twelve hours a day at his small hardware supply business. We weren't very close because he was never home.

The next few years I worked for a plant nursery. It was hard work and long hours and I didn't mind. But no matter how hard I worked I could never forget the accident.

This summer I made a big decision. I'm going back to school in the fall. It's going to be plenty rough because I'll be three years older than the other seniors. My classmates were in eighth grade when I was a junior. But I'll stick it out this time. I'll graduate and try to go on to college and make something of myself.

They say plastic surgery can do wonderful things. I pray for Cathy. I pray too for all the other pretty young girls who go out with hot-shot drivers.

I know one thing though. The kids in my town learned a lesson they'll never forget. I don't see much clowning around in cars any more. They all know that one slip, just one, can cause a tragedy.

I'll never forget mine. I can dig my fists in my eyes all I want, but I'll still see that smashed car and the bundle of white inside.

Editors' Note: Since the accident Cathy has spent two years in and out of hospitals. Her sight is badly impaired. She has undergone extensive plastic surgery, but doctors say she will bear lifelong scars. She has not been able to return to school.

* * * * *

SABBATH

A world without a sabbath would be like a man without a smile, like summer without flowers, and like a homestead without a garden. It is the most joyous day of the whole week.

--Henry Ward Beecher

* * * * *

A Sabbath well spent brings a week of content,
A new health for the joys of tomorrow.
But a Sabbath profaned -- whatever be gained --
Is a sure forerunner of sorrow.

--Matthew Hale

* * * * *

Mother's Day of Rest

Rising from her bed at dawn,
Mother got the breakfast on,
Laid out all the Sunday clothes,
Tied a shoelace, wiped a nose,
Got the children by their chairs,
So they could kneel for morning prayers.
Reminded Father time was fleeing
He must leave for Priesthood Meeting.
Combed and braided tangled hair
Dressed herself with Sabbath care
Prepared a roast for their return
And fondly prayed it would not burn.
Then nearly late as was the rule
She took her young to Sunday School
Returned from service with her brood
Fixed the meal and gave them food.
Reminded Dad while he was eating
That, he had another meeting.
Even then could not retire
Had to practice with the choir
Made a Sabbath call, and then,
Back she went to Church again.
Opened her book and sang with zest
"Beautiful Day of Peace and Rest."

--Virginia Maughan Kammeyer

* * * * *

A Standard For The Sabbath

Would you judge the lawfulness or unlawfulness of pleasure, then use this rule:

Whatever:
Weakens your reason,
Impairs the tenderness of your conscience,
Obscures your sense of God,
Takes off your relish of spiritual things,
Increases the authority of your body over your mind:
That thing to you is sin.

By this test one may readily detect when ever subtlety or plausibly temptation may be presented. So whenever specific problems arise as to what we should do or may do on the Sabbath, each individual may decide for himself by testing the activity by the above or other suitable standard. This leaves the burden of decision just where the Lord intended it to be -- on the shoulders of each individual.

--Susannah Wesley

* * * * *

The Lost Day

One time, in a large city, a great many people all lost the same thing at about the same time, and the loss was very keenly felt. The peculiar thing about the whole situation, however, was that the people were not quite sure what it was that was gone. They only knew that something they had loved and needed to make them happy had disappeared and must be found.

"Perhaps," they said, "It is the joy of good hard work that we have lost. We may be thinking too much of how many hours we work and the profits we make and not of the satisfaction that comes from work well done. Let us forget ourselves in our work."

So the people in the great city went to work early in the morning and worked until very late at night. Each one put his whole heart into his work and many fine things were accomplished; but the people were not happy. They were dull and tired. The something was still lost.

"It must be pleasure we have lost," they said. "We need some new ways to have fun." So men went to work creating new entertainments for them. Great resorts and dance halls and theaters ran night and day while the people tried to find happiness in drinking and dancing, but there was none. There were only poor, tired, bored people, seeking for pleasure they couldn't find.

At last there came to this big city a humble old man. He chose a small house on the outskirts of the city. And he watched the people around him hurrying through every minute of every day, trying to find happiness in faster cars and bigger houses. He himself lived a simple life, and yet his eyes held a constant brightness and peace and joy that the people had long been trying to recover. So at last they came to him to discover his secret if they could, and to find out what it was that they had lost. And the old man said, "Yes, I can see what it is you have lost. You have no Sunday."

The people thought he didn't know what he was talking about. They brought their calendars to show him. "See here: Friday, Saturday, Sunday. We have Sunday the same as everyone else. The calendar says so."

"Ah," replied the old man, "but you have lost the spirit of the Sabbath. This is not really a Sunday at all, for you have not made it the Lord's Day and because of that you have no longer the feeling of His nearness to you. You have not made it a day of prayerful meditation and so you go on blindly, not knowing why you are living. You have not made it a day of rest, and so all days are the same to you and your minds and bodies grow weary of living. Had you kept the Sabbath as you should, you would have had a day in which to think of helping others, a chance to grow closer to your families, and an opportunity to read good books and think on life."

Then the people began to see that they had lost the spirit of the Sabbath indeed, and they resolved to spend it as they once had long ago, in going to church to worship God and learn of His ways; in visiting with their families; in resting from the regular routine of their lives; and in looking at the many good things that God had given them.

There were some who were afraid that they might lose the Sabbath again and they said, "Tell us what things we must not do on the Sabbath lest we lose it."

And the old man answered, "That I cannot do, but ask yourself these two questions: First: Is it restful? And second: Does it help me think of the Lord? And if in your hearts you feel the thing is in keeping with His Holy Spirit, you will not do wrong."

And so the people in the great city remembered what he had told them. Once more on one day out of seven they worshipped together and rested from their labors, and they found joy.

--Bula Fish Garrett

* * * * *

SACRAMENT

The Bridge

There once was a big turntable bridge which spanned a large river. During most of the day the bridge sat with its length running up and down the river parallel with the banks, allowing ships to pass through freely on both sides of the bridge. But at certain times each day, a train would come alone, and the bridge would be turned sideways across the river allowing the train to cross. The bridge was just wide enough for a train to cross it.

A switchman sat in a small shack on one side of the river where he operated the controls to turn the bridge and lock it into place as the train passed. One evening as the switchman was waiting for the last train of the day to come, he looked off into the distance through the dimming twilight, and caught sight of the train's light. He stepped to the controls and waited until the train was within a prescribed distance when he was to turn the bridge. He turned the bridge into position for the train to cross, and moved the lever to lock the bridge into position, but to his horror, he found the locking control didn't work. If the bridge was not locked securely into position it would wobble back and forth at the ends when the train came onto it, causing the train to jump the track and go crashing into the river. This would be a passenger train with many people aboard.

He left the bridge turned across the river, and hurried across the bridge to the other side of the river where there was a lever which he could use to operate the lock manually. He would have to hold the lever back firmly as the train passed. He could hear the rumble of the train now, and he took hold of the lever and leaned backward to apply his weight to it, locking the bridge. He kept applying the pressure to keep the mechanism locked. Many lives depended on this man's strength.

Then, coming across the bridge from the direction of his control shack, he heard a sound that made his blood run cold! -- "Daddy, where are you?" His four-year-old son was crossing the bridge to look for him. His first impulse was to cry out to the child, "Run! Run!" but the train was too close; the tiny legs would never make it across the bridge in time. The man almost left the lever to run and snatch up his son and carry him to safety, but he realized he could not get back to the lever. Either the people on the train or his little son must die.

He took just a moment to make his decision. The train sped swiftly and safely on its way, and no one aboard was even aware of the tiny, broken body thrown mercilessly into the river by the onrushing train. Nor were they aware of the pitiful figure of a sobbing man, still clinging tightly to the locked lever long after the train had passed. They didn't see him walking home more slowly than he has ever walked -- to tell his wife how he had sacrificed their son.

Now if you can comprehend the emotions which went through this man's heart, you can begin to understand the feelings of our Heavenly Father when he sacrificed His son to bridge the gap between us and eternal life. Can there be any wonder that He caused the earth to tremble and the skies to darken when His Son died? And how does He feel when we speed along through life without giving a thought to what was done for us through Jesus? When was the last time you thanked Him for the sacrifice of His Son?

* * * * *

Significance of the Sacrament

One night after a date, after his buddy had let him out, and he was coming up the drive toward his darkened frame house, Bill became alarmed. He could smell smoke. Running closer, he could see that smoke was pouring from the kitchen window. Through the front room window he could see that flames were leaking through the kitchen and dining room wall.

Bill burst open the front door and wisely slammed it behind him to keep from creating more draft. Holding his handkerchief over his mouth and nose, he darted through the smoke-filled dining room, into the hall, and on into his father and mother's bedroom. With the door closed behind him, he threw open the windows, kicked out the screen and screamed, "Mom, Dad, get out of here; the place is on fire; I'll get the kids."

Then leaving his half-awakened father and mother to crawl out the window by themselves, Bill hurried into the bathroom, wet down a towel, tied it around his face, and rushed back into the hall to grope his way through the billows of smoke to the stairs. Upstairs asleep were his five-year-old twin sisters, Jan and Jane, and his fourteen and ten-year-old brothers, Bob and Jimmy.

Bill started up. The stair treads were already on fire, but he was used to those stairs; he took them two and three at a time. So up he sprang. On the first two jumps the treads held, but the burning wood on the third gave way, and Bill fell into the mass of flames below that was eating away the supporting lumber. Only the fact that he had hold of the handrail saved him.

With every ounce of strength and that old football fight, Bill pulled himself up. His trousers were aflame, but he could not stop there to put them out. He fought his way forward, grasping the stair rail with one hand and clawing at the smouldering stair carpet with the other. The wet towel mask had fallen off, and he thought he would choke. The climb to the top seemed an agonizing eternity, though it was not over two or three minutes at the most.

Finally, at the head of the stairs he rolled on the carpet and beat out his flaming clothes with his seared hands. His legs were burned and barked raw from his fall through the stairs. His torture was terrible, and he thought he would pass out. But, calling even on strength that he didn't have, and with his whole soul groaning in prayer, he half staggered and half dragged himself to the bedroom of his two brothers. Bill had thought fast; he would wake the two boys first and get them to climb out on the roof over the porch through their window, and then he would get the twins and pass them out to the boys.

Into the boys' bedroom he stumbled. He screamed with all the hoarse voice he had left, rolled the sleepy heads out of bed and pushed them towards the window. "The house is on fire; get out on the roof," he moaned. "I'm getting the twins."

Back into the upstairs hall he went and down to the twins' bedroom. He knew it would be nip and tuck to make it, but his love for those blue-eyed little sweethearts drove him on. The floor was already crackling with flames. Bill gingerly tiptoed across the burning area, entered the twins' room, tucked one sleeping little girl under each arm, and came back out into the hall. Here both his clothes and the children's nightgowns caught fire. Bill held on to the now crying twins for dear life. As he made it back to the boys' room and closed the door against the flames in the hall, he muttered a prayer of thanks. He passed the twins out the window to the boys on the roof, who immediately began to smother the flames on their nightgowns. Finally, Bill hauled himself through the window and onto the porch roof as the flames were starting to eat through the hall door.

By this time the shrill whine of a fire engine could be heard approaching the house and neighbors were gathering on the lawn below. Some of the neighbors were restraining Bill's father from trying to re-enter the raging house. Bill's distraught mother was sobbing and praying, "Dear God, help Bill make it."

The fire engine skidded to a screeching halt in the drive. The hose was unrolled, and a spotlight found the boys and the twins on the roof. Immediately, the firemen began spraying a stream of water on the wall beneath them. The water cooled the area so that some of the firemen and Bill's dad could get near enough to catch the twins as Bob and Jimmy tossed them into their waiting arms. Then Bob and Jimmy jumped into the stretched out net. But poor Bill, without the strength for anything of a jump, tumbled off into the arms of his father, who jumped in to break the fall when he saw that his son was not going to make the net.

They could see that Bill was really hurt. The firemen quickly cut off his smoldering clothing, wrapped him in a blanket, and rushed him to the hospital.

At the hospital the doctors shook their heads when they saw Bill. Third degree burns covered his legs and most of his body. His flesh was scraped raw from his fall through the stairs. His left hand was like seared raw meat from clutching at the burning stair treads and carpet in pulling himself out of the trap. His hair and eyebrows were singed off. The twins had been burned some, too, when their night clothing caught fire, but they were nothing to compare with Bill.

Bill lay in agony in the hospital for days fighting for his life. His family and friends kept a constant vigil at the bedside of this wonderful hero. Finally, Bill's great heart could stand the struggle no more, and he died amid cries of anguished pain but with a smile on his lips.

His family was heart broken, but what gratitude they felt to think that he had been able to save the other children. Bob and Jimmy cried and said they wished they had died in the fire and Bill had been saved. The twins were too young to realize that the big brother whom they adored would not be around any longer to tease them and to hug them playfully.

Bill was buried in the city cemetery in the family plot next to his grandparents. The funeral had been a sad service but full of sweet comfort. School was closed that afternoon, and it seemed as if the whole town turned out. Everyone was moved to tears with the realizations of the heroism of Bill in giving his life for his family.

Well, time went by but it seemed as if no one ever got tired of talking about Bill and his sacrifice. Especially on Memorial Day, as friends and relatives met at the graveside, they discussed the suffering Bill had gone through for his brothers and sisters. Even years later Bob, Jim, Jan and Jane would unashamedly shed tears when they recalled what Bill had gone through for them.

Bill's brothers and sisters grew up and had children of their own. More years passed and some of these children became teenagers. These teenagers had heard the story about Bill and his suffering to save the lives of their parents, and they knew if it hadn't been for Bill they would not be -- at least with that family.

Then one particular Memorial Day, when the whole family of Bill was gathered at the graveside, Bill's father and mother were now old grandparents, and they were sitting around with Bob, Jim and the twin sisters, discussing Bill and that dreadful night. The elderly mother and the twins still could not help shed a tear or two over Bill. But the grandchildren saw Memorial Day only as a time to get together and compare notes.

On this day, as the family met, the teenagers were particularly active and were chatting and engaging in horseplay. They actually grew loud and boisterous.

Two of the cousins began to tussel right on the grave. Three of the girl cousins, in their giggling chatter were leaning against Bill's tombstone. And the younger kids were running around all over the place, having a great time.

I wonder how it made those parents feel to see their children so disrespectful at the graveside of Bill, their older brother, who had suffered so much for them? What if you had been one of those parents? How would you react in such a situation?

Your answers to these questions are probably quite varied. Some would feel that they had failed to teach them properly, others would want to make the youngsters feel very ashamed, and still others might knock a few heads together and punish them.

You may think what you like about those teenagers in this story, but the fact of the matter is that most of us are those teenagers who desecrate the grave of the older brother. Most people today are doing something even more serious and more upsetting than playing around on the grave of an earthly hero.

Whether we realize it or not, for those of us in the Church of Jesus Christ of Latter-day Saints every Sunday is a memorial day. Twice on every Sunday except Fast Sunday, and then once, we have a particular formalized period of time during which we are supposed to remember the specific sufferings of our Older Brother who died for all of us. And this Older Brother suffered far more than poor Bill of the story who died of third degree burns. This Older Brother of ours rescued us from a fate far worse than that of burning to death in a frame house.

Yes, Christ suffered greatly. An account of what they did to him goes as follows: "The Roman scourging he received, consisted of tying the victim's hands above his head, stripping him to the waist, and delivering forty lashes. It was very common if the victim died from this treatment alone and didn't require crucifixion. Jesus was given a mock robe, had thorns imbedded in His head, lashed and scourged, spat upon and humiliated, and then was nailed to a cross.

Death by crucifixion was at once the most lingering and most painful of all forms of execution. The victim lived in ever increasing torture, generally for many hours, sometimes for days. The spikes so cruelly driven through hands and feet penetrated and crushed sensitive nerves and quivering tendons, yet inflicted no mortal wound. The welcome relief of death came through the exhaustion caused by intense and unremitting pain, through inflammation of organs incident to the strained and unnatural posture of the body. Crucifixion caused the maximum possible pain. The square pointed spike driven through the wrist, to keep the flesh from tearing loose in the palms of the hands, was driven so as to pierce a great medium nerve between the muscle and bone.

This caused the muscles in the chest, throat, to contract until the victim almost suffocated and had to place all of his weight on the spike through his feet.

At about three in the afternoon, on the day Christ was crucified, a loud voice, surpassing the most anguished cry of physical suffering issued from the central cross on the Hill Calvary. It was the voice of Christ: "My God, my God, why hast thou forsaken me?" What mind of man can fathom the significance of that awful cry? It seems, that in addition to the fearful incident of crucifixion, the agony of Gethsemane had recurred, intensified beyond human power to endure. In that bitterest hour the dying Christ was alone, alone in most terrible reality. That the supreme sacrifice of the Son might be consummated in all its fullness, the Father seems to have withdrawn the support of His immediate presence leaving to the Savior of men the glory of complete victory over the forces of sin and death.

Later, realizing that He was no longer forsaken, but that His atoning sacrifice had been accepted by the Father, and that His mission in the flesh had been carried to glorious consummation, He exclaimed in a loud voice of holy triumph: "It is finished." In reverence, resignation, and relief, he addressed the Father saying: "Father, into thy hands I commend my spirit." He bowed His head, and voluntarily gave up His life.

Jesus Christ was dead. His life had not been taken from Him except as He had willed to permit. Sweet and welcome as would have been the relief of death in any of the earlier stages of His suffering from Gethsemane to the cross, He lived until all things were accomplished as had been appointed. In the latter days, the voice of the Lord Jesus has been heard affirming the actuality of His suffering and death, and the eternal purpose thereby accomplished. Hear and heed his words; "For, behold, the Lord your Redeemer suffered death in the flesh: wherefore, he suffered the pain of all men, that all men might repent and come unto Him."

Bruce R. McConkie has said: "Nothing in the entire plan of salvation compares in any way in importance with that most transcendent of all event, the atoning sacrifice of our Lord."

The Holy Ghost is willing and ready to bear witness of the Father and the Son and to sanctify the soul who will come unto Christ with a broken heart and a contrite spirit. The greatest guide into this path we have is the Sacrament. This holy ordinance of the Lord's Supper is available to the general membership of the Church, and yet Sunday after Sunday in ward after ward the Sacrament is partaken as a habit without real feeling on the part of many of the participants.

One priest, who had been studying the significance of the Sacrament, wrote a paper titled "Observations During the Sacrament Last Sunday." In it he said:

"I decided that I would just bow my head during the Sacrament and think about Jesus. Sometimes I felt a chill go up my spine which made me think the spirit of the Lord was really there. And I did pray that I might get a more full understanding of the Sacrament. I also thanked him that I was able to repent from sin and be saved and that we can be resurrected because Jesus made it come about. These aren't the exact words, but it is a general idea of what I was thankful for and would like to be blessed with.

"I was officiating at the Sacrament table; sometimes my mind would want to wander somewhat, such as I wonder what those people think of me up here with my head bowed, and I found out. Just after we finished the Sacrament, I said to the elbow that was helping, "Say, it sure is warm in here," and he said, "Yes, I guess so, anyway warm enough to make you go to sleep." And I wondered if everyone thought that.

"I noticed that when I would have to stand up and take the trays and put them on the table it seemed like everyone was looking at me and I felt a little self-conscious. But I hope that I can overcome this because I know it's the right thing to do. It seemed like to me that when I said the prayer on the water that the words meant more to me than ever before. So I know for a fact that it certainly does help to bow your head and thank the Lord for this wonderful gift which has been given to us.

"I didn't do too much observation of the people there; in fact, I didn't seem to want to; but that really got me when that fellow told me in so many words that I was asleep. This is the best experience I have had. I hope that I will get more out of the Sacrament each time I take it."

* * * * *

SERVICE

The greatest pleasure I know is to do a good action by stealth...and to have it found out by accident.

--Charles Lamb

* * * * *

Help thy brother's boat across, and lo -- Thy own has reached the shore.

--Hindu Proverb

* * * * *

What we have done for ourselves alone dies with us. What we have done for others and the world remains and is immortal.

--Albert Pipe

* * * * *

He who does a good turn should never remember it, but he who receives one, should never forget it.

* * * * *

There are those among us who are trying to serve the Lord without offending the devil.

* * * * *

There is no better exercise for the heart than reaching down and lifting someone up.

* * * * *

You are indeed charitable when you give, and while giving, turn your face away so that you may not see the shyness of the receiver.

--Gibran

* * * * *

This is sure; that, come what may, Who does God's work will get God's pay.

* * * * *

Every man goes down to his grave bearing in his hands only that which he has given away.

* * * * *

Those who bring sunshine to the lives of others, cannot keep it from themselves.

--Sir James Barnei

* * * * *

The service we render to others is really the rent we pay for our room on this earth.

* * * * *

In the Gospel, most of the blessings lie in the second mile.

* * * * *

What do we live for if not to make life less difficult for others?

--George Elliot

* * * * *

I shall pass through this world but once.
Any good therefore that I can do or any kindness
that I can show to any human being,
Let me do it now.
Let me not defer or neglect it for I shall not pass
this way again.

* * * * *

A Closing Thought

Did you ever stop to think
What makes a day seem bright?
It isn't just the bright sunshine,
Though, of course, that helps all right.
It's not just meeting friends you like.
Exchanging news, and jokes;
No sir, it's the little thoughtful things
You've done for other folks.

* * * * *

The Little Things

The little things are most worthwhile --
A quiet word, a look, a smile,
A listening ear that's quick to share
Another's thoughts, another's care...
Though sometimes they may seem quite small,
These little things mean most of all.

--Margaret Lindsey

* * * * *

Fellowship

A crumb will feed a little bird,
A thought prevent an angry word,
A seed bring forth many a flower,
A drop of rain foretell a shower.

A little cloud the sun will hide,
A dwarf may prove a giant's guide,
A narrow plank a safe bridge form,
A smile, some cheerless spirit warm.

* * * * *

A patient hand
A steadfast heart --
The worth of these we see.
Work is fun
Together done.
The hours pass in sweet remembrance.
This work we do
In love and sisterhood.

And you thought your reward
Awaited you in Heaven!
How little we understood,
For our reward
Was with us all the while
In contentment
For service given.

--Don Stevens

* * * * *

God -- let me be aware.
Let me not stumble blindly down the ways.
Just getting somehow safely through the days.
Not even wondering why it all was planned.
Eyes to the ground unseeking for the light.
Soul never aching for a wild-winged flight,
Please, keep me eager just to do my share.
God -- let me be aware.

God -- let me be aware.
Stab my soul fiercely with others' pain,
Let me walk seeing horror and stain.
Let my hands, groping, find other hands.
Give me the heart that divines, understands.
Give me the courage, wounded, to fight.
Flood me with knowledge, drench me in light.
Please -- keep me eager just to do my share.
God -- let me be aware.

--Miriam Teichner

* * * * *

The Kitchen Prayer

Lord of all pots and pans and things,
Since I've not time to be
A saint by doing lovely things
Or watching late with thee
Or dreaming in the dawn's light
Or storming heaven's gates,
Make ma a saint by getting meals
And washing up the plates.
Although I must have Martha's hands
I have a Mary mind,
And when I black the boots and shoes,
Thy sandals, Lord, I find.
I think of how they trod the earth
Each time I scrub the floor.
Accept this meditation, Lord,
I haven't time for more,
Warm all the kitchen with thy love
And light it with thy peace.
Forgive me all my worry
And make my grumblings cease.

Thou who didst love to give men food
In room or by the sea,
Accept this service that I do,
I do it unto thee.

* * * * *

Outlook

Forget each kindness that you do
As soon as you have done it
Forget the praise that falls to you
The moment you have won it
Forget the slander that you hear
Before you can repeat it
Forget each slight, each spite, each sneer
Wherever you may meet it.

Remember every kindness done
To you, whatever its measure
Remember praise by others won
And pass it on with pleasure
Remember every promise made
And keep it to the letter
Remember those who lend you aid
And be grateful, debtor.

Remember all the happiness
That comes your way in living
Forget each worry and distress
Be hopeful and forgiving
Remember good, remember truth
Remember heaven is above you
And you will find through age and youth
True joys and hearts to love you.

* * * * *

Leaning and Lifting

There are two kinds of people on earth today,
Just two kinds of people, no more, I say.
Not the saint and the sinner, for tis well understood
The good are half bad and the bad are half good;
Not the rich and the poor, for to count a man's wealth
You must first know the state of his conscience and health;

Not the humble and proud, for in life's little span
Who puts on vain airs is not counted a man;
Not the happy and sad, for the swift-flying years
Bring each man his laughter and each man his tears.

No! The two kinds of people on earth I mean
Are the people who lift and the people who lean.
Wherever you go you will find the world's masses
Are always divided in just these two classes;
And oddly enough you will find too, I ween,
There is only one lifter to twenty who lean.
In which class are you? Are you easing the load
Of overtaxed lifters who toil down the road?
Or, are you a leaner who lets others bear
Your portion of labor and worry and care?

--Ella Wheeler Wilcox

* * * * *

The King's Highway

Once a king had a great highway built for the members of his kingdom. After it was completed, but before it was opened to the public, the king decided to have a contest. He invited as many as desired to participate. Their challenge was to see who could travel the highway best.

On the day of the contest the people came. Some of them had fine chariots, some had fine clothing, fine hairdos, or great food. Some young men came in their track clothes and ran along the highway. People traveled the highway all day, but each one, when he arrived at the end, complained to the king that there was a large pile of rocks and debris left on the road at one spot, and this got in their way and hindered their travel.

At the end of the day, a lone traveler crossed the finish line and wearily walked over to the king. He was tired and dirty, but he addressed the king with great respect and handed him a bag of gold. He explained, "I stopped along the way to clear away a pile of rocks and debris that was blocking the road. This bag of gold was under it all, and I want you to return it to its rightful owner."

The king replied, "You are the rightful owner."

The traveler replied, "Oh no, this is not mine. I've never known such money."

"Oh yes," said the king, "you've earned this gold, for you won my contest. He who travels the road best is he who makes the road smoother for those who will follow."

* * * * *

SMILING

When you meet a person without a smile, give him one of yours.

* * * * *

A smile is a curve that can set a lot of things straight.

* * * * *

God gave all people in every nation the ability to smile and laugh in the same language.

* * * * *

A smile increases your face value.

* * * * *

Be sure to take a smile with you to your problems.

* * * * *

All the world is a camera -- smile please.

* * * * *

Nothing on earth can smile but man,
Not even the loveliest flower can
Nor bird, nor bee, nor butterfly,
Nothing, just nothing but you and I;

Nothing on earth that heals so much
As a simple smile its cheer and such
Nothing that heartens the soul of folk
When the day goes wrack, and the heart goes broke.

Nothing that lingers so tenderly
When lips that smile are a memory
Nothing that costs so little to give
Nothing so blest, for in smiles you live.

* * * * *

Smile

It's easy enough to be pleasant
When life flows like a song
But the man worthwhile
Is the man who can smile
When everything goes dead wrong
For the test of the heart is trouble
And it always comes with the years
And the smile that is worth the praises of earth
Is the smile that shines through tears.

It's easy enough to be virtuous
When nothing tempts you to stray
When without or within no voice of sin
Is luring your soul away
But it's only a negative virtue
Until it is tried by fire
And the life that is worth the honor of earth
Is the life that resists desire.

By the cynic, the sad, the fallen
Who had no strength of the strife
The world's highway is cumbered today
They make up the item of life
But the virtue that conquers passion
And sorrow that hides in a smile
It is these that are worth the homage of earth
For we find them but once in awhile.

--Ella Wheeler Wilcox

* * * * *

SUCCESS

No age or time of life, no position or circumstance, has a monopoly on success. Any age is the right age to start doing.

--Gerard

* * * * *

One of the biggest troubles with success these days is that its recipe is about the same as that for a nervous breakdown.

--Powerfax

* * * * *

The Lord gave us two ends to use; one to think with, the other to sit on. Which one we use will determine how well we do in life. In other words, heads you win, tails you lose.

* * * * *

The greatest of human possessions are a well-trained mind, a body to match, and a love of achievement, without which a man is old before his time.

--Unknown

* * * * *

Success usually is a plant of slow growth although its flowering may seem sudden.

--B. C. Forbes

* * * * *

Success in life is a matter not so much of talent or opportunity as of concentration and perseverance.

--Charles Wendte

* * * * *

Success comes in cans...not in can'ts.

--Dirk Vander Lende

* * * * *

A man may fail many times, but he isn't a failure until he begins to blame somebody else.

* * * * *

By others' faults wise men correct their own.

* * * * *

Success is never found at the top of the hill if the duties at the bottom of the hill are neglected.

* * * * *

All men are born equal, but some outgrow it.

* * * * *

Success is measured in terms of preparedness for eternity.

* * * * *

Sometimes a noble failure serves the world as faithfully as a distinguished success.

* * * * *

Success consists of getting up just one more time than you fall.

* * * * *

You're on the road to success when you realize that failure is merely a detour.

* * * * *

Success is the art of making mistakes when no one is around to notice them.

* * * * *

No one has success unless he abound in life...in the getting up each day with a thirst for the challenges thereof...in the thrilling at the beauty of the world... in the love of people...and a closeness with God...in filling his niche by working at his task -- whether it is rescuing a team from defeat or a soul from the depth.

* * * * *

Success is not a matter of position or possessions. It is a frame of mind. It is the satisfied feeling of service rendered and a life spent in a worthwhile way. There have been rich men, important men, whose lives were complete failure. And there have been poor men whom the ages have delighted to honor.

--Stephen M. Paulson

* * * * *

The best way to get ahead in the world is by learning to conquer difficulties by hard work and by cooperation with our fellow men.

* * * * *

No man has ever climbed the ladder of success with his hands in his pockets.

* * * * *

There are two kinds of men who never amount to much. Those who cannot do what they are told, and those who can do nothing else.

* * * * *

It is well to remember that an indolent person did not discover the telephone. And an indolent person did not learn to control steam. And an indolent person did not discover the power of gasoline, nor learn how to harness the great Niagara Falls.

The men who have accomplished most in the world were persons who had ambition and a goal, and worked long and hard to attain it.

--Samscripts

* * * * *

If man is to achieve lasting greatness he must have a God-centered life. Remember personal achievement is bought at the price of work and sacrifice.

* * * * *

When Failure Strikes

When failure smites a soul to earth
His faith will stand him up again,
And give him courage to go forth
In service to his fellow men.

* * * * *

Your Goal

Be the soul you wish to be, start this very minute.
Mark your goal with courage, and stick until you win it.

* * * * *

To A Loser

It takes a lot of courage, in games of work and play,
To take defeat while cheering the team that won today.
It is a noble winner whose heart and lips can say,
I'll work until I conquer and win the game someday.

* * * * *

A Victory

Forgetting takes strength and courage
Whenever a wrong is done.
With forgiveness and forgetting
A victory is won.

* * * * *

Make A Start

The world needs countless things,
And you will be the man
To add a priceless gift --
If you decide you can.
Dream on and let your courage
Awake and make a start,
And bring the richness out
That's hidden in your heart.

* * * * *

The Only Real Way To Achieve Success

I would like to reiterate that I sincerely believe the only real way to achieve success -- no matter what business you are in -- is through discipline. You must determine what degree of success you are going to obtain and then discipline yourself to working habits that will lead to your goals. If you do this, then everything will fall into place. Enthusiasm will be kindled, ideas will spring up, knowledge will be accumulated...and the sales will roll in.

It's not how much you know, but rather, how well you put what you know into action!

* * * * *

Achievement

Michael J. Dowling was a young man who fell from a wagon in a blizzard in Michigan when he was fourteen years of age. Before his parents discovered that he had fallen from the rear of the wagon, he had been frostbitten. His right leg was amputated almost to the hip, his left leg above the knee; his right arm was amputated; his left hand was amputated; Not much future for a young lad like that was there? Do you know what he did? He went to the board of county commissioners and he told them that if they would educate him he would pay back every penny.

During World War I, Mr. Dowling, who was at that time president of one of the largest banks in St. Paul, went to Europe to visit the soldiers -- to visit those who were wounded...Upon one occasion he was in a large hotel in London, and he had before him the wounded soldiers in their wheelchairs. They were in the lobby, and he was up on the mezzanine floor. As he started to speak, he minimized the seriousness of their wounds, the fact that one had lost an eye, another had lost an arm, etc., were no grounds for complaint. And he got these fellows so wrought up that they started to boo him. Then he walked over to the stairway and down the stairs toward the lobby, telling them as he walked how fortunate they were, and they continued booing.

Finally, he sat down on one of the steps and took off his right leg. And he kept on talking and telling them how well off they were. Well, they calmed down a little bit, but they still resented his remarks. Then he took off his left leg. Well, the booing stopped then. But before he arrived at the bottom of the stairs, he had taken off his right arm and flipped off his left hand, and there he sat -- just the stump of a body.

Michael Dowling was the president of one of the biggest banks in St. Paul. He had married and was the father of five children -- He finally died as the result of the strength he gave in encouraging the wounded soldiers of World War I.

--Matthew Cowley

* * * * *

Are You One Of The Priceless Few?

I am on a voyage of discovery. I search for those of you who will go on a great adventure. I am looking for you, one of the audacious few, who will face life courageously, ready to strike straight at the heart of anything that is keeping you from your best; you intrepid ones behind whom the world moves forward. To you, I am going to unfold a secret power that but few know how to use -- the secret power of daring and sharing which carries with it tremendous responsibilities. Once you have it, you can never be the same again. Once it is yours, you can never rest until you have given it to others. And the more you give away the greater becomes your capacity to give. Deep down in the very fibre of your being you must light an urge that can never be put out. It will catch this side of your life, then that side. It will widen your horizon. It will light up unknown reserves and discover new capacities for living and growing. It will become, if you don't look out, a mighty conflagration that will consume your every waking hour. And to its blazing glory a thousand other lives will come for light and warmth and power.

It is going to take courage to let this urge possess you. My life in business and my contacts with young people have convinced me that the world is full of unused talents and latent ability. The reason these talents lie buried is that the individual hasn't the courage to dig them up and use them. Everybody should be doing better than he is, but only a few dare. Prospectors for gold tell us that gold is where they find it. It may be in a bed of a river or on the mountain top. And prospectors for courage tell us the same thing. The one who dares may be found in a cottage or in a castle. But wherever you live, whoever you are, whatever you have or have not -- if you dare, you are challenged to enlist in a great cause.

H. G. Wells tells how every human being can determine whether he has really succeeded in life. He says: "Wealthy, notoriety, place, and power are no measure of success whatever. The only true measure of success is the ratio between what we might have done and what we might have been on the one hand, and the thing we have made and the thing we have made of ourselves on the other."

I want you to start a crusade in your life -- to dare to be your best. I maintain that you are a better, more capable person than you have demonstrated so far. The only reason you are not the person you should be is you don't dare to be. Once you dare, once you stop drifting with the crowd and face life courageously life takes on a new significance. New forces take shape within you. New powers harness themselves for your service.

Who wants to do unimportant and uninteresting things? Who even wants to gratify an ambition that has grown into a passion for fame and fortune? To desire something permanent in life, to develop your gifts to the largest possible use -- that's your dare. You have a wealth of possibilities, but maybe up to this time you have lacked a definite aim. You have a gun and plenty of ammunition. And now I dare you to aim at something worthy of the best that is in you.

--William H. Danforth

* * * * *

TEACHING

Education is learning the rules, experience is learning the exceptions.

* * * * *

That which we learn pleasantly we retain.

* * * * *

You cannot teach a man anything. You can only help him to find it within himself.

--Galileo

* * * * *

An individual learns best those things that he wants to learn...

...best those things he is able to do.
...best those things that tie in with what is familiar to him.
...most effectively those things that make sense to him.
...best when he takes an active part in the learning process.
...most effectively when he knows what he is doing.
...best when he gets satisfaction out of the learning process.

* * * * *

At The Crossroads

He stood at the crossroads all alone
The sunrise in his face;
He had no thought for the world unknown,
He was set for a manly race.

But the road stretched east and the road stretched west,
And the boy knew not which road was best,
So he strolled on the road that led him down,
And he lost the race and the victor's crown.
He was caught at last in an angry snare,
Because no one stood at the crossroads there
To show him the better road.

Another day at the self-same place,
A boy with high hopes stood.
He, too, was set for a manly race,
He, too, was seeking the things that were good.

But one was there who the roads did know,
And that one showed him which way to go;
So he turned from the road that would lead him down,
And he won the race and the victor's crown.
He walks today the highway fair,
Because one stood at the crossroads there,
To show him the better road.

* * * * *

It is the spirit that maketh alive. I know that you must test, grade, measure, counsel, guide, individualize, generalize, nationalize, Americanize, Christianize, humanize, intellectualize, spiritualize; that you must classify on proper social levels, vocational levels, intelligence levels, maturity levels, psychological levels; that you must adjust the misadjusted, adjust the maladjusted, and the utterly unadjustable; that you must not only be a teacher but a psychologist, a psychiatrist, a sociologist, a progressivist, a modernist and a fundamentalist, and a 100 percent Americanist -- all of this you must be, and more! But forget it! Chuck it! And once a day, if possible, just be the simple, honest, loving human thing that God made you, and let children be the human things that God made them, and between the three of you -- you and the child and God -- the divine thing called teaching will now and then get done.

--Dallas Lore Sharp

* * * * *

I have taught in high school for ten years. During that time I have given assignments, among others, to a murderer, an evangelist, a pugilist, a thief and an imbecile.

The murderer was a quiet little boy who sat on the front seat and regarded me with pale blue eyes; the evangelist, easily the most popular boy in the school, had the lead in the junior play; the pugilist lounged by the window and let loose at intervals a laugh that startled even the geraniums; the thief was a gay-hearted Lothario with a song on his lips; and the imbecile, a soft-eyes little animal seeking the shadows.

The murderer awaits death in the state penitentiary; the evangelist has lain a year now in the village church yard; the pugilist lost an eye in a brawl in Hong Kong; the thief, by standing on tiptoe, can see the windows of my room from the county jail; and the once gentle-eyed little moron beats his head against a padded wall in the state asylum.

All of these pupils once sat in my room, sat, and looked at me gravely across worn brown desks.

I must have been a great help to those pupils -- I taught them the rhyming scheme of the Elizabethan sonnet and how to diagram a complex sentence.

* * * * *

A Parable

I took a little child's hand in mine. He and I were to walk together for a while. I was to lead him to the Father. It was a task that overcame me, so awful was the responsibility. And so I talked to the child only of the Father. I painted the sternness of His face were the child to do something to displease him. I spoke of the child's goodness as something that would appease the Father's wrath. He walked under the tall trees. I said that the Father had power to send them crashing down, struck by his thunderbolts. We walked in the sunshine, I told him of the greatness of the Father who made the burning, blazing sun. And one twilight we met the Father. The child hid behind me. He was afraid, he would not take the Father's hand; I was between the child and the Father. I wondered, I had been so conscientious, so serious.

I took a little child's hand in mine. I was to lead him to the Father. I felt burdened with a multiplicity of the things I had to teach him. We did not ramble, we hastened from one spot to another spot. At one moment we compared the leaves of the different trees. In the next we were examining a bird's nest. While the child was questioning me about it, I hurried him away to chase a butterfly. When he chanced to fall asleep I awakened him, lest he should miss something I wished him to see. We spoke to the Father, oh, yes, often and rapidly. I poured into his ears all the stories he ought to know, but we were interrupted often by the wind a blowing, of which we must trace its source. And then, in the twilight, we met the Father. The child merely glanced at him and then his gaze wandered in a dozen directions. The Father stretched out his hand; the child was not interested enough to take it. Feverish spots burned in his cheeks. He dropped exhausted to the ground and fell asleep. Again I was between the child and the Father. I wondered, I had taught him so many things.

I took a little child's hand to lead him to the Father. My heart was full of gratitude for the glad privilege. We walked slowly. I suited my steps to the short steps of the child. We spoke of the things the child noticed. Sometimes we picked the Father's flowers and stroked their soft petals and loved their bright colors. Sometimes it was one of the Father's birds. We wondered, elated at the care it gave its young. Often we told stories of the Father. I told them to the child and the child told them again to me. We rest, leaning against one of the Father's trees, and letting his cool air cool our brows, and never speaking. And then, in the twilight, we met the Father. The child's eyes shone. He looked lovingly, trustingly, eagerly up to the

Father's face. He put his hand into the Father's hand. I was for the moment forgotten. I was content.

* * * * *

A Parable: The Talker, The Entertainer, The Teacher

And it came to pass...

That three Latter-day Saints went out from their homes and made way to the chapel at the appointed hour, where they had been called to teach. One was a TALKER, the second an ENTERTAINER, and the third a TEACHER. All three bore strong testimonies of the Gospel and had a sincere desire to build testimonies in their learners.

The TALKER came well prepared, cited scriptures, read from books, and verily beseeched his learners with many words. For a few, the words fell on fertile soil and they went straightway from the class greatly enriched. For the many, the words were not enough and visions of roasts in the oven, skiing on powdered slopes, and the excitement of bright colors and taffetas, silks and laces gradually drowned out the words, words, words, until they had comfortably become a part of the background making way for more pressing matters.

The ENTERTAINER, familiar with the effect of some talkers on some learners, bore testimony; cited scriptures; showed pictures, maps, charts, filmstrips, films; played tapes and records. Surely the learners' interest was captured by the wonders of the instructional media. Roasts, skis, and apparel became of little concern and the hour of instruction was all too soon over. The learners left the ENTERTAINER and went their various ways only to be dismayed by the proverbial question, "Well, what did you learn today?" They were unable to answer because the instructional materials were used for the wrong reasons and the learners' recollection of the lesson was now without form and void -- so much gloss and tinsel, without real substance.

The third Latter-day Saint, the TEACHER, bore no stronger testimony than the others nor was he any more dedicated to his calling. He just realized that if his learners didn't actually change their behavior, increase their testimonies, and start living richer and more productive lives, he had failed. He faced his many communication problems squarely and he defined his instructional objectives. He used a variety of instructional materials for the right reasons... to overcome the barriers to effective communication and to reach his objectives. He used tape recordings to bring general authorities into his classroom in order to reach the inactive and the active members at the same time, for he has both in his class. When appropriate he used the motion picture to dramatize important ideas and the chalkboard for key scriptures. In order to communicate with both the learner who attends under social pressure and the class member who is sincerely interested, he used these and other instructional materials to reach the new convert as well as the returned missionary, for he knows that they will greatly increase learning as well as interest. And his learners went out into the land for another week, filled with the spirit, their lives enriched, and with a feeling that they really learned, and for the present they were satisfied with their new knowledge and insight.

* * * * *

The Teacher

The teacher looked ahead with misgivings but with hope.
Would the way be smooth or rough?
Would it end in success or failure?
The teacher stood and looked and wondered.
And a voice said, answering: "There will be no end."

And the teacher smiled and said:
"I know it will end. I may teach one year, two years,
Or possibly many more years
But this I know: Someday it will end."
And the teacher went forward to teach.

Those who gathered around the teacher had need to learn.
And the teacher looked into their eyes and desired to fill their needs
And taught them with mind and heart and voice --
A mind filled with knowledge from continued study,
A voice speaking this knowledge in wisdom,
And a heart filling the mind and voice with
Conviction and power.
The teacher learned from mistakes made
And received happiness from lessons taught with inspiration.

Then life changed, and the teacher could not teach.
"It has ended," said the teacher, continuing on the road
Of life. "This is really the end of my teaching."
And the teacher believed this until a person of good position
Stood and said: "I am here because this teacher
Taught me thus."
And the teacher was happy and said, "It was not the end back there --
This is the end.
And it could not have ended better.
I am glad I taught in love and faith and prayer."

Time passed; and the teacher grew old and slept and awakened and
Stood before the Maker.

And the teacher looked and was surprised, for there
Stood also those who had been taught.
And He before whom they stood questioned them and then
Sent them to a high place.

And the teacher said, "It was not the end back there --
This is the end. And it is a more glorious end than
I ever could have hoped for."
And joy filled the teacher's heart, as a great celestial light.

And the teacher looked ahead of those who had been taught
And saw the continued steps of progress and work before each one
And then said: "This is not the end -- there is no end.
I have just realized, there is no end to my teachings!"

And a voice spoke: "When first you were called to teach, I tried to warn you
Of your great responsibility.
But you can be thankful you taught well,
In humility, in faith, in testimony --
For there is no end to your teachings."

--Goldie B. Despain

* * * * *

TESTIMONY

I hope you will excuse me if the tears fall, but sometimes I like to water my testimony -- it helps it to grow.

* * * * *

Witness Testifies That The Book Of Mormon Is True

May it please the court and gentlemen of the jury: my brother attorney on the other side has charged me with connection with Joseph Smith and the golden Bible. The responsibility has been placed upon me, and I cannot escape reply.

Before God and man I dare not deny what I have said, and what my testimony contains as written and printed on the front page of the Book of Mormon. May it please your honor and gentlemen of the jury, this I say, I saw the angel and heard his voice -- how can I deny it.

It happened in the daytime when the sun was shining brightly in the firmament; not at night when I was asleep. The glorious messenger from heaven, dressed in white, standing above the ground, in a glory I have never seen anything to compare with -- the sun insignificant in comparison -- told us if we denied that testimony there is no forgiveness in this life or in the world to come.

Now how can I deny it -- I dare not: I will not.

--Oliver Cowdery

* * * * *

The Spirit Giveth Light

I had not traveled but a short time to testify to the people, before I learned this one fact, that you might prove doctrine from the Bible until dooms day and it would merely convince a people, but would not convert them. You might read the Bible from Genesis to Revelation and prove every iota that you advance and that alone would have no converting influence by or upon this people. Nothing short of a testimony by the power of the Holy Ghost would bring light and knowledge to them, bring them in their hearts to repentance. Nothing short of that will ever do.

--Brigham Young

* * * * *

Sometimes during solitude I hear truth spoken with clarity and freshness; uncolored and untranslated it speaks from within myself in a language original but inarticulate, heard only with the soul, and I realize I brought it with me, never taught it, nor can I efficiently teach it to another.

--Hugh B. Brown

* * * * *

The Footprints Of God

A devout believer in God and an atheist were engaged in conversation. Bluntly the atheist said, after seeing the believer kneel in prayer -- "Did you ever see God, hear, or put out your hand and touch Him?" The answer came, no. Then he said, "Well, you're a fool person to believe in a God you never saw, heard or touched." But the conversation did not continue, as they retired for the night.

The next morning they arose before sun-up and the believer said, "There was a wolf around the tent during the night." Immediately the atheist asked the same questions. "Did you see the wolf, hear him, or put out your hand and touch him?" Again, the answer was no. The atheist was convinced that he was truly a strange man. But the believer pointed out the footprints to prove the wolf's recent presence. So also, just then the sun came up and the believer reverently said, "Behold the footprints of God."

* * * * *

THANKSGIVING

We thank Thee for our daily bread;
For faith by which the soul is fed;
For burdens given us to bear;
For hope that lifts the heart's despair.

We thank Thee, Lord, for eyes to see
The truth that makes, and keeps, men free;
For faults -- and for the strength to mend them;
For dreams -- and courage to defend them.

We have so much to thank Thee for,
Dear Lord; we beg but one boon more:
Peace in the hearts of all men living,
Peace in the whole world this Thanksgiving.

--Joseph Auslander

* * * * *

Thanks For My Voice

"This morning I would like to thank my Heavenly Father for my voice. No, I don't have a beautiful voice for singing, nor the type for speaking that holds audiences spellbound, as many do. But I do have a voice. It is an instrument I might use to teach the Gospel of Jesus Christ -- one that I might use to sing hymns and praise to my Father in Heaven; an instrument I might use when I stand upon my feet to tell the world that I know we are engaged in the work of the true church of Jesus Christ.

Yes, the Lord has been very good to us. He has given each one a voice, a talent, but if it is to become a great talent we must cultivate it. The Lord can't do that for us. First, we must realize that in our voice lies a talent, appreciate it and then go to work.

I am reminded of the story of a man who had lived fifty-six years. He had sailed along very smoothly through life with no tragic upsets. He had everything that money could buy. He owed no one and no one owed him, or so he thought.

One morning he woke up with a bad case of laryngitis and blaming it on the cold he had the previous week, began taking all kinds of cough syrup but to no avail. His voice grew steadily worse. At times it would boomerang back upon his ears, loud and harsh. At other times it would fade away. He was aware of his associates straining to grasp his words. Finally he consulted a physician. After many tests and x-rays were taken, the man was told that because of a dreaded disease, his vocal cords would have to be completely removed if they were to save his life.

This news came as a great blow, but not in full force until the night before the operation as he lay in bed thinking about it. Just imagine! No more Good Mornings or Good Evenings; no more cheery Hello's, just a nod of the head. No more laughter would ripple through his throat when he saw something he was amused at, and enjoyed. Just a smile on his lips -- not even a song could ever be sung; and he thought, how could a man live for fifty odd years and never realize how very precious the gifts are that God has given him, until they are to be taken away."

--Thelma Brown

* * * * *

TIME

The supply of time is a daily miracle. Each day twenty-four hours are given to us to do with as we wish. It is the most precious possession we have, so live it daily and take advantage of every opportunity.

* * * * *

Just as your fortune depends upon how your money is invested, so the success of your life depends upon how your time is invested.

--Leone Kester

* * * * *

Spare moments are the gold dust of time.

* * * * *

Everything comes to him who hustles while he waits.

--Thomas Edison

* * * * *

Our Wish To You

In the coming year -- may you have --
Enough happiness to keep you sweet.
Enough trials to keep you strong.
Enough sorrow to keep you human.
Enough hope to keep you happy.
Enough failure to keep you humble.
Enough success to keep you eager.
Enough friends to give you comfort.
Enough wealth to meet your needs.
Enough enthusiasm to look forward.
Enough faith to banish depression.
Enough determination to make each day a better day
than yesterday.

* * * * *

Take Time

Take time to work with love,
It is the assurance of success.
Take time for joyous play,
It is the secret of renewing youth.
Take time to think creatively,
It is the foundation of wisdom.
Take time to love your fellow men,
It is the gateway to heaven.
Take time each day for silence,
It is the storehouse of God.
Take time to worship God,
It is the highway of peace.

* * * * *

A Prayer For Today

This is the beginning of a new day. God has given me this day to use as I will. I can waste it -- or use it for good, but what I do today is important, because I am exchanging a day of my life for it! When tomorrow comes, this day will be gone forever, leaving in its place something that I have traded for it. I want it to be gain, and not loss; good, and not evil; success, and not failure; in order that I shall not regret the price that I have paid for it.

--Dr. Heartsill Wilson

* * * * *

Has anyone seen a tall little lad
And a wee winsome lass of four?
'Twas only today, barefooted and brown,
They played by my kitchen door.
'Twas only today -- or was it a year?
It couldn't be twenty, I know.
They were calling for me to come out and play,
But I was too busy to go.
Too busy with sweeping and dusting to play
And now they have silently wandered away.

If perchance you hear of this tall little lad
And this wee winsome lass of four,
Oh, tell me I pray.
To find them again I would journey this wide world o'er.

Somewhere, I'm sure, they are playing a game,
And should they be calling for me
To come out and join them,
Oh, tell them I'm coming as fast as can be!
For there's never a house might hold me today
Should I hear them call me to join in their play.

--Author Unknown

* * * * *

Your Next Twelve Hours

Just for today -- I will try to live through this day only and not tackle my whole life problem at once. I can do something for twelve hours that would appall me if I felt that I had to keep it up for a lifetime.

Just for today -- I will be happy. This assumes to be true what Abraham Lincoln said, "That most folks are happy as they make up their minds to be."

Just for today -- I will try to strengthen my mind. I will study. I will learn something useful. I will not be a mental loafer. I will read something that requires effort, thought and concentration.

Just for today -- I will adjust myself to what is, and not try to adjust everything to my own desires. I will take luck as it comes, and fit myself to it.

Just for today -- I will exercise my soul in three ways: I will do somebody a good turn, and not get found out. I will do at least two things I don't want to do -- just for exercise. I will not show anyone that my feelings are hurt; they may be hurt, but today I will not show it.

Just for today -- I will be agreeable. I will look as well as I can, dress becomingly, talk low, act courteously, criticize not one bit, not find fault with anything and not try to improve or regulate anybody except myself.

Just for today -- I will remember that language is the dress of my thoughts. Everytime I speak I will remember that my mind is on parade. I will recall that someone said, "You can always tell what kind of wheels are a man's head by the spokes that come out of his mouth."

Just for today -- I will have a program. I may not follow it exactly but I will have it. I will save myself from two pests: hurry and indecision.

Just for today -- I will have a quiet half hour all by myself, and relax. During this half hour, sometime, I will try to get a better perspective of my life.

Just for today -- I will be unafraid. Especially I will not be afraid to enjoy what is beautiful, and to believe that as I give to the world, so the world will give to me.

* * * * *

Everyone Cries, "There Wasn't Time"

Time.

It hangs heavy for the bored, eludes the busy, flies by for the young and runs out for the aged.

Time.

We talk about it like it's a manufactured commodity that some can afford, others can't; some can reproduce, others waste.

We crave it. We curse it. We kill it. We abuse it. Is it a friend? Or an enemy? I suspect we know very little about it. To know it at all, and its potential, perhaps we should view it through a child's eyes.

"When I was young Daddy was going to throw me up in the air and catch me and I would giggle until I couldn't giggle anymore, but he had to change the furnace filter, and there wasn't time."

"When I was young, Mama was going to read me a story and I was going to turn the pages and pretend I could read, but she had to wax the bathroom and there wasn't time."

"When I was young Daddy was going to come to school and watch me in a play. I was the fourth Wise Man (in case one of the three got sick), but he had an appointment to have his car tuned up and it took longer than he thought and there was no time."

"When I was young, Grandma and Grandad were going to come for Christmas to see the expression on my face when I got my first bike, but Grandma didn't know who she could get to feed the dogs and Grandad didn't like the cold weather and besides, they didn't have the time."

"When I was young, Mama was going to listen to me read my essay on "What I Want To Be When I Grow Up," but she was in the middle of the Monday Night Movie and Gregory Peck was always one of her favorites and there wasn't time."

"When I was older Dad and I were going fishing one weekend, just the two of us, and we were going to pitch a tent and fry fish with the heads on them like they do in the flashlight ads, but at the last minute he had to fertilize the grass and there wasn't time."

"When I was older, the whole family was always going to pose together for our Christmas card, but my brother had ball practice, my sister had her hair up, Dad was watching the Colts and Mom had to wax the bathroom. There wasn't time."

"When I grew up and left home to be married, I was going to sit down with Mom and Dad and tell them I loved them and I would miss them. But Hank (He's my best man and a real clown) was honking the horn in front of the house, so there wasn't time."

--Erma Bombeck

* * * * *

TITHING

It doesn't take money to pay tithing -- it takes faith.

--Robert L. Simpson

* * * * *

Foxtail

Karlton came home feeling pretty low. For days he had planned on his trip to settle tithes...Just think of a boy of ten who had $15.97 to pay in tithing!

When he arrived at the office, it was crowded. There were money and checks on the tables in piles. His small contribution made no showing at all. Worse of it all, the clerk who took his money had to ask his name. What should have been a great event had been a disappointment. He had been embarrassed and ill-at-ease. It seemed like a whole year's work had gone to waste.

"Mother," he said when he arrived home, "no one cared whether I paid my tithing or not. They didn't even know my name and seemed glad when I was out of the way. I could have gone to a lot of shows for fifteen dollars."

Mrs. Bidgood was troubled by his attitude and left off washing dishes. As she dried her hands, she was thinking how to meet this apparent slight. "Son, how old are you?" she asked.

"I'm nearly eleven." He straightened up an inch taller.

"Just as I thought. You're almost grown up, so I must tell you that the man spoiled you with kindness every time you brought a few pennies for tithing. He is a very busy man and spends lots of time for us." She knew that her boy had been taught why he should give a tenth of his earnings. She must find something else that would illustrate the law.

"One day many years ago," she said, "your great-great-grandfather, Carl, sat in his little rock house and looked out its one small window. He was very lonely because his wife had died and left him with five small children. He had to earn the living, do the cooking, wash the clothes, do the ironing, and a hundred other things each day. He had finally decided to give the baby girl to his sister, and he felt bad to think of parting with her. But he could not take care of baby and do all the other things. Besides this, he couldn't speak English very well. He was a Norwegian shoemaker who had joined the church and was now trying to farm. It was such a struggle that one winter they had lived on bread and roots of sego lilies, with now and then a piece of mutton that some neighbor gave them.

"While Carl was thinking of his troubles, his pet sheep came up to the window and put its nose up to be petted. 'Aha,' said Carl, 'you want a crust of bread.' He went to the wall and took down a flour sack half full of crusts that had been saved and dried. The sheep ate the bread and waited for more. Carl started to laugh. He remembered that they had been out of bread that morning, but there was bread two or three days old. And to think he would forget the sack. Now they could have bread soup for supper, and the boys would love it.

"Just then Christian came rushing in and scared the sheep away. 'The team is hooked up, Father. Where shall we get the hay for tithing?'

"Carl turned toward his boy. He must teach him a good lesson in tithing. This was more important than bread or anything right now.

"'Ve owe vone big load of hay, and I vant you boys should go in de soutvest corner of de field vere de vild hay is much finer and not coarse. Be sure you get no foxtail hay. We must give de best to de Lord. Remember, no foxtail.'

"Years later, one of Carl's boys told me that that was the best sermon on tithing that had been preached. Because when he and your great-great-grandfather drove into the tithing yard, the first thing they noticed was that some of the hay there had lots of foxtail in it. They were proud that even though they had no bread to eat, their father didn't pick out the coarse swampy hay for tithing.

"After they unloaded, another wagon moved up and covered their good hay so that no one ever knew about it but the boys. And the man didn't come out and tell them what fine boys they were for working so hard to bring in the hay."

Karlton looked at his mother in silence. Then he smiled, "Golly, Mom, I don't know if $15.97 is so much after all. If I was starving, I don't know if I could do like that or not. I'd feel like selling the hay and buying food."

Mrs. Bidgood saw that her boy was smiling again, "Whenever it seems hard to pay my tithes," she concluded, "I always think of 'remember, no foxtail,' and then it is easy."

--Eugene Olsen

* * * * *

I have found a great many people who do not know what their tithing is. I have never met people of that kind but that I believe if I were in partnership with them and they had a tenth interest in that partnership, they would know pretty well what part their tenth was. I do not think they would have any difficulty whatever in finding how much I owed them. So, I am inclined to think that if we wanted to, we would have no difficulty in finding out what is one-tenth of our income, and that is what we owe the Lord -- no difficulty whatever.

--Heber J. Grant

* * * * *

It is generally understood that in figuring one-tenth of one's income that in certain cases one needs merely to push the decimal point over one place to the left and he will know the correct amount to pay as a tithe. In other cases, however, before the tithing is figured, there may be legitimate deductions made from the wages or income, which deductions constitute the actual expenses involved in making the money and thereby producing the increase. However, if there ever are questions regarding the deductions ...favor the Lord instead of yourself. By so doing you are on the safe side. It would be far better to pay a little extra tithing than it would be to be guilty of robbing God.

--Milton R. Hunter

* * * * *

God's Money

Let me start out with a story of a great furniture manufacturer of Grand Rapids, Michigan. He was starting over in life. His first attempted business had not been a success. The tiny string of credit which he had to depend upon in his new venture was made up of the faith of a few close friends rather than the calculated mathematical confidence of banks.

One day he walked slowly through the empty rooms of the little factory. He was alone in the building. As yet the machinery was not in place. When he came to a remote corner of one of the upper floors, he knelt, closed his eyes, and prayed.

Then he got up and went out into the world again and began his hard business fight. The machinery came at last, and he started to make furniture. He borrowed; his improving business records strengthened his credit.

But there was a mystery about him in the fields of credit. Although he began to look more and more safe to the credit man, he seemed to insist on giving money away. While he was borrowing, he gave. Sometimes he said "no" to those who asked for financial aid for religious or philanthropic purposes. But when he did say "yes," he said it with an alacrity that astonished the recipient. He did not give money to foolish ventures or to unsound enterprises, but it was a puzzling thing to the bankers to have him borrow from them while he was giving money freely to help others who were finding the world a hard place in which to live.

His business grew; within a few years it became well-established; his furniture became known to the trade for its honest quality. At last, there came a time when borrowing was no longer necessary.

His tiny string of credit had become a thousand-stranded cable; he was one of the marked successes in the furniture world.

When he died, after a well-rounded life, the mystery of his gifts was explained. It seemed that during all his business career he had considered that the money which he borrowed, the money which he earned, and the money which he gave away was not his own money at all; it was God's money.

Over his casket, that day of the funeral, the clergyman of the church which he had attended told the story.

"I have carried a secret about our friend," ran the gist of the clergyman's story, "which I have never been able to reveal until now. He asked me never to tell it while he was alive."

"When he was making his second start in life, so he told me, he knelt in an empty room in his new factory; and he told God that he wanted to take Him into partnership, that one-tenth of all the earnings should go to Him, and that he would use the money in all his business ventures as if it were God's money."

--Ernest L. Wilkinson

* * * * *

VALUES

The trouble with most of us is that we would rather be ruined by praise than saved by criticism.

--Norman Vincent Peale

* * * * *

It is something to be able to paint a particular picture, or to carve a statue, and so to make a few objects beautiful; but it is far more glorious to carve and paint the very atmosphere through which we look -- to affect the quality of the day -- that is the highest of the arts.

--Henry Thoreau

* * * * *

It is better to be right and alone than to be wrong and have company.

* * * * *

Don't give away your future just to make an hour more stimulating.

* * * * *

The city of Happiness is found in the State of Mind.

* * * * *

Life is interesting only to the interested.

* * * * *

A man's mind is like a garden, which may be intelligently cultivated or allowed to run wild; but whether cultivated or neglected, it must, and will, bring forth. If no useful seeds are put into it, then an abundance of useless weed seeds will fall therein, and will continue to produce their kind.

* * * * *

I often think no man is worth his salt until he has lost and won battles for a principle.

--John Marsh

* * * * *

Do not spend money for that which is of no worth, nor your labor for that which cannot satisfy.

* * * * *

It is a good thing to have money and the things that money can buy, but it is good, too, to check up once in awhile and make sure we haven't lost the things money can't buy.

* * * * *

President McKay's Rules For Living

1. Develop yourself by self-discipline.
2. Joy comes through creation, sorrow through destruction.
3. Do things that are hard to do.
4. Entertain upbuilding thoughts. What you think about when you do not have to think shows what you really are.
5. Do your best this hour, and you will do better the next.
6. Be true to those who trust you.
7. True friends enrich life. If you would have friends, be one.
8. Pray for wisdom, courage and a kind heart.
9. Give heed to God's messages through inspiration. If self-indulgence, jealousy, avarice or worry have deadened your responses, pray to the Lord to wipe out those impediments.
10. Faith is the foundation of all things -- including happiness.

* * * * *

The following statement by John D. Rockefeller, Jr., is inscribed on a tablet in Rockefeller Center, New York:

I Believe

I believe in the supreme worth of the individual and in his right to life, liberty, and the pursuit of happiness.

I believe that every right implies a responsibility; every opportunity, an obligation; every possession, a duty.

I believe that the law was made for man and not man for the law; that government is the servant of the people and not their master.

I believe in the dignity of labor, whether with head or hand; that the world owes every man an opportunity to make a living.

I believe that thrift is essential to well-ordered living and that economy is a prime requisite of a sound financial structure, whether in government, business or personal affairs.

I believe that truth and justice are fundamental to an enduring social order.

I believe in the sacredness of a promise, that a man's word should be as good as his bond; that character -- not wealth or power or position -- is of supreme worth.

I believe that the rendering of useful service is the common duty of mankind and that only in the purifying fire of sacrifice is the dross of selfishness consumed and the greatness of the human soul set free.

I believe in an all-wise and all-loving God, named by whatever name, and that the individual's highest fulfillment, greatest happiness, and widest usefulness are to be found in living in harmony with His will.

I believe that love is the greatest thing in the world; that it alone can overcome hate; that right can and will triumph over might.

* * * * *

Wealth

Wealth is not the things we own, a stately house upon a hill, paintings and tapestries or servants taught to do one's will. In luxury a man may dwell as lonely as in a prison cell.

Wealth is not a plentive purse, the bonds that one has stored away, boastful balance in the bank, jewelled baubles fools display. The things that really gratify are things that money cannot buy.

Wealth is health, a cheerful heart, an ear that hears a robin's song, a mind content, some treasured friends, fragrant memories lingering long.

Living is an inward art, all lasting wealth is in the heart.

--Alfred Walton

* * * * *

If You Could See God

If you could see God, what would you see?
A beautiful sunset in a sparkling sea?
Or is He the moon or the warm sunlight?
The trees, the mountains, or stars in the night?
Or the miracle love of a growing boy,
While parents look on with delighted joy?
No, these are creations of heaven and earth
By God who was born of humble birth.

The architect builds, but greater is he
Than the building he builds of wood from a tree.
The earth and the heavens were made by God
And surely this Builder is greater than sod.
Children are born to look like you
So we as God's children must look like Him too.
Yes, when you see God what will you see?
Not a mountain, the sunlight or a growing tree --
But a heavenly Man is what you'll see
A man, like the Master of Galilee.

--Monte C. Scoville

* * * * *

The Path That Leads To Nowhere

There's a path that leads to nowhere
In a meadow that I know,
Where an inland river rises
And the stream is still and slow;
There it wanders under willows
And beneath the silver green
Of the birches' silent shadows
Where the early violets lean.

Other pathways lead to Somewhere,
But the one I love so well
Had no end and no beginning --
Just the beauty of the dell,

Just the windflowers and the lillies,
Yellow striped as adder's tongue,
Seem to satisfy my pathway
As it winds their sweets among.

There I go to meet the Springtime,
When the meadow is aglow,
Marigolds amid the marshes,
And the stream is still and slow;
There I find my fair oasis,
And with carefree feet I tread
For the pathway leads to Nowhere,
And the blue is overhead.

All the ways that lead to Somewhere
Echo with the hurrying feet
Of the Struggling and the Striving,
But the way I find so sweet
Bids me dream and bids me linger --
Joy and Beauty are its goal;
On the path that leads to Nowhere
I have sometimes found my soul.

--Corinne Roosevelt Robinson

* * * * *

In the summer of 1962 an event happened in Salt Lake City and Grantsville, Utah, that shocked and shook the entire community. Four young people, two boys and two girls, all L.D.S., were out all night long, drinking and driving. They took a deserted back road off the main highway. Car trouble of some kind stopped them. One boy decided to hike to find help. The girls and other boy stayed in the car. This boy, being drunk got abusive to the girls and they ran from him. He grabbed up a hammer and took after the girls. He beat them insensibly, dragged their bodies into the brush and covered them with rocks, old pieces of tin and brush. Then he took off.

The young fellow who went for help returned with the police to the car, found them gone and the search began. The girls' bodies were found. One was dead, the other survived after a long period in the hospital. This girl wrote the following poem for the friend who did not live.

If I Could Change That Night

If I could only change that night,
A night that left a mark of blight.
A mark that never will erase,
Not from the heart or from the face.

It all began if the truth were known
When we left our home, to be on our own.
Two foolish girls who thought they knew
All about life, and boy friends too.

If every girl could know my fate,
They'd watch and pray before it was too late.
But listen as I recount our tale
Which led to death and a boy in jail.

We walked down town to see the sights,
When a car pulled up with two shiny lights,
Two boys were soon along our side,
They asked us nicely if we wanted a ride.

At first we didn't know whether to go,
For these were boys we didn't know.
But just this once we got into their car.
Went to a drive-in, and then to a bar.

The boy who drove had himself a drink,
I guess he got so he couldn't think.
We drove in the night, to the Nevada line,
They took us out to wine and dine.

Coming back we drove off the road,
Got stuck and scared, so we started to run
And here is where terrible tragedy won.

One boy took a hammer and beat us on the head,
Bruised and bleeding, left us for dead
Then he covered us up with weeds
So no one would know of his terrible deeds.

Now could I change that fateful day,
To all I would have this to say:
I'd never leave my home until,
I'd asked the Lord if it was His will.

I'd never be a pick-up girl
I'd never drive all night for a whirl.
I'd always follow the Temple goal,
I'd want to have a clean, pure soul.

But now I know it is too late,
For death has closed his final gate,
Now I think...and wish I'd been,
A girl who would have avoided this sin.

But may each girl let me give
This poem's thought so she might live.
Remember all these things I've said;
For I forgot...and now I'm dead.

* * * * *

By My Actions I Will Prove My Allegiance To The Kingdom Of God

If I can live my day so that each minute
Will add a new enrichment to my youth,
And stand strong for my church and all that's in it,
And by my actions demonstrate its truth;
If I can live above all filth and crudeness,
And make my life a pure and happy one,
And yet avoid all haughtiness and rudeness --
Find joy in life instead of merely fun;

If, when I'm asked to carry out a duty
Right from my heart I can declare, "I'll try!"
And in my work find all its hidden beauty;
And thus increase my powers as days go by;
If I can pay my tithing -- not for showing --
Nor with a grudging spirit nor a whine --
Pay all my offerings, oh! so gladly, knowing
The fraction that I pay back isn't mine;

If I can fill each day with pleasant greetings,
And spread about some happy thought or song;
Be present and on time at all my meetings,
And help push every worthy work along;
If I can serve and learn its fullest meaning,
Say, "Gladly," when I'm asked to work or teach;
If I can learn to lift instead of leaning,
If I can always practice what I preach;

If I can make old folks and children love me,
And keep my faith in God a-burning bright;
Believe in those that He has placed above me,
And know that they're directing me a-right;
If I can really prove my soul courageous,
And in a battle triumph over sin;
If I can know ambition is contagious --
That if I work the rest will soon "fall in;"

If I can pray and know that God will heed me,
If I have asked with an unselfish heart;
Can be on hand when e'er my church may need me,
Be ready and so glad to do my part;
If I can say "no" with power undaunted
When asked to stoop to something low or wrong;
But if for some good cause my help is wanted,
Can make the "yes" I say be just as strong;

If I can use the life of our great Savior
As my ideal in everything I do,
And prove to all the world by my behavior,
That I am with my church right through and through;
If I can look for good instead of weakness,
And really be successful in my search --
If I can do all this with love and meekness,
Then I have proved allegiance to my church.

--Author Unknown

* * * * *

In Ancient Greece there were "oracles" -- people who answered questions for the populace -- answers which were supposed to come "from the Gods." The answers the oracles gave were supposed to be always true answers.

One boy said to another, "I am going to make the oracle lie. I'm going to catch a bird and hold it in my hand. Then I'm going to say to the oracle, 'What do I have in my hand?' He will of course answer, 'A bird.' Then I'll say, 'Is it alive or dead?' If the oracle says, 'It's alive' I'll squeeze it in my hands until it is dead -- that way the oracle will have lied. If he says, 'It's dead' I'll let it loose from my hands to show it is alive. Either way the oracle will have lied."

The boy did as he said he would. He caught a bird, held it in his hand and went to the oracle. He said, "What do I have in my hand?" The oracle answered, "A bird." The boy said, "Is it alive or dead?" The wise oracle answered, "That is entirely up to you."

This is true of all things in our lives. We can have an "alive, active" testimony, for instance, or we can have a "dead, inactive" one. We can be "active" in the work of the Lord or we can be "inactive." It's <u>entirely up to us.</u>

* * * * *

When Charlemagne lay dying in the year 814, he commanded that instead of being buried horizontally like ordinary mortals, a magnificent subterranean throne room should be prepared, and that, dressed in his coronation robes, he should be seated in death upon a marble stone. His command was literally obeyed, and for more than three centuries, the magnificent remained undisturbed. The Emperor Fredrick the First, Fredrick Barbarossa, ordered that the gorgeous cavern should be opened. And there, surely enough, was the spacious stone room with its ornate furnishings; and there surely enough was all that remained of Charlemagne seated in dreadful silence upon it.

A discovery was made for which the investigators were unprepared. For, on the knees of the splendidly robed skeleton an open Bible reposed. A bony finger pointed to the text: "What shall profit a man if he shall gain the whole world and lose his own soul?" The question comes to mind, who placed the Bible on the dead king's knees, and what prompted this action.

--F. W. Boreham

* * * * *

When I am tempted to listen to hot, egotistic voices within my own heart; when it seems that love can never win but always loses; when it seems as though humility is ruthlessly trodden down by those who pass over it on their way to their own selfish ambitions; when it seems as though God cannot possibly triumph; when pity and love and mercy and kindness and tenderness are weakness; when it seems as though greatness is only possessed by those who know how to grab, and have the power to snatch at it, no matter what the cost to others -- ah, yes, when voices sound in my own heart which say you must play for your own hand, you must think of number one, you must not let yourself be trodden down -- when I am thus tempted, my God may I hear in imagination the tinkling of water, poured into a basin, and see, as in a vision, the Son of God washing the disciples' feet.

--Leslie D. Weatherhead

* * * * *

A kind philosopher went into the hills each day to study nature that he might be nearer unto God. Then each evening on his return, he gathered the people of the village about him to impart unto them the lesson he had learned. As in all good things, there arises skepticisms; for one morning, before he departed, one of his potential friends asked him to bring back a hawthorn twig. Another asked him to bring back a rose, and a third asked him to bring a lily. The kind philosopher assented to the requests of these three friends.

As the day wore on and the evening let down her curtain, the three stood by to receive their gifts from nature. As they took them in their hands, the first said: "Here is a dead leaf on my hawthorn twig." The second murmured: "Here is a thorn on my rose." and the third cried out and said: "Yes, and here is some dirt on the root of my lily." The kind philosopher took them back, took the dead leaf from the hawthorn twig and placed it in the first friend's hand. Likewise the thorn and the dirt from the rose and lily. Then he said: "You have what attracted you first. I will keep the hawthorn twig, the rose and the lily for the beauty I see in them."

Those who grow most perfectly in life and in the service of the Lord are the men and women who find only that which is good in others.

* * * * *

The Pardoner's Tale

Three young rioters were in a tavern when they saw a funeral cortege passing. They inquired about the corpse and were told that he was a victim of a marauding killer who had slain many in a neighboring valley and of whom everyone had a deadly fear. The rioters asked his name.

His name was Death, and no one in the world could overcome him, they were told.

Boastful with drink, the rioters vowed they could vanquish him, and they started toward the valley he had devastated.

Soon they met an old man coming from the valley. They asked how he had escaped. He told them he was old and wanted to die, but Death ignored him. They thought the old man must be a spy -- an accomplice of the slayer.

They asked him where they could find the fiend and were told to follow a crooked road up to a hilltop where they would find Death under a tree.

They hurried on and found the tree, but what they saw under it was gold -- bushels of gold coins. That sight made them forget their quest. Their one thought was to possess that wealth. But now to take it in broad daylight without being detected was a problem. Finally, they decided that one of them should go to the town for wine and bread while the others guarded the treasure. Then in the darkness of night they could take it away.

They drew cuts to see which should go. The lot fell to the youngest. As soon as he was gone, the other two began considering how much more each would have if the hoard was divided by two instead of three. Their covetousness incited plans for murder. They plotted to kill their companion when he returned.

Meanwhile, the youngest meditated on how wonderful it would be to possess all that wealth for himself. He thought of a way to do it. He procured three bottles of wine and some poison. The poison he put in the two bottles of wine intended for his companions.

When he returned to the tree, he was killed and left lying beside the gold. The murderers then sat down to drink their wine and to wait for darkness. But in a few moments, they, too,were lying dead beside their victim.

The old man was right. The three young men had found Death under the tree, beside that which they had coveted.

--Geoffrey Chaucer

* * * * *

The Boy With Many Recommendations

When a merchant had hired an office boy out of fifty applicants who answered his advertisement, a friend asked:

"How did you come to select that fellow? He didn't have a single recommendation

"He had a great many," replied the merchant. "He wiped his feet when he came in; and he closed the door after him, showing that he is careful. He gave up his seat to a lame old man, showing that he is kind and thoughtful. He took off his cap when he came in and answered my questions promptly and respectfully, showing that he is polite and gentlemanly. He picked up a book which I had purposely laid on the floor and replaced it on the table, while all the rest of the boys stepped over it or shoved it aside. And he waited his turn quietly, instead of pushing or crowding. When I talked to him, I noticed that his clothes were carefully brushed, his hair in nice order, and his teeth as white as milk; and when he wrote his name, I noticed that his fingernails were clean, instead of being tipped with jet like those of that handsome little fellow in the blue jacket. Don't you call all these things letters of recommendation? I do; and I would give more for what I can tell about a boy by using my eyes ten minutes than for all the letters of recommendation he can give me."

A mother who is teaching her boy good manners and habits of self-respect may be providing him with a capital more substantial than a bank account.

I have known a good many boys and some men who make fun of those who take care to dress tidily and attractively. Yet young people who have a little pride in making themselves presentable, and whose faces are often wreathed in loving, happy smiles, are most likely to make friends.

Not long ago a prominent business firm discharged their manager because he was never tidy in his personal appearance. When they advertised they received forty applications for the place; yet only one young man was asked to call again.

"Did you observe his neatly fitting shirt and necktie?" asked one of the partners after he had gone, "how nicely his boots were polished, and how tidy he was?"

The young man's references were looked up, and he was engaged the next morning. Several of the others might have been better men for the position, but a first impression is lasting.

In this land of opportunity the cases are very rare where the poorest boy or man ever needs to appear to poor advantage. A man's clothes may be thread-bare and even patched; but if they are well brushed and if he is clean himself, he will command the respect of everyone.

--Author Unknown

* * * * *

The Nice Elephant

Charlie was the kind of guy who didn't appreciate the delicious feeling of doing some things slowly. He didn't know that some matters scream to be accomplished in a leisurely manner. Things like eating a parfait. Or watching a child at play. Or kissing his wife when he left the house every morning on his way to work. Sure, a lot of people said Charlie got more accomplished than others. He was a moderately successful businessman with too much of the stuff called nervous energy.

"Slow down, Charlie," a friend would say. "You're forgetting how to live." What the friend didn't realize was that Charlie had never known how.

Charlie's oldest boy was playing high school basketball, but Charlie had seen him play only once. "Too many meetings that interfere," Charlie apologized. His eleven-year-old daughter asked him to promise he'd be at her piano recital. Charlie promised. But he found himself taking an out-of-town business trip on the little girl's big night. A man has to make a living, right?

One evening after dinner, Charlie felt a pain in his stomach. It wasn't much at first. But it got worse. Betty, Charlie's wife, called the doctor when Charlie's face went gray. When the doctor told Charlie he was going to the hospital, Charlie didn't want to go. The pain got worse about that time, so Charlie didn't argue.

The doctor stuck some wires on various places around Charlie's body and watched as a needle moved up and down a piece of paper. They stuck a needle in Charlie's arm and told him not to even so much as sit up in bed. Charlie thought this was a lot of hogwash, but the pain in his chest...

The next day, Charlie gathered he'd had a heart attack. It was something that would take weeks, maybe months, to get over. He'd have to lie in bed until the heart mended itself. It scared Charlie, so he minded the doctor.

Betty stayed with Charlie during these three weeks in the hospital, and for the first time in their eighteen years of married life, they became pals. They talked about little things. Charlie watched Betty as she went around the room straightening flowers in the vases, and it was like spotting her for the first time. After that, he spent long minutes just looking into her eyes, and Betty blushed. They were like eighteen-year-olds again.

When Charlie came home, he talked over every single play of the basketball season with his boy. Often, when he would hear his daughter practicing at the piano, he would turn to Betty and, with a note of surprise in his voice, say: "Hey, that kid's pretty good!"

Charlie's strength came back and he went to work again. When he met friends on the street, they would stop him and invariably say something like: "Hey, Charlie! Good to see you back on the job! Heart attack, eh? Say, that's bad. They tell me there's nothing as painful as having the old elephant on your chest. That's real bad."

And Charlie would smile and invariably reply something like: "Don't feel sorry for me, chum. That heart attack was the best thing that ever happened to me."

* * * * *

Sweeping Out The Cobwebs

You don't have to return to a neglected or vacated house to find cobwebs -- the spiders are busy all the time. After all, they have more time than we do, and, too, they have their houses to build.

Nevertheless, as I was sweeping the cobwebs from my ceiling, I conceived another household sermonette.

It might be a good idea to start sweeping a few cobwebs, not only from our ceiling, but from our lives, to clear our vision to the beauty of God's world.

There are endless cobwebs -- ignorance, temper, stubbornness, procrastination, neglect, laziness, impatience, exasperation -- you could go on and on.

Does the cobweb of ignorance keep you from enjoying the great achievements of man? Does it make you accept less than your due on earth because you don't really understand the scriptures?

Can you observe the beauty of a sunset till it stirs you inside and sends chills up your spine, or does the cobweb of impatience cause you to see only the passing of time and a late appointment?

Can you respond to the joy of your son making his first home run, or have you shackled yourself with the cobweb of stubbornness and insist that he wipe his muddy shoes first, and so spoil a magic moment?

Did you cheer up a lonely neighbor as you promised, or are you enmeshed in the cobweb of procrastination -- you too have much to do, you haven't the time -- there is shopping and cleaning and children and meetings?

Can you give your Relief Society lesson with true inspiration, or is it clouded by the cobwebs of neglect and preparation and research?

When your husband looks as if he is carrying a problem, do you draw him out to see if you can help, or do you let your cobweb of impatience for getting household things done interfere?

Do you waste precious time complaining about the torn ironing cover, a lost hammer, a cracked window, rather than admit that the cobweb of neglect has entangled your action?

Let us dispel these cobwebs of ignorance with learning. Our Church sponsors this. There are excellent opportunities. Relief Society meetings are an excellent beginning. Dispel the cobweb of temper with control, the cobweb of procrastination with action, stubbornness with a consideration for others, neglect with interest, impatience with patience, laziness with activity, and exasperation with inspiration.

What are your cobwebs? List them, and one by one dissolve them with your own dissolving agent.

To help us the beauty of God's world to see --
Sweep out the cobwebs wherever they may be.

* * * * *

Youth
(An Allegory)

Womanhood was happy; she didn't even know exactly why, but something inside of her seemed to be singing for joy as she skipped gaily down the road of life, shirt tail out and levis rolled to the knees.

She was, she knew, growing up, and sometimes she consciously tried to slow down her tomboy gait and move with the dignified, grown-up step of a lady. She would quickly give up the attempt, however, and scurry on, clacking her bubble gum noisily. She was engrossed in blowing an enormous bubble when she first saw him looking at her. Suddenly she became very self-conscious; and she realized, almost ruefully, that she was now too big for bubble gum.

"Hi." he said.

"Hi."

When they met again it was in the halls of Hometown High. Womanhood's hair was no longer in pigtails. She was still very young, but she had somehow become quite beautiful. She moved with such an easy grace that it was a joy to behold her. Mostly she wore pretty flared skirts and soft blouses now and a touch of lipstick, and a very radiant smile. He, too, had grown taller. His shoulders were broad and his muscled arms bronzed from a summer's hard work outdoors. She learned that his name was Manliness and that he was a very popular fellow.

"Hello again," he said.

"Hello."

"I say, how about a movie?"

"I'll have to ask my mother."

Mother, of course, was reluctant; but, as mothers, must, she one by one withdrew her apron strings. Soon Womanhood and Manliness were seeing each other often. They attended movies and school parties together, and sometimes he even walked her home from school -- a little self-conscious at first about carrying her books, but gradually with a more possessive air.

They often talked together, as good friends will, about their hopes and aspirations, about their precious dreams of the future. She told him that she one day wanted a fine strong husband to love, and a home to care for, and children to rear. He spoke of a college career in athletics, with maybe a little study on the side, of a mission, and then a loving wife and family. Then she confided in him. "You know, I have something in my possession that is infinitely precious. It is a jewel more radiant than rubies, more sparkling than diamonds. It is a thing which has been given to me to guard and protect, to keep lustrous and beautiful. I am told that there are people in the world who would take it from me, but I shall guard it well. It is the priceless pearl of Virtue."

"Ah," he said, "I am bigger and stronger than you are. I shall help you to protect it; never fear. I, too, have something which I honor above all. It is a wonderful God-given gift which gives me an advantage over the world at large. It is the Priesthood."

Womanhood squeezed his hand a little and looked up at him. "I shall do all I can to honor that Priesthood, too." she said.

For some time now they had noticed a tall handsome stranger in their neighborhood, but always they had seen him at a distance. He had been in the back seat of the school bus the evening they returned late from a music festival, and they had seen him on an isolated park bench once when they walked home from a movie. Then one night when Manliness had been permitted the use of the family car, the stranger approached them directly. They were ready to go in after a pleasant evening of dancing when he tapped on the window. He was extremely handsome, and he had a very winning way. He introduced himself as Temptation. Manliness didn't exactly trust him, and Womanhood, in spite of her fascination, felt a little wary, too. But his was a very convincing line of reasoning: "There's no harm in showing your affection, is there? Get hep, kids, this is 1973. Are you too old fashioned or something? For Pete's sake, all the kids do it. What's the matter, boy, why don't you act like a man?"

Manliness bristled a little. He reached over and pulled Womanhood close to him. It made her feel kind of good inside. She snuggled still closer and laid her head comfortably on his shoulder.

Temptation visited them often after that and taught them to like being very close to one another, to enjoy kisses, and caresses. Sometimes they almost recognized him for the treacherous fellow he is, but he would smile so innocently and assure them of his good intentions with such earnestness that they continued to trust him. Once a terrible thought came to Womanhood, "What if he's courting our favor so he can steal my pearl?" She voiced her fear to Manliness, but he only scoffed at her.

"I can take care of you," he said. "Don't forget, I have the power of the Priesthood."

Ah -- had Womanhood but scrutinized her pearl, she would have found it less lustrous, slightly tarnished already. And had Manliness taken a few moments to be honest with himself he would have realized that his Priesthood was not as readily available for the use as it had once been.

Their fascinating friend continued to smile upon them and reward them with pleasure, but when he was out of their sight he would rub his hands together with satisfaction and chuckle wickedly to himself.

One afternoon while walking briskly down the Avenue of Folly, Manliness heard an old friend call to him. He didn't want to see him and pretended to not hear, but the older man was persistent. At length Manliness turned and greeted him, "Hello Wisdom. What do you want?"

"Don't greet me so coldly, my son. Haven't I heretofore been your best friend? Wisdom and Manliness should always go together you know."

"Excuse me, but I'm in rather a hurry, and I..."

"Slow down a moment, my boy, and hear me. I have observed of late that you and your beautiful companion have been seeing a great deal of that smooth salesman down the street. Temptation, I think he's called. He means to do you harm, my boy."

"Nonsense, Wisdom. You can see for yourself I'm much bigger and stronger than he is. I can take care of him if he gets out of line."

"He won't play fair, boy. He's out to trick you."

"I'm not afraid, old man. Good day."

But all the rest of the day Manliness had the peskiest brat in the neighborhood tagging him around. "Ny-ah, ny-ah. Manliness isn't your name at all; it's weakness. You're a weakling!"

"For Pete's sake! Keep still and mind your own business."

"Ya don't respect your girl friend. Ya don't respect your girl friend."

"Oh, I do! I have every respect for Womanhood."

"You sure don't show it. You let that slick bird Temptation lead you around by the nose just because he's got fancy pants and smooth talk."

"Oh, Conscience, pipe down. Go on and leave me alone!"

When he and Womanhood were alone that night, she confided in him. "Oh, dear, I paid a call on my true friend, Good Judgment, today. She frankly doesn't approve of some of the things we have been doing lately. She says we are risking both my pearl of Virtue and your claim to Priesthood. I argued with her, but somehow I can't forget what she said -- that we should save our caresses and kisses until -- until -- well, you know..."

Manliness said nothing for a thoughtful moment and then answered, "Wisdom and Good Judgment must have got together. I guess, to be honest, I feel the same way you do."

Whereupon he released her from his embrace and turned the car around. They drove away from the Road of Disaster where Temptation stood in the shadows beckoning them; and, although they didn't even realize it, the straight well-lighted boulevard onto which they turned would lead Manliness and Womanhood with their priceless treasures of Priesthood and Virtue to the Temple of God.

--LaFond P. Hall

* * * * *

WOMAN

There is a woman at the beginning of all great things.

--Lamartine

* * * * *

Reason Men Marry: It's the tender moments that a woman creates in the life of a man that he can't create for himself.

* * * * *

She is not made to be the admiration of all, but the happiness of one.

--Burke

* * * * *

A woman's mind is cleaner than a man's: she changes it more often.

* * * * *

Girls are like angels -- always up in the air, harping, and never an earthly thing to wear!

* * * * *

Girls who try to be walking dictionaries should remember that reference books are never taken out.

* * * * *

Please, God, help me never to rush the years,
And let my heart remain a little girl's
So that it may know only April tears
With tiny rosebud dreams deep in its furls.
Let my life be a brand new party dress
That I may wear with pride where e'er I go...
Help me to keep my tiptoe eagerness
And be a place where loveliness may grow.
I guess one wish could cover every other
If you would just help me grow up to be
The kind of daughter that my dad and mother
Were dreaming of when they first ordered me. Amen.

--Kathryn Kay

* * * * *

If

If you can hear the whispering about you and never yield to deal in whispers too,
If you can bravely smile when loved ones doubt you,
And never doubt, in turn, what loved ones do;
If you can keep a sweet and gentle spirit in spite of fame, fortune, rank or place
And though you win your goal or only merit, you can win with praise or lose
with equal grace.
If you can meet with unbelief, believing,
And hallow in your heart a simple creed.
If you can meet deception, undeceiving and learn to look to God for all you need,
If you can be what a girl should be to mothers,
And be unto the others as you'd have the others be unto you -- no more and
yet no less.
If you can keep within your heart the power to say that firm, unconquerable "no"
If you brave a present shadowed hour rather than yield to build a future woe.
If you can love, yet not let loving master, but keep yourself within your own
self's clasp
And not let dreaming lead you to disaster.
Nor petty fascination lose your grip
If you can lock your heart on confidence, nor ever needlessly in turn confide.
If you can put behind you all pretenses of mock humility or foolish pride;
If you can keep the simple homely virtue of walking right with God,
Then have no fear that anything in all the world can hurt you,
And, which is more, you'll be a woman, dear.

--J. P. McEvay

* * * * *

A girl, a daughter, a sister, a young lady, a bride, a mother, a woman, a grandmother -- all of womanhood, glorified -- born to be something special and to do something special with your life. You have a special obligation in life -- to be an example to all the world in your high goals, actions, attitudes, and accomplishments.

You have a special assignment in life -- to live life fully -- developing all possible talents, studying diligently, gaining wisdom and knowledge.

You have a special place in life -- to bring happiness, laughter, and fun to those around you.

You have a special role in life -- to be an efficient, charming, wise wife and mother -- a helpmeet in honoring the Priesthood of God. You have a special mission in life -- to be you -- a Latter-day Saint girl -- happy, considerate, clean, modest, honest, obedient.

You have a special place in life -- to be a queen in the Kingdom of God.

You are special -- you are you -- a beautiful, beloved girl -- a Latter-day Saint girl, the most important girl in the world.

--Florence Jacobsen

* * * * *

Lest We Forget

She came tonight as I sat alone
The girl that I used to be...
And she gazed at me with her earnest eye
And questioned reproachfully:

Have you forgotten the many plans
And hopes that I had for you?
The great career, the splendid fame
All wonderful things to do?

Where is the mansion of stately height
With all of its gardens rare?
The silken robes that I dreamed for you
And the jewels for your hair?

And as she spoke, I was very sad,
For I wanted her pleased with me...
This slender girl from the shadowy past
The girl that I used to be.

So gently arising, I took her hand,
And guided her up the stair
Where peacefully sleeping, my babies lay
Innocent, sweet and fair.

And I told her that these are my only gems,
And precious they are to me;
That silken robe is my motherhood
Of costly simplicity.

And my mansion of stately height is love,
And the only career I know;
Is serving each day in these sheltering walls
For the dear ones who come and go.

And as I spoke to my shadowy guest,
She smiled through her tears at me;
And I saw that the woman that I am now
Pleased the girl that I used to be...

--Author Unknown

* * * * *

Lollipops and Lipstick

Have you ever noticed what happens to girls?
They start out in braids and end up in curls.
They wear pins in their diapers and bows in their hair,
Then pins on their sweaters, their beaus put them there.

As kids they wear petticoats starched full and frilly,
But soon yearn for slinky things -- the other's too silly.
Healthy as children, they eat every day,
Then stop altogether to control what they weigh.

With youthful energy they make mud pies
Later transfer the recipe to face, neck and eyes.
When asked to perform as children, they're mute,
Yet their control of the telephone becomes absolute.

Little girls love dolls, candy and toys
But bigger girls love mostly just boys.
When little, girls rely on what parents do for them.
But soon like it better to completely ignore them.

They go on for years caring not about looks,
Then have nothing to wear with clothes falling from hooks.
In winter you simply can't get stockings on them,
Then before they're thirteen, expensive nylons they don them.

As kids, hair is something that stays in its place
Then later looks as if set to be launched into space.
Make-up is another of those things that changes;
From nothing at all to face mask it ranges.

At play their energies unbounded rage
At school they're fatigued after reading one page.
They have time for play, for TV and for eating,
But talk about work, they'd prefer a good beating.

Then a pimple appears and shatters that bubble.
The boys they ignore, they simply abhor them.
Then wake up one day and do naught but adore them.
One minute they're babies, such gay little elves,
The next they are making just feminine noise.

They leave skates, dolls and childhood behind
When loftier pursuits overtake the mind.
Preoccupation with boys, looks and learning
Is the fire with which these new damsels are burning.
And parents take note the metamorphosis so quick
From girls sucking lollipops to wearing lipstick.

These lipstick'ed ladies we honor tonight
With word and with song we'll do it up right.
For their honors, accomplishments and talents we praise 'em.
And give thanks for the endurance of parents who raise 'em.

* * * * *

When the souls shall return to the presence of the Father of all, the worthy mothers will be there to welcome their worthy children; and with humble pride born of righteous achievement, they will revenently bow and humbly speak:

Father, we come back to thee with the righteous souls whole earthly bodies thou lettest us to build, "bone of our bone, flesh of our flesh," all to thine everlasting honor and glory and to our blessing and exaltation forever.

Blessed were our wombs for they bore children, even as thou didst command, in the image of thine Only Begotten, who is in the image of thee.

Great is the joy of this the end of our labors, for these souls have been saved with eternal life.

Blessed were we in our example set, for thou gavest us the power to live worthily; in the teaching of thy children, thou didst give us a goodly measure of wisdom.

Blessed were we in our understanding, for thou didst cause the Holy Ghost to enlighten our minds.

Blessed were we in our living, for thou didst give us patience and kindliness, and forgiving natures, with charity and unbounded love.

Blessed were we that thou didst send these spirits to the bodies which we by thy power fashioned, for they were choice spirits.

Blessed were we in their companionship, for they were loving and kind, respectful and obedient to us.

Blessed were we in the mortal fathers of our children's bodies, for they gave us comfort and help, and love and kindness unmeasured, and likewise walked worthily before thee.

Our souls cry out to thee, our Father, in worship of thee for thou hast been with us from the beginning and hast covenanted to be with us during all eternity. Honor and glory and love to thee forever, and forever.

Well done, thou good and faithful handmaids, enter thou into the rest I have prepared for those who builded the mortal temples in which dwelt the spirits I created, that they might keep their second estate, for without the keeping of their second estate they could not have "glory added upon their heads forever and ever."

And then the priesthood will wish to proclaim their debt to these their helpmeets without whom the priesthood could not have worked out their destiny.

These wives and mothers in Israel, are your rewards and your destinies. And your offspring, saved and exalted in the presence of God, will never forget you, will ever bless you, and will sing hymns of eternal gratitude for the bodies you gave them and taught them to make the temples of the Spirit of God.

God be thanked for the knowledge he has given us of all this.

* * * * *

So came Eve, an helpmeet to the priesthood mission of Adam -- Eve the last created being in the creation of the world, without whom the whole creation of the world and all that was in the world would have been in vain and the purposes of God have come to naught. Receiving her, Adam took her in purity, took her, radiant and divinely faithful, into the Garden he had dressed and kept for her, into the bridal home he had built, into the Garden that from then till now had been the symbol of heaven and earth, there to begin together their earthly life, that was finally to bring the opportunity for salvation and exaltation to the untold myriads of spirits then waiting for the mortal tabernacles these two were to make it possible for them to possess.

The Only Begotten had fashioned the world, had filled it with beautiful flowers and lofty forests, with grasses and grains, and multitudes of living creatures; Adam had had some part in this. But the key to the glorious arch of temporal earthly creation for man was still missing. So Eve came to build, to organize, through the power of the Father, the bodies of mortal man, to be a creator of bodies under the faculties given her by the Priesthood of God, so that God's design and the Great Plan might meet fruition.

This was her calling; this was her blessing, bestowed by the priesthood. This is the place of our wives and of our mothers in the Eternal Plan. They are not the bearers of the priesthood; they are not charged with carrying out the duties and functions of the priesthood; nor are they laden with its responsibilities; they are builders and organizers under its power, and partakers of its blessings, possessing the complement of the priesthood powers and possessing a function as divinely called, as eternally important in its place as the priesthood itself.

The crowning glory of motherhood came to the daughters of Eve, when, in Bethlehem, there was born to Mary of Nazareth a mortal, the Christ child, begotten of the Father.

* * * * *

My Dream Girl

We'll be in love some day, you and I; but I'm not sure I know you now. Some day, somewhere, we will discover each other.

I'm fresh home from the mission field, still feeling the way only a returned missionary can feel, still floating on memories too new to dim, and dream girl, I'm looking for you.

Two years ago I was one of the boys, running the race of popularity -- more concerned with sharp styles and good looking cars than anything else. Along with the few serious moments given to Sunday School, there was all the frolic of the modern merry-go-round. Girls then were fun, not for keeps. If they could dance and had pretty eyes or a cute smile, I had an occasional "case" on them. But marriage seemed a long way off.

Then came the call, the farewell, the field. I was a missionary. There was the humbling realization of my greenishness and the regrets that I hadn't spent more hours gaining an understanding of the plan of living. I worked and studied and prayed. With new understanding of the precepts of Christ came new determination to live them, and what had been a vague inner assurance became a burning testimony.

I began tasting what is only a word until you do taste it -- Joy -- and exalted happiness that dwarfed the passing pleasures I had thought so desirable only yesterday. I began to comprehend the deeper significance of love and marriage and the family. I began thinking serious thoughts about the girl of the future -- and about you, dream girl, -- wondering, like all who are young where you were and how I would know you.

I met people, I was startled by their kind of life -- by their kind of marriage and home. Doors opened, revealing husbands and wives whose faces showed bitterness and disillusionment. I saw neglectful parents and neglected children. I saw a ten-year-old who preferred the gloom of a pool hall to arguments at home. I heard a mother try to explain to her tiny daughter why daddy, who had been drunk for three days, wasn't home for dinner. I saw a husband and wife treat each other like enemies and their home like a prison. For the first time in my life, I realized that marriage could be misery.

How different was the home of the young Latter-day Saint couple I met. Love for each other and for the Gospel was in their every act. I saw them hold family prayers even though their family consisted so far of only one toddling two-year-old, a baby boy who one day asked his mother, who was lying pale on the couch, "Sick Mommie?" and when he somehow understood that she was, fell to his knees and began praying for her. I could see the love in that family's eyes and felt the happiness, yes the joy in their home.

Before my eyes was the contrast -- the contrast between couples who with differing attitudes and opposing religions, married in the world's way and couples who with common ideals and common purposes married in the divine way. I realize now that the advice of church leaders, to marry in the Church and in the temples, was wisdom. I know that it was inspired by God.

And so, dream girl, I thought of you. You, I told myself, would know what I know. You would want to share the joy that would come from walking through life with the Lord at our side. You would want to go to the Temple. You would want to be a Mother. You would want to be a Queen of the greatest kingdom of earth -- the home.

I brought home with me the knowledge that the Gospel is essential to true happiness, and part of the Gospel is you.

I don't want to lose that knowledge, dream girl, because if I do, I will lose everything -- my title to happiness and my right to marry you. But not wanting is not enough. There are things I know I must do and things I must not. For one thing, I know that association with evil leads to acceptance of evil. The best way for me to remain clean and faithful is to associate with young men and women who are clean and faithful.

And so I am not interested in the girl who gives her lips freely, the girl who is immodest in dress and conduct. I'm not interested in the girl who changes her standards to fit her company, the girl who can see nothing wrong with an occasional drink or occasional immorality. My mission taught me that a lot of what we youth like to call broadmindedness is evil, and that phrase, "just once won't matter," can be traced to the prince of lies. I'm not looking for you among questionnable companions. I'm not looking for you at shady parties -- because you will not be there.

You will not be the kind of a girl who cares nothing and knows nothing about homemaking. Marriage will bring us face to face with the down-to-earth problems of living. There will be meals to prepare and dishes to wash, clothes to care for, and dirt to battle. There will be budgeting and sacrificing. There will be all the cares and responsibilities of parenthood. Going through the Temple is not a magic solution of the problems of life. It is their beginning. And that's why we both must spend some time preparing for the responsibilities we will carry as parents.

Neither of us will be perfect, dream girl. But we will love each other for what we want to be as well as for what we are. And when we don't see eye to eye, we'll kneel hand in hand and seek the inspiration of the Father. So there you are in my dreams.

There will not be many tomorrows until we meet, and when we do, I will enjoy dating and dancing, still laugh with you, still relish good clean fun. But I will sense the inner part of you, too. I will feel your faith and your love for God.

I will not be concerned with your popularity as much as with your spirituality; with your face and figure as much as with your ideas and ideals; with your ability to dance as much as with your ability to make a home. I will see you as my future queen, and I will wonder:

1. Is she close enough to the Lord to want a Temple marriage?

2. Will she make our house into a home -- and want to bring children into it?

3. Does she know enough of money and its value to help us move forward financially, enough of culture and education to teach our children to love the good and beautiful in life?

4. Can I picture us dreaming and working together, sharing the bumps and stumps as well as the successes?

5. Can I picture us kneeling together in harmony, thanking the Lord for each other?

And you will wonder about me in the same way.

Because we know what we know and feel what we feel, love and marriage will be sacred to us. And if we keep ourselves unspotted from the world, if we prepare for each other -- and if we pray to Him who knows our hearts -- we will be brought together. When that day comes, I will find it easy to love you, because, dream girl, the Lord loves you.

* * * * *

WORD OF WISDOM

A Bar

The name of each saloon is bar,
The fittest of its names by far
A bar to heaven, a door to Hell
Whoever named it named it well
A bar to manliness and wealth
A door to want and broken health
A bar to honor, pride, and fame
A door to grief, and sin, and shame
A bar to hopes, a bar to prayer
A door to darkness and despair
A bar to an honest useful life
A door to brawler, senseless stuff
A bar to all that's true and right
A door to every drunkard's grave
A bar to joys the home imparts
A door to tears and aching heart
A bar to heaven, a door to Hell
Whoever named it named it well

* * * * *

A Judge's Lecture

Dear Abby:

Recently, a seventeen-year-old Florida boy pleaded guilty to possessing hallucinogenic drugs. He had also been charged with violence toward a Miami Beach police officer.

Judge Alfonso Sepe sentenced the youth to one year in the County Stockade and four years probation. The comments of the Judge so impressed me that I ordered the transcript from the Court Reporter so that I may read it to my own children.

Your column is so widely read I am sending you the"lecture" Judge Sepe gave that boy in the presence of the grieving parents. I hope you will publish it and give it the national forum I think it deserves.

Sincerely,

Mrs. A. L. Gates

Judge Sepe spoke directly to the youth and said, "Do you know who is going to serve that year? Not you; your mother and father will serve that year.

"That is what's wrong. THEY get sentenced. They get sentenced for a lifetime.

"You serve a year. Your body is in the stockade for a year, but their souls are tormented for a lifetime. Why? Because you are a selfish, spoiled boy, that's why.

"There is no punishment in the world that I could inflict upon you that could in any way compensate for what you are doing to your mother and father. I have not spent five cents raising you. I didn't know you from Adam. But your mother and father have put their lives, their hearts, their sweat, their money and everything else they have into bringing you up. And now they have to sit in this courtroom and listen to a total stranger who had nothing to do with your upbringing scold you and put you in jail.

"This is at a time when phony kids your age are yelling, 'You adults have your alcohol, we want our drugs; you have polluted our water and our air, you have polluted this and that,' and all the rest of the garbage that comes our of your mouths.

"Meanwhile, you put yourselves above everybody else. I feel sorry for you.

"I want you to think of this for one year, and reason why I say it:

"If you are sick, a doctor will treat you and he won't be on drugs. The lawyer who represents you won't be high on drugs, and the people in whose custody you'll be won't be on drugs.

"Your astronauts are not on drugs, and your President is not, and your legislators are not.

"And your engineers who build the bridges that you drive across and the tunnels that you drive through are not on drugs, and those who build the planes that you fly in and the cars that you drive are not.

"Neither are those who build the bathrooms that you stink up with your lousy, rotten drugs.

"None of them have been on drugs, and this is because of people like your mother and father.

"But in the world of the future," Sepe went on, "the same may not be true. Teachers, doctors, lawyers, legislators -- products of the new drug-oriented generation -- may well be high as kites.

"You won't know whom to send your child to, or whom to trust your life to."

Sepe sighed and closed the case file.

"Let's see what kind of world you leave to your children," he said, "before you talk about the world that we left to ours."

--Abigail Van Buren

* * * * *

WORK

Too many young people itch for what they want without scratching for it.

--Tim D. Taylor

* * * * *

If you want to keep ahead of Satan, you have to work like him.

* * * * *

Enthusiasm -- the difference between a puddle and a geyser.

* * * * *

The bee that gets the honey doesn't hang around the hive.

* * * * *

Work is the yeast that raises your dough.

* * * * *

If we work upon marble it will perish
If we work upon brass time will efface it
If we work upon immortal souls
If we imbue them with principles
With the just fear of the Creator and love of fellowmen
We engrave on those tablets something which will
brighten all eternity.

--Daniel Webster

* * * * *

'Twas Ever Thus

Current newsletter of a local church congregation offers the following variations on an old theme:

Church membership, 525; non-resident members, 59; balance left to do the work, 466.

Elderly folk who have done their share in the past, 58; balance left to do the work, 408.

Sick and shut-ins, 58; balance left to do the work, 350. Inactive members, 106; balance left to do the work, 244.

Christmas and Easter members, 58; balance left to do the work, 186. Alibiers, 58; balance left to do the work, 128.

Members who are too tired and already overworked, 58; balance left to do the work, 70. Members too busy somewhere else, 68; balance left to do the work, 2.

Just YOU and ME -- and Brother, you'd better get busy, because it's too much for me!

* * * * *

Begin; to have begun is half the work. Let the half still remain; again begin this and thou wilt have done all.

--Ausonius

* * * * *

All growth depends upon activity. There is no development physically or intellectually without effort, and effort means work. Work is not a curse; it is the prerogative of intelligence, the only means to manhood, and the measure of civilization.

--Calvin Coolidge

* * * * *

There is, in the invisible universe, that which takes up what we initiate and fulfills it according to its kind. The seed of desire or faith or action sets forth on its processes under the care of universal law, and arrives at its destined development. Men are planting those seeds all the time. The man who is diligent in the planting of good seed will find after awhile that he always has something coming to fulfillment, to fruition. And as the period of waiting is filled with labor, there is no fruitless waiting. Learning, laboring, and waiting are the ingredients of achievements. As Henry Wadsworth Longfellow wrote:

"Still achieving,
Still pursuing
Learn to labour
And to wait."

--Henry Ford

* * * * *

It is a good safe rule to sojourn in every place, as if you meant to spend your life there, never omitting an opportunity of doing a kindness, or speaking a true word, or making a friend.

--John Ruskin

* * * * *

Sir Walter Scott wrote to his son Charles:

"I cannot too much impress on your mind that labor is the condition which God has imposed on us in every station in life; there's nothing worth having that can be had without it, from the bread which the peasant wins with the sweat of his brow, to the sports by which the rich man must get rid of his boredom. As for knowledge, it can no more be planted in the human mind without labor, than a field of wheat can be produced without the previous use of the plow. Labor, therefore, my dear boy, and improve the time. In youth, our steps are light, and our minds are receptive, and knowledge is easily laid up, but if we neglect our spring, our summer will be useless and contemptible, our harvest will be chaff, and our winter of old age unrespected and desolate."

* * * * *

Let us realize that the privilege to work is a gift, the power to work is a blessing, the love of work is success. Genius undoubtedly is little more than the capacity for hard, sustained work.

--David O. McKay

* * * * *

Who? Mx?

Xvxn though my typxwritxr is an old modxl.
It works quitx wxll, xxcxpt for onx of thx kxys.
Thxrx arx forty-onx kxyx that function, but
Just onx kxy not working makxs thx diffxrxncx.

Somxtimxs it sxxms that an organization is
Likx my typxwritxr -- that not all of thx kxy
Pxoplx arx working propxrly.

You may say, "Wxll, I am only onx pxrson:
I don't makx or brxak an organization."
But a succxssful organization, to bx xffxctivx,
Rxquirxs thx activx participation of xvxry mxmbxr.

So thx nxxt timx you think that your xfforts arx not
Nxxdxd, rxmxmbxr my old typxwritxr and say to
Yoursxlf, "I am a vxry kxy pxrson in our organization,
And I am nxxdxd vxry much!"

* * * * *

If you work for a man, in heaven's name work for him.
Speak well of him and the institution he represents.
If you must growl, condemn and eternally find fault,
resign your position.
And when you are on the outside, damn to your heart's
content.
But as long as you are part of the institution, do not
condemn it.
If you do, the first high wind that comes along will
blow you away,
And probably you will never know why.
Remember, an ounce of loyalty is worth a pound of cleverness.

* * * * *

A Short Course in Human Relations:

The six most important words: "I admit I made a mistake"

The five most important words: "You did a good job"

The four most important words: "What is your opinion?"

The three most important words: "If you please"

The two most important words: "Thank you"

The one most important word: "We"

The least important word: "I"

* * * * *

WORK FOR THE DEAD

The greatest responsibility in this world that God had laid upon us is to seek after our dead.

--Joseph Smith, Jr.

* * * * *

Every father and mother has a great responsibility resting upon them to redeem their dead. Do not neglect it. You will have sorrow if you do. Any man will who neglects the redemption of his dead that he has power to officiate for here. When you get to the other side of the veil, if you have entered into these temples and redeemed your progenitors by the ordinances of the House of God, you will hold the keys of their redemption from eternity to eternity. Do not neglect this!

--Wilford Woodruff

* * * * *

Concerning the work for the dead, he (Joseph Smith) said that in the resurrection those who had been worked for would fall at the feet of those who had done their work, kiss their feet, embrace their knees and manifest the most equisite gratitude.

--Horace Cummings

* * * * *

...When we have the privilege of building up Zion, the time will come for saviors to come up on Mount Zion. Some of those who are not in mortality will come along and say, "Here are a thousand names I wish you to attend to in this temple, and when you have got through with them I will give you another thousand;" and the Elders of Israel and their wives will go forth to officiate for their forefathers, the men for the men and the women for the women.

--Brigham Young

* * * * *

And when you have been diligent, and have procured all the information within your reach, and have gone into the holy Temple of the Most High, and done what is required of the living for the dead, then God will show you, by his

Prophets and Seers, and by holy messengers and angels, the genealogies of your fathers, back from generation to generation, unto the beginning, or unto the time when the powers, and keys, and ordinances of the Priesthood were upon the earth.

--Orson Pratt

* * * * *

The Saints have not too much time to save and redeem their dead, and gather together their living relatives, that they may be saved also, before the earth will be smitten, and the consumption decreed falls upon the world... If the whole Church should go to with all their might to save their dead, seal their posterity, and gather their living friends, and spend none of their time in behalf of the world, they would hardly get through before night would come, when no man can work; and my only trouble at the present time is concerning ourselves, that the Saints will be divided, broken up, and scattered, before we get our salvation secure; for there are so many fools in the world for the devil to operate upon, it gives him the advantage oftentimes.

--Joseph Smith, Jr.

* * * * *

Temple Dawn

Rays of the shining dawn glowed softly,
Upon the dome of the Temple,
Rising serene,
High upon the holy hill of Jerusalem.

Palm trees and olive branches
Laced patterns against the sky
As birds stirred in their branches
Filling the air with pulsing hymns of joy
To welcome the new day.

To the Temple came those whose names,
Through the subtle transition of time
Have become familiar to us:
Mary, Martha, Hannah, Rachel, Elizabeth,
Beloved names dear to us,
As we turn the pages of Scriptures,
Names recorded with careful scribing
Upon the records of the Temple.

Today, I too, have placed my feet in holy places.
Today, too, my name is scribed in holy records,
Today, too, I have been obedient.

--Helen E. Schlie

* * * * *

A Cry From The Dead

Must I, behind locked doors, forever wait
While you, who are on earth, procrastinate?
Work which would set me free?
Must I cry out, unheard, forevermore,
And wait, in vain, behind this bleak, barred door
Because you would not see?

Must I, who once held loved ones tenderly,
Stretch out my arms through all eternity,
While others move ahead?
Must I not know the joy of being sealed
By this great power God has now revealed
Because you failed your dead?

When I dwelt on the earth as mortal man,
The Lord had not revealed his Gospel Plan,
Which I accept as true.
I would have done my own work had I known,
And would not now be waiting here alone,
Depending on you.

Please hear my voice before it is too late,
For you, and yours, will one day share my fate,
If you heed not my plea,
For God has spoken in this latter day,
Commanding you to open the way,
To set your kindred free.

For in your day the Lord has plainly said,
That no man can be saved without his dead,
And so I call once more.
As I must look to my posterity,
So must they also have the need of me
To pass beyond the door.

--Clara Lewis Jennings

* * * * *

YOUTH

"The history of heroes is the history of the young," said Lord Beaconsfield. Here are some:

At sixteen, Victor Hugo was writing acceptably.
At seventeen, Leigh Hunt was a prolific writer of verse.
At eighteen, Alexander Hamilton commanded the attention of his country.
At nineteen, Stevenson carried in his head a well-developed steam engine; Washington Irving delighted the readers of the Morning Chronicle; Bryant had written "Thanatopsis"; Joan of Arc had led her country to a lasting victory; Washington was a major.
At twenty, King Alfred had begun one of the greatest reigns in England.
At twenty-one, Alexander had mounted the throne.
At thirty-three, Christ had descended from the Father, had completed the plan of salvation for mankind, had died, been buried, had risen from the grave, and had ascended to the right hand of the Father.

--Frank H. Leavell

* * * * *

Wanted

Wanted: Youth who will listen to counsel of those who have lived life and who know the joys of conformity and the sorrows of disobedience.

Wanted: Youth who live their lives unfettered by the faddish fads; uninfluenced by the idiosyncrasies of the "odd balls" and the eccentric would be leaders.

Wanted: Young folks who will not, like sheep, jump over the cliff merely because the whole band before them have leaped to destruction below; but youth who stand "by their guns" yielding only to those social and crowd pressures which wisdom labels proper.

Wanted: Youth who will resist all anti-social influences antagonistic to proper development; youth who will lead in proper dance patterns and foster group activities for many of the teenage years.

Wanted: Youth who will be the masters rather than slaves of styles, customs and mores, unimpeded by their eccentric deviating demands -- bright youth who will maintain a middle-of-the-road course in modest make-up, hairdo's, dress, talk, dance, and dates, avoiding the shackles of the radical extremes.

Wanted: Youth, who, though out-numbered in the group, dare to stand firm for the principle even through criticism or taunting.

Wanted: Youth who have the moral stamina to turn the tables, proving the eccentric, the extremist, the deviate, as the subnormal.

Wanted: A young generation who will yield to NO unrighteous pressures; surrender to NO cheap practices; submit to NO immoral activities. Youth who will die before sacrificing honor and virtue!

--Spencer W. Kimball

* * * * *

The Peeled Zero

Lissen son, you been away to college
An you got a lot of what you calls knowledge.

But boy, that ain't knowledge...that's just book learnin'.
Knowledge is what your heart knows concernin
Folks and lovin' and livin'.

You may think you's what they calls a ay-the-ist,
Or a egg-nog-tie; now I don't know what a nog is,
But I knows a egg when I sees one, and I knows a bad egg when I sees it
An there's somethin' in this room that ain't perfume.

You say the Good Book is full of contradictions.
In fact, that it begins with a contradiction
Because it says, "In the beginnin' was the Word,"
And that a word can't come out of nothin'.

Boy, I just been a listenin' to a mighty lot of words comin' out of nothin'.
Because nothin' is you in your present frame of mind.

Ya know what you reminds me of?
In arithmetic they's got a little figure they calls a zeero.
A zeero is nothin' with a line around it.
An that's your present frame of mind.

An you know what's happened to you?
You was up in the corner zeeroin' at the top of your voice
You was zeeroin' at all the pretty girls passin' by, now mind Ya, I don't blame you for that.
But that ol' devil comes up behind you, an just like slippin the skin off a grape, he skins that line from around that zeero.

An ya know's what's left?
...A peeled zeero. Yessir, a peeled zeero.
Just a big bunch of bare nothin' without even it's underwear.

An there ain't nothin' in this world so cold and dismal an lonesome
As a peeled zeero. Nothin' around it... nothin' in front of it...
Nothin' behind it...and given off nothin' in jus every direction...

I tells Ya what Ya gotta do, boy...cause you's in a bad way.
Ya gotta get ya some faith.

But how's you gonna get what you ain't got and don't believe in anyhow?
I tell you, boy...you's done it before.

Remember when you was a little shaver? You went out to the ole
Swimmin' hole with the other boys.
You sits on the bank skeered stiff of that ole deep-lookin' water,
Cause you knows you can't swim.
But the other boys is in there snortin' and havin' fun, and you
Wants to be in the swim too.
That's just plain human.

Finally you puts your toe in, then ya gets knee-deep, and finally you dunks.
It ain't so bad. But still ya knows you don't know how to swim.

You goes in for several days, and don't nobody know the time between
When you can't and when you can swim.
But the next time you goes in, you takes a deep breath and submits
Yourself to the elements.
And you swims.

Boy, what a sensation. You's the swimminest boy in that whole puddle.

Then you tries to get the other boys to try, cause that's gettin'
Faith in a big way...you wants to share it...everywhere...

Then you know what happens? That old peeled zeero begins developin'
A skin around it again.
And you begins growin' up...

The old fat sides of that zeero begins slimmin' down...as the hot air
Leaks out of it...until there ain't no space between them sides,
And they soon lengthens right out into a straight up-and-down line.
An you know what that straight line is?

It's the word I.

Remember how Jesus said, "Before Abraham was, I am?"
Well, now you's got the first part of "I am."
When you get the "am" part, you'll be a man-grown.

You'll be worth talkin' with then. Come back and see me.
In the meantime, God bless you, boy...and go get them shoes
Shined...Ya hear?

* * * * *

An Open Letter

We read a statement in the Press made by one young man: "Everyone knows there is too much drinking in this country, but what can you do about it? Everybody knows the morals of this country are going down the drain."

We believe we have the answer to the young man's question. We believe it is time our generation stopped self-righteously deploring this state of the nation or irresponsibly contributing to it. The time has come to change it.

We represent hundreds of young Americans across the nation who have committed their lives to create a new society in America and the world with the global program of Moral Re-Armament.

We are in revolt against a society which creates the climate of immaturity and lawlessness that leads to such a debacle and to such a cynical statement. We have got to stop it.

We are in revolt against the gutlessness of "good" Americans who lack the courage to explode the corruption existing in all levels of our society, who sit silently while one woman forced God out of our schools, who permit the men committed to atheism and anti-God to proceed unchecked, who proclaim one set of standards and live another.

We are in revolt against the line of the "new morality" which is forced down our throats by books, magazines, television, films, professors and some church men. Sex, violence, lust and godliness are taking over the nation. When venereal disease among young Americans rises 130 percent between the years 1956 and 1961, when 13,000,000 children come from broken homes -- who is responsible? We are.

Where are the young Americans who will pay the price in their own lives to stand up for what is right in the country? Where are the fighting Americans who will cure the hatred, bitterness, impurity and selfishness which divide families, destroy races, deaden youth, split nations? The free world looks to us for leadership. The captive world looks to us to make freedom a reality again. We know that if America fails, the world fails.

We are out to build a nation where families teach mankind how to live together, where industry -- management and labor -- teach the whole world how to work together, where all races, colors and classes learn together with all nations how to lead the whole world forward. We are out to create a force of young Americans more dedicated to building a world that works. Not Communist or Materialist. We will create an America to whom the whole world will turn and say, "That is the way men are meant to live."

We believe in modern America. We believe she will rise to the challenge of the times. We believe she will demonstrate the great reality that free men will accept of their own accord the discipline to be governed by God, so that millions on the earth will never be ruled by tyrants. The challenge facing the American youth is not to go backward to the decadence that destroyed the Roman Empire, but to go forward to the revolution of Moral Re-Armament. We can rebuild the modern world. Let us go forward to absolute moral standards for all men everywhere: Absolute honesty, purity, unselfishness and love, not as an end in themselves, but as a means for giving us the energy, the maturity, the responsibility, the clarity that will take humanity forward to the next stage in human evolution.

--Advertisement in the Daily
Universe, BYU

* * * * *